IT'S TIME TO GIV
A SECOND Th

DID YOU KNOW...

- Toxins in commonplace items such as carpeting and shower curtains may be contributing to memory loss over time?

- Overexpos
  deodorant

- Lavender

- A cooked
  ing foggy?

- The essent
  ness?

- Eating foo
  may help

- Certain pr
  ically affe

"Insightful, i
tive about m
this book."

"Packed wit
practical."

"Females ho
men. Now D
cognitive decline.

—Dharma Singh Khalsa, M.D
   president/medical director, Alzheimer's
   Prevention Foundation, and
   author of *Brain Longevity*

FEMALE
and
FORGETFUL

A SIX-STEP PROGRAM
to Help
RESTORE
Your
MEMORY
and
SHARPEN
Your
MIND

Elisa Lottor, Ph.D., N.D.
and Nancy P. Bruning

A Lynn Sonberg Book

WARNER BOOKS

An AOL Time Warner Company

Warner Books, Inc., 1271 Avenue of the Americas, New York, NY 10020
Visit our Web site at www.twbookmark.com.

 An AOL Time Warner Company

Printed in the United States of America
First Printing: March 2002
10 9 8 7 6 5 4 3

Library of Congress Cataloging-in-Publication Data

Lottor, Elisa.
    Female and forgetful : a six-step program to restore your memory and sharpen your mind. / Elisa Lottor and Nancy P. Bruning.
        p. cm.
    Includes bibliographic references and index.
    ISBN 0-446-67743-4
    1. Memory—Age factors.   2. Mnemonics.   3. Women—Psychology.   I. Bruning, Nancy.   II. Title.

    BF378.A33 L38 2001
    153.1'25'082—dc21   2001026879

Text design by Meryl Sussman Levavi/Digitext
Cover design and illustration by Brigid Pearson

This book is dedicated to

The pioneers (both here and gone) in natural medicine who risked their professional standing to blaze new paths in the fields of complementary/alternative medicine in treating the person, not the disease, who believed cures should be quick and medicines safe and found in nature.

All my patients, past and present, who continue to be my greatest teachers and inspiration.

My parents, Beckie and David Tacher (the tiny couple). Thank you for all of the sacrifices that you made. And thank you for your continued wisdom and guidance.

My husband, Mike Lottor, who continues to stand by me and makes all things possible.

My little girl, Resolina, who makes every day a joy.

Acknowledgments

My thanks to the many thoughtful, articulate women who talked to me at length about their memory problems. Names and personal details have been changed to protect their privacy.

I would like to acknowledge the following people, who, through the years, have continued to support me in every possible way, through education, patient referrals, information encouragement, and help:

Michael Leb, M.D., and Fran Leb
David Wong, M.D.
Richard Farr
Steve and Kimberly Litvak and the Whole Santa
    Monica Homeopathic Pharmacy family

Don Tyson of Montiff—Don Tyson's Advanced
  Neutraceuticals
Thorne Research
The Life Extension Foundation
Terrace International Distributors
Julian Whitaker, M.D., of the Whitaker Wellness
  Institute
Kathie Preisont
Patricia O'Donnell, R.N.P.
Harlan Carey and Pam Healy of Total Remedy
  (formerly Apothecary)
Nancy Bruning
Lynn Sonberg
And all my friends and professional associates

Important Note

This book is for informational purposes only. It is not intended to take the place of medical advice from a trained medical professional. Readers are advised to consult a physician or other qualified health professional regarding treatment of their health problems or before acting on any of the information or advice in this book.

This book provides selected information about memory loss. Research about this complex subject is ongoing and subject to conflicting interpretations. As a result, there is no guarantee that what we know about this subject won't change with time.

In order to protect the identity of the women whose stories appear in this book, we have changed names and in some cases created composites.

The mail order offer contained in the back of this book is solely the responsibility of the Life Extension Foundation. Warner Books, Inc., its affiliates, and the authors shall have no liability whatsoever in connection with such cffer.

Contents

Part Two
Dr. Lottor's Six-Step Program 109

Introduction

"Some days I walk down the hallway at work and suddenly forget where I'm going. For the life of me, I can't recall whether I was going to speak to a colleague or to the bathroom. If I'm lucky, the empty coffee mug in my hand will remind me that I was going for a refill. What's wrong with me?"

"Last week as I drove home from work, I felt unusually relaxed. The car seemed so quiet and I was really enjoying listening to the segment on National Public Radio. As I got off the freeway, it occurred to me—it was so quiet because there were no kids in the car! I'd forgotten to pick them up from school. Am I going to get Alzheimer's like my mother?"

"It's so embarrassing. I've always been a great public speaker, but lately I find myself lost—completely at sea—in the middle of a sentence. Sometimes it's just the next word that's gone; other times I haven't the slightest idea about what I've been saying, or why, or where I'm going with it. I don't know how much longer I can go on like this. There's only so much covering up I can manage."

All across America, women are misplacing keys and cars, losing their train of thought, and walking into rooms only to discover they haven't a clue as to why they entered them. Company presidents and sales managers are missing appointments, speaking in fractured sentences, and groping for the next word. Mothers are forgetting the names of their children, culture mavens are forgetting the names of their favorite actors and authors, and everyone is forgetting the names of people they were just introduced to five seconds ago.

As a naturopathic doctor, I have been working with midlife women for seventeen years. Without question, one of the most common complaints I hear is about memory loss. These women are surprised, puzzled, concerned, and downright scared. They are surprised to be losing their capable brains along with their youthful looks; puzzled as to what, exactly, is happening and why; concerned that they will make fools of themselves and lose their jobs; scared that their symptoms may be those of a brain tumor or early signs of Alzheimer's disease. I understand how they feel, because I recently experienced memory impairment myself, around the time of menopause. This, of course, sparked my interest in finding natural solutions. I did intensive research into dietary, nutritional, and other lifestyle components; I investigated herbs and other botanicals. I finally created a program that worked for me. I have been offering individualized versions of this program to my patients with superb results, and am now offering it to you in *Female and Forgetful.*

For many women, forgetfulness is a mere nuisance. But for many women, memory loss can go beyond the embarrassing and inconvenient and into the realm of the dangerous. Some are forgetting to pick up their children, forgetting to shut off the oven when they leave the house, and crashing into other cars when they forget to put their cars in "park." They are working doubly hard to maintain productivity on the job and are worried that their livelihoods are in jeopardy. What may have started out as a mere nuisance has come to have a huge impact on their lives, their self-image, and their self-esteem.

If you have been noticing problems with memory, concentration, and learning, this is the book for you. I know that you are hungry for information, reassurance, and ways to overcome your difficulties. *Female and Forgetful,* the first book to focus exclusively on memory loss in women, will satisfy you on all three counts. In this book, I combine my medical expertise with the expertise of a veteran writer who has authored or co-authored twenty books on health and healing, including a book on menopause. Together we have created an easy-to-read book that not only accurately portrays what it is like to be a woman living through the experience of memory loss, but also offers an individualized, holistic program that you can use to help slow, halt, and possibly reverse this debilitating condition.

Memory Loss in Females

Of course, as men age, they too experience problems with forgetfulness. Women, however, experience memory loss differently, both physiologically and psychologically. Women are more likely to be aware of and troubled by the problem than men, and they want to do something about it. They tend to pay more attention to their bodies as well, because, even though men have cycles, too, women's cycles are more pronounced and culturally and personally acknowledged. They have more dramatic symptoms and are more sensitive to changes in their minds and bodies. They are more health-conscious, and more likely to buy books and take self-help courses. Now that PMS and menopause are no longer taboo, women with memory problems are coming out of the closet in droves and demanding solutions. As is the case with heart disease, cancer, depression, and other diseases and conditions, women need and deserve their own book on memory loss.

Science is starting to understand and pay attention to the physiological differences between the sexes and how they influence health. Factors specific to women in memory loss are

- Anatomy
- Estrogen

- Stress
- Nutrition
- Other factors such as biochemical illnesses, including depression

ANATOMY

Women's brains are not the same anatomically as men's, and perhaps this is why studies show that men and women experience memory loss in very different ways. As they age, men are prone to tissue loss in the front and temporal lobes, areas that are associated with thinking and feeling. But women tend to lose tissue in the hippocampus and parietal areas—parts of the brain associated with memory and visual and spatial abilities. While both sexes can experience all types of memory loss, these findings suggest that women tend to lose their memory more often than men, and that memory related to sight and space suffer most. There are other anatomical differences as well. For example, women have more connections between the two halves of the brain, suggesting a mechanism for women's intuition and also a possible mechanism for compensating for memory loss. (For more on this, see chapter 1.)

ESTROGEN

Estrogen has many far-reaching effects beyond those related to sex and reproduction. This powerful hormone affects every organ of the body, including the brain. Women have five times as much estrogen as men do, and experience dramatic swings in hormones at key points in their lives; thus, their skills are noticeably affected during those times. Many of my patients complain of decreased memory and brain function after pregnancy and during menopause, points at which their hormone balance changes.

However, just taking estrogen won't solve the problem. Clinically known as "age-related cognitive decline" or "age-associated memory impairment," memory loss often becomes apparent around the same time that women notice symptoms of menopause. Since there is scientific evidence that estrogen is needed for healthy brain function, it's easy to assume that forgetfulness is simply another menopause symptom. That's why, if they address memory loss at all, many conventional doctors are prescribing estrogen replacement therapy for women who complain of this problem. If only it were so simple!

Unfortunately, for most women estrogen pills or patches are not a panacea—I have seen many women patients on estrogen improve their memories only somewhat, or not at all. And for many women, artificial estrogen is not appealing—they just don't like the idea of taking a synthetic substance. Often they cannot or will not tolerate the side effects. In others, it is medically too risky; these serious medical risks, such as increased risk of cancer or stroke, are discussed in the book. In any event, brain physiology is far too complex for estrogen—or any one treatment—to be the whole answer. Estrogen is not the only way to affect the brain. Just as we must look to additional therapies to prevent and treat heart disease and osteoporosis, so we must let go of the magic-bullet mentality for memory problems. (I discuss the possible role of estrogen more fully in chapter 2.)

STRESS

Both sexes suffer from stress, but female stress is of a different quality and plays a larger role as a cause of memory loss. Chronic stress affects all the body organs, including the brain, in part by affecting estrogen metabolism. Is it any wonder women are forgetting where they left their briefcases and their children?

Stress is particularly taxing on a midlife woman who may be at the peak of her career, juggling a myriad of relationships and responsibilities, taking care of a spouse, young children or teenagers, and perhaps elderly parents. The sheer mental and emotional overload of daily life is an immense burden on today's too-busy, overloaded women. There's just too much going on, too much information to assimilate, and too many tasks to keep track of.

When mental capacity starts slipping, we take it as a personal failing; we fear being stereotyped as an incapable, empty-headed ditz. In addition, a failing memory is firmly entrenched in our culture as a sign of aging, and it is harder for women to accept growing older—physically or mentally—because of societal pressures. We are all Ginger Rogers, as they say, "doing the same thing as Fred Astaire, only backward and in high heels." (For more on this issue, see chapter 3.)

NUTRITION

When you look at nationwide nutrition surveys, women fare worse than men in many categories. Many women are simply not getting a sufficient supply of the nutrients needed by the brain to create and use neurotransmitters (chemical messengers of the brain) or to repair and maintain nerve cells. In their need to rush to the next task, these women grab fast food. Women, much more than men, are chronic dieters, starving themselves or following fad diets that completely eliminate an entire food group. This type of eating deprives the brain of adequate amounts of protein or carbohydrate, needed to maintain brain function. By skimping on foods high in B vitamins and antioxidant nutrients, these women are failing to protect themselves against atherosclerosis and damage due to free radicals, which deprive the brain of oxygen and nutrients and kill brain cells. (For more on nutrition, see chapter 4.)

OTHER FACTORS

Twice as many women as men suffer from depression, and depression impairs memory, attention, concentration, and speed of thinking. More women than men suffer from brain-fogging conditions such as chronic fatigue, low blood sugar, and thyroid imbalances. Poor circulation due to atherosclerosis is another contributing factor that is largely ignored, especially in women. Poor circulation deprives the brain of blood and, therefore, of the oxygen and nutrients it needs. (For more information, see chapter 5.)

These factors are the main causes of memory loss in women. The first half of this book explores each of the factors in depth, and teaches you how to identify your individual needs; the second half presents my breakthrough, all-natural program designed to combat the factors' effects.

Why My All-Natural Program Works

There has been astounding progress in the scientific understanding of the brain during the last several decades. Scientists now have insight into the way the brain allows us to form, store, and retrieve memories. We are unlocking the biochemical mysteries buried deep inside the brain and finding ways to alter brain chemistry in order to improve memory function. One promising avenue is through so-called "smart drugs." Another popular remedy for women is estrogen replacement therapy. But smart drugs need more study and should be taken only under a doctor's strict supervision, and estrogen is not appropriate for all women and may not even solve the problem.

Despite these advances, there is still no magic-bullet solution for memory loss. Besides, forgetfulness itself is not a medical condition, and it doesn't require harsh medicines. A safer, and more effective, way is through medicines and approaches that use substances found in nature that encourage your body to restore itself. Many women find these approaches intrinsically more appealing, but don't know how to choose between them, or how to put them all together into a program that works and makes sense.

The answer is a comprehensive plan that considers all the factors related to memory loss. That is what I provide for my patients, and that is what I provide for you in *Female and Forgetful*. It is an individualized, holistic approach that includes diet, nutritional supplements, exercise, and stress reduction, as well as all-natural brain boosters, and it is the wisest, safest, and most effective way to manage your mind. The natural therapies that comprise my program are gentle on the body but can powerfully affect brain chemistry.

Here's a brief list of problem areas that contribute to memory loss, and the solutions my program offers:

Nutritional deficiencies/ imbalances	Proper diet and nutrition
Estrogen imbalance	Natural therapies, including soy, herbs, botanicals, exercise, stress reduction
Stress	Herbs and behavioral changes
Poor circulation	Nutritional supplements, exercise, diet, and nutrition
Low blood sugar	Nutritional supplements, exercise, diet, and nutrition

Female and Forgetful provides you with a program designed to help you help yourself. It allows you to understand your type of memory loss and its causes, providing a firm foundation for individualizing the Six-Step Program. By gently adjusting your brain chemistry, you can restore your memories, regain your mental acuity, and live life to its fullest. My goal in writing this book is to offer hope, help, and empathy to women who are experiencing memory decline. The Six-Step Program has helped many women get back what they have lost and allowed them to live full, productive lives. Wouldn't you like to join them?

Understanding Memory Loss in Women

CHAPTER 1

What Is Memory?

The Anatomy

of Forgetfulness

*W*hile scientists debate the subtleties of the categories of memory loss, women march through my office with a litany of complaints. Often the first thing they notice is that they are forgetting names of someone they've just been introduced to in a business or social situation. This is one of the most common and most infuriatingly embarrassing scenarios. Leah, who works for a major university, finds she must constantly cope with looking ridiculous before the student body. "I'm often introduced to students, and I frequently cannot remember their faces or their names," she says. "I find myself in situations where it's clear that I've met a student before and we've talked with each other, but I have absolutely no recollection of the face, let alone the name. It's very embarrassing."

Many women tell me they need to write everything down at work, or they forget it. Anna, who works as an admissions nurse for rehabilitation says, "I get patients who've suffered anything from a stroke to massive trauma. My job involves a lot of detail work and a lot of memory. I was really good at this before. Now I have to write everything down! Insurers ask me 'How far is the patient walking?' and I'll say, 'Wait a minute. I have to look at the PT notes,' even though I just read them a minute ago!"

Just as our bodies lose strength, energy, and flexibility over the years, so may our brains. Dendrites can shrink in size and number, neurons can be damaged and die, and neurotransmitters dwindle and weaken. Some studies show that starting at age forty or fifty, your brain loses about 2 percent of its weight every ten years, much of it in the *hippocampus,* the memory center of the brain. However, according to PET (positron emission transmission) scans, a type of X-ray image, done by Dr. Stanley Rapoport at the National Institute on Aging, the average brain loses only 10 percent of its mass between ages twenty and seventy. Some experiments do show that this shrinkage (however much it is) translates into failing memory. For example, when people ranging in age from twenty to ninety were tested with a series of numbers and letters, it was found that younger people were able to remember and reverse the series more quickly.

Sometimes the befuddledness resembles learning disorders or attention deficit disorders. It's particularly devastating for women with high-powered jobs who are used to being sharp and focused, and instead find their mind hopping around like a flea on a kitten. Zelda, a fifty-one-year-old computer programmer, describes it this way: "I used to be able to focus on a task and everything else would fade into the background. Now my brain can't sweep the other things aside." Anna observes, "My son has ADD and sometimes I wonder if I have ADD, too. But of course I didn't just get ADD! Still, the symptoms seem so similar. He is not focused or able to pay attention. He doesn't remember things. Unfortunately, I feel a real kinship with him because I'm the same way!"

New research, however, suggests the picture is not that bleak, and other studies show that age-related cognitive decline does not afflict everyone. For example, when older people are compared with twenty-year-olds, over one-third of the older folks could remember names and events in their lives as well as the young ones. The Seattle Longitudinal Studies (which followed a large group of people over a long period of time) are also encouraging. They show that although perceptual speed and numerical ability reached their peak in persons in their mid-twenties, verbal and reasoning ability held until those people were in their seventies and eighties—provided they remained in good health. People with health problems, such as cardiovascular disease, were eight times more likely to lose brainpower. Another large study of about 6,000 older people published in the *Journal of the American Medical Association* in 1999 found that 70 percent of the subjects experienced no decline in cognitive abilities during the length of the ten-year study.

When considering these somewhat contradictory

studies, two things are clear: First, serious problems with memory and cognition are not inevitable. And second, people with healthy bodies also tend to have healthy brains. That's why we all know older people who are still sharp as tacks who would, in fact, put many younger people to shame in the Jeopardy game show of life. It is not "normal" to become senile as we age, any more than it is "normal" to become obese, hunched over, sedentary, arthritic, or depressed. Patients will come to me complaining of memory loss, and when I interview them carefully, I find that there are all sorts of other things that are bothering them—low energy, digestive problems, fitful sleep, mood swings. This tells me that we need to work on their overall health and lifestyle habits. Invariably, when we bring them up to better health, these symptoms improve along with their memory problems.

Although it may be normal to lose some brain cells, it seems that most dwindling brainpower is due to cells losing power and function. The signals are not getting through. In the parlance of E-commerce, the "bricks" are not the problem—it's the "clicks" that need to be serviced. This can result in subtle changes, noticeable to you and you alone. Perhaps you are not as fluidly creative as you used to be—how can you assemble your knowledge in a new way if you have trouble recalling and focusing on what you know? You may have difficulty with memorization, or with learning something new. You may take longer to do complex tasks and become confused and inefficient when multitasking. Your faulty memory, in fact, is only one aspect of overall cognitive decline.

Bonnie, a Unit systems administrator, says, "I've

always prided myself on my memory; it's what I've built my career upon. In my field you just don't go to school and then come out and put it into practice. You keep on learning because nothing stays the same. I can't really afford to be less than I was. I need to be more. So, after my hysterectomy I decided to take a couple of classes to prepare myself for an installation of a new system. Because memory loss is subtle in the beginning, it seemed that everything was fine in the classes. I took the amount of notes that I normally take. But once the course was completed, I had no memory of what I did in those classes at all. My books tell me I was there. I must have been there. But I have absolutely no clue as to what those classes consisted of."

Memory is not just remembering the name of the President or what you ate for breakfast. It is remembering your train of thought, where you are, where you are going and why, and what you are doing at any given moment. It is remembering how to put a sentence together, spell a word, balance your checkbook, turn on your computer, and what someone has just said. But many women complain that they are sometimes unable to do these things. They are suddenly rereading things over and over in order to get the meaning, not finding things that are right in front of them, stashing their socks in the freezer, calling their sons by their husband's name, and becoming clumsy, awkward, and, for lack of a better word, "ditzy."

You need memory to hold on to your thoughts and ideas long enough to organize them. But if they slip away like quicksilver before you have the chance to arrange them in a logical sequence, your ability to communicate your thoughts to others breaks down. Zelda says, "I used to be able to store the whole task in my head from start to finish, with one thought progressing to the next. I could count on being able to have a thought and hang on to it while I was thinking the next thought and the next thought, and so on, in branches all over the place. That doesn't happen anymore. Now when I start thinking about a task, I have the original thought, go on to the next thought, and then branch out maybe into a few more, only to find that the original thought is gone. So then I have to go back and start with the original thought, but then I go there and lose it again. I keep going around in circles with my thoughts . . . It's very hard to think something through. I can't hold on to the thought long enough to get through a line of reasoning. It's like my memory span has been cut short."

Memory retrieval also slows down as we age, but this doesn't mean the memories aren't still there. We just need to work at it harder. Often, the information we are looking for is the name of someone or something—a place, a book title. As one woman puts it, "The lapse of memory gnaws at me for hours, sometimes days; it's like struggling to open a locked door. And then, when I'm not even trying to remember, the door flings open and the name pops into my head and I feel so relieved." Somehow, all that time our brains are trying to locate the memory.

My co-author calls this the "three o'clock in the morning Glenn Close phenomenon." She and her friend Fanny were talking about the movies and their favorite actresses. Neither one could remember the name of an actress who was in *The Big Chill*. They went through the list of her other movies, confirmed that she had had a child late in life, described the myriad of hairstyles she had sported in films, and could see her face and her expressions as clear as day. But they absolutely could not think of her name. In the middle of the night the name came to Nancy. She waited until morning to call Fanny and spoke only two words into her answering machine: "Glenn Close." Somehow, all that time, her brain was at work trying to locate the memory.

And then there is what women call "brain fog," and its cousin "brain fatigue." This state of mind seems to be a kind of temporary loss of short-term memory, and is sometimes also related to an inability to focus and pay attention. It feels like being drugged—similar to being stoned, confused, disoriented, and dissociated without the accompanying pleasurable high. Deborah describes it as "trying to think underwater" and says it's "like someone had turned my thinking down to lowest speed." Diane says her head feels "empty, depleted" and that she feels "easily overwhelmed." Michelle says that her "head feels cloudy" and that she is "easily distracted and needs to concentrate really hard to focus and be accurate"; she usually has brain fog and dizziness together. Some women say they simply "can't think" or "can't think straight."

Female and Forgetful

To my knowledge, there are no studies that compare the ways in which the loss of cognitive function varies between men and women. But as I stated in the introduction, there are indications that women experience memory loss differently than men. Their brains differ anatomically, and this alone suggests profound possibilities of uniqueness. Other factors such as stress, nutrition, and hormonal influences also set women's forgetfulness apart from men's.

As they age, men and women lose tissue in distinct parts of the brain, and thus may experience dissimilar types of memory loss. Studies also suggest that men and women use their brains differently. For example, females generally have thicker, more developed left cerebral hemispheres, while males usually have thicker, more developed right hemispheres. What might these discrepancies mean? For one thing, they may explain why females often learn to speak at a younger age and remain better at language skills throughout life, and why males excel at spatial skills, such as map reading and navigation. In addition, the bridge between the brain's two hemispheres appears to be thicker and larger in women. This suggests that the two halves of the female brain generally communicate better with each other, and that men's brains are more specialized.

The structure of women's brains may explain why women are more intuitive, since they may be more naturally adept at coordinating logic with emotion. Men may be more naturally able to compartmentalize information and thinking; perhaps this ability to isolate problems enables them to solve certain problems better. This in turn may also explain why males tend to excel in math, mechanics, and engineering. On the other hand, males are more prone to dyslexia and hyperactivity because these conditions are made worse by a weak communications bridge between the hemispheres. Men also have a harder time recovering from stroke and other brain injuries because they are less able to let the uninjured half take over these lost functions. However, women tend to suffer from dementia more than men do; possibly because women have fewer brain cells to begin with, so when cells die it has a greater impact.

There are other differences that we've all noticed in real life, and that have been confirmed by scientific testing. It's long been recognized that men tend to have a better sense of direction and can decipher maps better—tasks that require spatial reasoning. Anatomically speaking, this also makes sense. Men, on average, have 13 percent more neurons in the outer layer of the brain, but women have a similar percentage of cells that are responsible for communication between nerve cells. The researchers conclude that, in men, the extra cells may contribute to greater spatial reasoning, or that men may have more of a certain type of brain cell devoted to this type of thinking. Men's brains may have more cells, but women's brains have better wiring.

Hope: Your Plastic Brain

Fortunately, your brain has an amazing capacity to continue to change and grow throughout your whole life—this ability is called *plasticity*. Until recently, scientists thought that humans did not grow new brain cells. They thought that only fetuses could grow brain cells and the rest of us were stuck with the brain cells with which we were born. But the world of neuroscience was pleasantly shocked when researchers at Princeton University discovered in 1998 that monkeys could grow new memory cells. While we do not yet have any accepted way of stimulating the growth of new brain cells in humans, this exciting news suggests that what has been lost can be replaced, at least in part. For now, we can protect and support the cells that exist so they perform to their full potential and do not die off.

Another type of plasticity is called *redundant circuitry,* or *multiple mapping.* We know about this thanks to increasingly sophisticated imaging technology, which has rendered the brain less mysterious than when it was hidden behind an impenetrable skull. Using a PET (positron emission transmission) scan, we are now able to see a representation of the brain in action in a living, breathing, thinking, remembering person. We can actually see which parts of the brain are active during certain processes, including memory, and we now know that each memory is stored in several areas throughout the brain. This means that each area could serve as the springboard to remembering aspects of a memory. This is nature's way of making it difficult for you to lose a memory completely, because this memory is stored in many widely separated storage areas. Plasticity allows the brain to re-route pathways through a different neuron, should a particular cell die.

We also know that *dendrites* (your brain's receiving stations) can grow and extend throughout your life. The creation of new dendrites that connect with other brain cells makes for richer and more complex memory pathways. The more connections, the better your brain works. These extra branches may help to compensate for the loss of individual cells. Think of the network of neurons in your brain as a grid of city streets. A city grid has many intersections, options, and detours, so if one path is blocked, there is always an alternate route. This means that once a connection is broken, it is not broken permanently—another can replace it. That's how people with strokes or head trauma can recover from brain damage—their cells grow new dendrites, enabling them to relearn how to talk and walk. It is also what makes it possible for people in their fifties, sixties, seventies, and beyond to learn to play piano, do the tango, speak Italian, and surf the Web.

The Inner Workings of the Female Mind

Until you began having problems with your memory, you probably didn't give your brain a second thought. If you think the Internet or a computer is incredible, consider that your brain is even more vast and complex. Your brain is the most complicated entity in the entire known universe! Think about it—your brain is the very organ that makes you aware that you are having trouble thinking. Together with the rest of your nervous system, the brain forms an elaborate network over which communications, thoughts, and feelings flow faster than the brain itself can fathom.

Imagine a tree with long roots, a sturdy trunk, and limbs that reach out into ever-smaller branches. Now imagine a veritable forest of 100 billion trees with branches that communicate with one another, sending and receiving uncountable numbers of messages every minute of every day. This gigantic forest is your brain, and the trees are your brain cells, which are the seat of your memory, your mind, and—some would say—your essence and your consciousness.

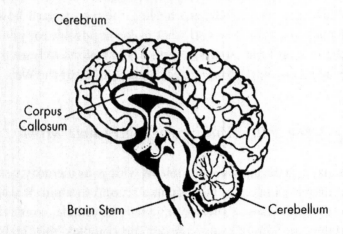

INSIDE YOUR BRAIN

Cerebrum

Corpus Callosum

Brain Stem

Cerebellum

Fig. 1 The Major Parts of the Brain

Your brain has three main parts and two hemispheres each divided into four lobes. All the parts act together to create and store memory and thoughts.

Brain stem. This was the first part of the brain to evolve among animals on earth; it is also known as the reptilian brain. The brain stem doesn't think or feel, but it's a crucial part of your brain nevertheless because it relays information from your five senses and controls basic body functions, such as breathing and heartbeat.

So, what happens when our brain cells fail, when communications between them misfire? Why do you misplace your keys, have trouble adapting to a new computer program at work, or forget your train of thought mid-sentence? Is a dimming memory an inevitable part of getting older? What kind of memory does aging affect most and which is the first kind to go? And, most importantly,

---

Cerebellum. This part is in charge of muscle coordination and body movement, and is where you store memory for movement. When you walk or dance or ride a bike or swim, you are drawing on your cerebellum. It's not surprising that athletes and dancers have very well developed cerebellums.

Cerebrum. The largest and most developed part of your brain. The cerebrum is divided into two halves or hemispheres, which make it look like a big walnut. The two hemispheres have different functions. The left side of the cerebrum emphasizes logic, analytic thinking, and written and verbal language. The right side of the cerebrum is more involved in creative and imaginative thought processes, nonverbal communication, and spatial organization. Right and left hemispheres are connected to each other by a structure called the *corpus callosum,* a band of nerve fibers that enables the two halves to communicate with each other.

Lobes. Each hemisphere of the cerebrum is further divided into four lobes. The *frontal lobes* do most of your abstract thinking, such as math and problem solving, and are the primary seat of your memory. The *parietal lobes* help process information taken in by your senses. Your *occipital lobes* govern visual activity. *Temporal lobes* are near your temples and coordinate memory, hearing, and language.

how can becoming more knowledgeable about your brain help you to better understand why diet, nutritional supplements, herbs, exercise, and stress management are such potent tools for protecting and repairing your mind?

To tackle these questions about the causes of and treatments for memory failure, we first need a basic understanding of the various components of our brains and brain cells (see the box on page 14).

What Is Memory?

Every moment we live, our memories are working. Memory can be thought of as both a process and a result of a process. It is the act of registering, storing, and recalling information, and it is the thing being stored and recalled. Memory is what allows you to perceive, store, and access information you need to survive and enjoy life. Memory is the cornerstone of the learning process, which is what allows us to gain new knowledge, to grow in awareness, to acquire wisdom. Memory, the retention of that knowledge, influences how you feel, make decisions, and express yourself. Memory is our rock; it grounds us in the world and gives us a position in relation to the past, places us in the present, and tells us that there is a future. And memory is what allows you to understand this sentence by remembering the words long enough to give the sentence meaning.

But how does your brain form and store so many memories? And how does it retrieve them when you want it to? To answer these questions, we need to think microscopically for a moment. Your brain is composed of specialized cells called nerve cells, or *neurons*. (See the box on page 18.) Scientists estimate that the average person has approximately 100 billion nerve cells—that's half of all the nerve cells in your body. Neurons differ from other cells because they alone can receive electrochemical impulses and currents and transmit them to other neurons. Each neuron in your brain links up with up to 10,000 other neurons, forming complex neuron pathways of communication. Our memories and other thought processes depend on the ebb and flow of these electrochemical currents, much like our bodies depend on the flow of blood.

A memory begins with a stimulus—something you perceive with your five senses. Your sense organs pick up a message and send it along a pathway of nerves to your brain. Once it has been received by a neuron's dendrite, the message enters the cell body. An electrical charge pushes the message through the cell body and the cell's axon. Then the message is transmitted by the axon to the dendrite of a neighboring neuron. This process gets repeated from neuron to neuron until the message reaches its destination, each neuron sending the message to another neuron via axon, neurotransmitter (brain chemical), and dendrite.

But each neuron can retain only a tiny fragment of a memory. So, the entire memory is stored in a network of memory traces, or long chains of nerves that snake through the brain. Each bit of memory is laid down or created when your senses pick up a signal from your environment—a sound, color or shape, a texture, taste, or

ANATOMY OF A NEURON

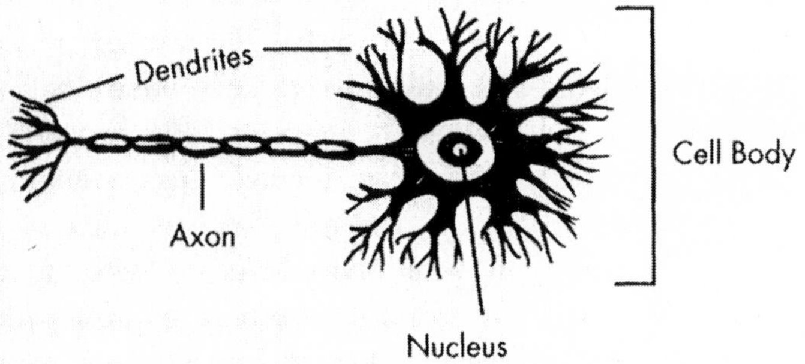

Fig. 2 The Major Parts of the Brain Cell

There are three major parts to each neuron: the cell body and two types of extensions. Each one plays its role in enabling you to process the billions of memories and thoughts that occur every moment of your life.

Cell body. Among other things, this part contains the nucleus—the "command center" or processing station that regulates

odor—that is carried along a chain of neurons by chemical and electrical forces. We don't know exactly how this occurs, but the most recent theory is that in the process, the RNA (ribonucleic acid) or genetic material in the neuron gets changed and holds the codes for that memory. Memory is the billions of neurons communicating with each other through these electrical and chemical signals. Neurons, with their thread-like projections, form a dense adaptable network in your brain. The more stimulation in your environment, and the more memories you store, the larger, richer, and more complex the dendrite branches.

memory flow and the genetic code for each cell. It also contains the tiny power centers (mitochondria) that produce energy from oxygen and blood sugar to fuel your thought and memory activity. The cell body is like the trunk of a tree from which the dendrite branches emerge.

Dendrites. Each neuron has several dendrites, the gossamer projections that are like the branches of a tree. Dendrites are the neuron's "receiving stations," and each one has thousands of tiny spires or filaments that help to receive the electrical messages that eventually create memory.

Axon. Although each neuron has many dendrites, or "receiving stations," it has but one axon, the "sending station," whose job it is to pass the electrical message to a neighboring neuron's dendrite. A single axon may be as long as three feet, or more. Fortunately, the axon is protected by a layer of cells called the *myelin sheath,* which insulates the axon to minimize the risk of losing electrical messages, and also makes message transmission faster.

Needless to say, the ability of your neurons to communicate across the *synapse,* or the tiny space between the axon and dendrite, determines the speed and clarity of the messages being sent. Like a faulty or overloaded connection between a plug and an electrical outlet, a compromised synapse can dim your thinking bulb or short out your memory circuits. This might seem a precarious and fragile way to transmit messages. Why not just connect the nerve cells like a web or a net so the messages can pass through directly without depending on a chemical molecule to bridge the gap? The advantage to this setup is that it allows for a tremendous amount of versa-

NEUROTRANSMITTERS AND
OTHER BRAIN CHEMICALS

There is a microscopic gap between the end of one axon and the end of the dendrite next to it. This gap is called a synapse, and electrical messages are carried across it via biochemicals called *neurotransmitters*. These specialized chemicals are stored at the end of each axon. To send a message, the axon releases a precise amount of a specific neurotransmitter. The chemical finds its way across the synapse and binds to special structures on the neighboring dendrite, called *receptors*. Scientists estimate that there may be as many as 100 different neurotransmitter chemicals. So far, however, we have only identified about fifty. Each of these amazing biochemicals must be present in just the right amounts at just the right time for your brain to work properly. If your supply of neurotransmitters fails or even diminishes, so does your ability to remember and think. Riding shotgun to the neurotransmitters are other chemicals, primarily neurohormones (hormones that affect the brain), that help the memory cells do their jobs. The brain chemicals you will be hearing about most often are the following:

Acetylcholine. This neurotransmitter is the most important chemical involved in memory, concentration, and thinking.

tility and flexibility. Without the gaps and neurotransmitter bridges, your brain would not have the potential to adapt to the new information you continually take in from your constantly changing environment. Your brain was designed to be flexible, and to create and store different types of memories for different lengths of time.

Dopamine. A major neurotransmitter, this chemical has many functions in the brain, including memory. It stimulates your ability to learn and is also involved in muscle control and regulates feelings of pleasure and pain, moods, and libido.

Serotonin. Another major neurotransmitter, and a key chemical in memory and learning functions; it is also involved in appetite, sleep, mood, sexual desire, and behavior. The popular antidepressant drug Prozac works by elevating your brain's level of serotonin. L-tryptophan, an amino acid, is the major building block for serotonin.

Adrenaline. This hormone is released by the adrenal glands, and gives a burst of mental and physical energy.

Norepinephrine. This hormone enlarges your memory storage capacity, causes your brain to be more alert, and stimulates mood-elevating brain chemicals called *endorphins*. Both cocaine and coffee influence your mood by affecting norepinephrine.

Estrogen, progesterone, and testosterone. Scientists have recently discovered that these "sex hormones" affect many organ systems, including the brain, but are still not sure how.

Types of Memory

Have you ever noticed, even before you began having memory problems, that certain memories penetrated deep into your mind and stayed there? But other experiences and information just "went in one ear and out the other"? What is the difference between recalling the name of someone you have just been introduced to, remembering the various components of a project at work, and knowing how to tie your shoe? Obviously, there are different types of memories. The two basic types of memory are *short-term memory* and *long-term memory.* Memory is part of *cognition,* a general term that refers to the ability to know, which includes all types of perceiving, recognizing, thinking, learning, reasoning, problem solving, imagining, mental clarity, and the ability to concentrate and focus.

Short-Term Memory

You may not realize it, but there are a couple of types of short-term memory. The most transient type of short-term memory is sometimes referred to as "immediate memory" or "working memory." As the name implies, working memory is the memory you are working with at the moment. It lasts only a few seconds or less and consists of the newest, moment-to-moment information you need to keep in mind for the task or situation at hand. You discard this memory so quickly it may not even seem like a memory. For example, you use this type of memory when you are driving through an intersection and need to juggle several pieces of information to make snap decisions, such as your position and speed, the position and speed of other cars, and the presence of pedestrians. Another example is when you hear "I-17" at a Bingo game and remember it long enough to cover that number on your Bingo card. People naturally vary in what they retain for immediate use. Often when you have trouble with this type of memory, it is a matter of lack of concentration and focus. Working memory is of a fluid, flash-in-the-pan quality that melts into nothingness for good reason. If every single one of your experiences became a permanent inhabitant, your brain circuits would eventually become overcrowded with information you really don't need.

The other type of short-term memory, on the other hand, lasts several minutes, hours, and days, and comes in to play when working memory wouldn't last long enough. It is still temporary, but makes a deeper impression because it is more important in the larger scheme of things. You use short-term memory, for example, when you remember that there is road construction this week in order to make sure to take a different route to work. The name of someone you are introduced to at a party is also parked temporarily in short-term memory, because you will only need it for the party's duration.

Long-Term Memory

Long-term memory is the type that can stay with us throughout life. This is information that you have decided is important enough to keep—information that you will need to recall and use often in the foreseeable future. This is the type of memory you draw upon to remember that we drive on the right side of the road in this country, and that in your city you can or can't make a right turn on a red light. Other examples are the names of your friends and relatives, locations of important places and things, plus information you learned in school or on the job. The name of someone you meet at a party may become a long-term memory if you decide to make that person an ongoing part of your life. Although it is called "long-term," this type of memory is not permanent. And although it tends to stay intact in most people, much of what we learn can grow dim and vague unless we actively use it.

Some experts make a further distinction between recent long-term memory and "remote" or "vital" memory. The latter are core memories that are so deeply etched into your being that they are a part of you—information such as what a cookie is, how to put on a shoe, the words to a childhood prayer or lullaby that you pass on to your own children, and the name of your country, your mother, or your first dog. They give continuity to your life and help form your unique personality.

To remember is human. Bill Thies, Ph.D., vice president of medical and scientific affairs for the Alzheimer's Association says, "We expect people to integrate memory with behavior—that's probably the single most striking ability of the human organism. It's what separates us from other animals. Our behavior is frequently driven by our memory and we've gotten to the point now where we not only use our own memories, but we use other people's memories. We write books, we collect them in a library, we have a kind of internal Internet that allows us to go get other people's memories and information. This is an indication of how much we depend on past experience to manage our current behavior."

Turning Short-Term into Long-Term

Short-term memories get placed in limbo or a holding pattern, hovering there until we tell them to get lost or until we decide to pass them to another place in the brain for more permanent storage as a long-term memory. Short-term memory is sometimes likened to the temporary impression you make when typing a document into a computer. It remains long enough for you to print it out, but disappears unless you elect to "save" it, in which case it is stored, much like long-term memory. Short-term memories are recorded in your neural circuit, but result in relatively minor, shallow changes in the cells. Some researchers believe that short-term memory is processed in a single system or location in the brain. Long-term memories are more solidly imprinted and result in deeper, more significant changes in the cells, and are also stored in many places in the brain; they are rich in associations, providing many pathways for retrieval.

One way to etch a short-term memory more permanently in your brain is through sheer willpower, determination, and work, by studying and repeating it over and over to yourself. Another mechanism involves attaching strong emotions to the memory. When emotions are involved, another part of the brain, called the *limbic system,* comes in. This is the part of your brain that governs emotions and decides what's important and what is not. Located deep inside your cerebrum, this cluster of structures is linked with emotions and feelings. If an emotion is attached to a memory, the memory is more powerful.

Your emotion causes norepinephrine to be released, which fixes the memory strongly in your brain, so you are likely to remember it and be able to recall it more vividly for a longer period of time. Therefore the limbic system has a tremendous amount of influence on your ability to remember and recall things. A key part of the limbic system is the *hippocampus,* the brain's primary memory control center. If you are having problems with short-term memory, your hippocampus is involved; this part of the brain seems most vulnerable to damage by excess stress hormones in anyone, male or female, regardless of age.

Our memories, our thoughts, are not just a *part* of ourselves—they seem to *be* ourselves. These are the most intimate, powerful, and creative inner processes we experience. They are powerful in spite of their wispy, transient, intangible, elusive, invisible nature. Like digestion, circulation, breathing, and reproduction, our memories and thoughts have a physical basis. And thus we can protect and restore memory and thinking with physical means—food, nutrients, herbs. By furnishing the brain with the right materials and environment, my program not only helps prevent brain cell death, but also helps to forge new connections between cells. So, although our brains, like our bodies, were not designed to last forever, the mental changes we undergo need not be dramatic—if we stay healthy and supply the brain with the protection and raw materials it needs. As you'll see, you can get back your brain, your memory, your thoughts . . . yourself.

CHAPTER 2

It's Not Just My Hormones!

"Menopause problems are bad enough! You have these horrible symptoms that make you feel weird and old. *Then* you lose your mind! It stinks!"

*A*s this Internet posting exemplifies, when a woman of a certain age becomes forgetful, it's tempting to chalk it up to "getting old" or "hormones" or "menopause." Many of the women who come to me with typical menopause symptoms of hot flashes, fatigue, insomnia, mood swings, and loss of sex drive also complain of memory loss and cognitive problems. So it's easy to see why hormone imbalance gets the blame for these midlife symptoms, too. Although I think the estrogen connection has become overplayed as of late, there's an element of truth to the association. Recent studies show that estrogen does have many effects on the brain, and thus needs to be considered a factor in at least some women's memory problems.

Mature women describe a constellation of mental symptoms, including feeling disorganized, being less able to handle stress, having difficulty thinking of words, and experiencing brain fog. These changes may be subtle and may or may not be apparent to anyone but themselves. These mind slippages often exacerbate feelings of low self-esteem due to other signs of aging, and often cause the most distress regarding on-the-job capabilities.

Lynn, for example, is a seasoned civil rights attorney. She laments the confused thinking and loss of concentration that she says make her less efficient and have become a major hurdle in her professional life. "As a lawyer, I need to have statute numbers at the tip of my tongue, I need to remember how to spell names, and know the citations for a law. Now I'm constantly referring to books and notes instead of being able to rely on my brain. Needless to say, this interrupts my flow of thought. My memory and concentration were always really good, so this has been very difficult to deal with."

She says she sometimes mails court papers from work without the attachments. "I've had to turn around and tell the clerk, so I could correct it," Lynn says. "I haven't missed any deadlines on cases, but it's been very close. I think I cover it up well enough so people don't know. It's part of being a lawyer that you don't want to show that you have any flaws at all." But in her private moments, when she is being honest with herself, Lynn thinks, "How am I practicing law? Can I even do this?"

Midlife women worry that they will be found out, that they will not be able to perform, that they will make some horrible mistake—or a million tiny ones—that will cost them their jobs. They are fearful that at their age, they will not find another job, and that they will not be able to support themselves or their families. Forgetful, slow, disorganized, inefficient women are often looked upon as dispensable, dead wood, even malingerers. Lisa recalls, "Before they fired me they called me to the personnel department because my level of work had slipped. I wasn't producing as much and it wasn't of the same quality. I was forgetting to do even simple things, like filing or making sure my boss had the right files for a meeting." Lisa tried keeping quiet about what was going on. But finally, she says, "They asked me if it was personal problems. And in the end, I just told them I was going through menopause. But they didn't believe me."

Women in their fifties describe mental lapses as having a "menopausal moment" or a "senior moment." But so many younger women are also having troubles that we also need to add to the list "peri-menopausal moment"— *peri-menopause* being the time of transition heading up to the menopause, which can begin as early as the mid-thirties and stretch out for ten years or more.

Mary, a working mother in her mid-thirties, has the beginnings of classic short-term memory loss. She finds she has to ask friends to remind her of things they have said, things she has said, and where and when they agreed to meet. Deborah, a forty-three-year-old stay-at-home mom, says, "I do all kinds of forgetful things. I'm one of those people who walks into a room and forgets why they went there. I sometimes walk into the bathroom, brush my hair, and completely forget to urinate, which is why I went there in the first place! I went shopping once and when I got home I was furious because the packer had not packed up my toilet paper or toothpaste in the bag. I found them a few days later in the freezer—obviously, where I had put them."

Shoshona is another case in point. She was forty-five years old when she started noticing the usual perimenopausal symptoms: "a lot of hot flashes, poor sleep, fatigue, uncomfortable sex"—along with long- and short-term memory problems. "And sometimes I just can't find the right word," she says. "At home my memory lapses are not a problem—my family loves me. But at work, it's embarrassing. It makes me feel incompetent." One incident in particular is burned into her mind. She recalls, "One day I was brimming over with exciting ideas to share with my boss. I called her to tell them to her, and all of a sudden I went blank. I could not remember even one of the brilliant ideas that I was so excited about two minutes before. I said I would call her back because I forgot what I was going to tell her. When I hung up the phone, I started to cry."

Hormone-related memory loss and other cognitive problems can occur even in relatively young women after delivering their babies. Sybil, for example, noticed problems concentrating immediately after the birth of her baby, which the nurse dismissed as the aftereffects of anesthesia, pain relievers, and fatigue. Sybil thought that sounded logical. "But within another month," she says, "I could not read. The words were all jumbled. That eventually straightened out, but to this day, I still have a problem. Words sometimes don't sink in or make sense to me. I have to go back and read things over and over. I never had to do that before. I have always loved to read, but I'm not reading as much as I was before." Nursing, which changes a woman's hormone balance, can also affect a new mother's mental acuity.

Estrogen and the Brain

Why should so many women start noticing lapses in their short-term memory around the times of hormone fluctuation, along with other more widely recognized symptoms, such as hot flashes and fatigue? Because although estrogen is thought of as a sex hormone, it has many far-reaching effects beyond those related to sex and reproduction.

This powerful hormone seems to affect every organ of the body, including the brain. Like the cells in the rest of your body, your brain has estrogen receptor sites. When these sites are activated by estrogen, they in turn activate processes that help the brain think and remember. Estrogen has been shown to affect the supply of important neurotransmitters, such as acetylcholine (a memory chemical), serotonin (a mood elevator), dopamine (needed for motor coordination), and noradrenaline (another mood-related chemical). It stimulates chemicals involved in nerve growth and promotes the uptake of glucose, which is used by the brain for fuel. Estrogen also acts as a protective antioxidant against free-radical damage, stimulates the brain's metabolism and the growth of dendrite branches, and modifies the harmful effects of stress on the hippocampus, the major memory center of the brain. Estrogen levels influence memory and learning as well as language skills, mood, and attention span.

On the other hand, studies that measure the actual effects of estrogen replacement therapy (ERT) on mental performance are inconclusive or contradictory. For example, a study of forty-six postmenopausal women conducted at Yale University used MRI (magnetic resonance imaging) technology to actually visualize the effects of estrogen on parts of the brain. The MRI showed that women on estrogen therapy had greater brain activity during memory tests than women who took a placebo. However, this did not translate into better scores on the memory tests.

Similarly, exciting research that suggested that estrogen therapy can improve recall in Alzheimer's patients has since been tempered by other, less positive studies. But researchers still hope that estrogen can perhaps help delay or prevent Alzheimer's in the first place. And a recent study by the National Heart, Lung, and Blood Institute found that women on ERT actually had more atrophy in their brain centers than women who did not take estrogen.

In another recent study, researchers at the University of Washington in Seattle surveyed more than 200 women averaging forty-seven years old, and divided them into three groups: early to middle peri-menopause; late peri-menopause to postmenopause; and women using hormone replacement. Surprisingly, the younger women— those in early and middle peri-menopause—and those using hormone therapy reported more memory problems than the older women in late peri-menopause or post-menopause. The author of the study, Nancy Fugate Woods, Ph.D., said, "This suggests that [memory difficulty] is a minor change, or that women learn to cope and become less anxious about it." It also suggests that peri-menopause can actually be the time that memory problems, and perhaps other changes, such as hot flashes and insomnia, bother women most. If estrogen is a factor, this theory makes sense because peri-menopause is the time when your body is going through the wildest and most unpredictable hormonal swings, swings that eventually settle down when you reach menopause. Interestingly, the Seattle study also found that poor health, depression, and high levels of stress were important factors related to the women's perceived memory loss.

Still, it's amazing that the possible estrogen connection has been overlooked and under-studied for such a long time. This is easier to understand if we consider the social, cultural, and medical climate in which we have been living. The fact is, we know very little about what happens to women and their hormones, especially in healthy, normal women. Medicine tends to focus on unhealthy women so they can be "fixed." You may be surprised to learn that there is little consensus among medical experts about the so-called "normal" highs and lows and timings of hormone balance.

For example, no one can agree on what a normal menopause is, whether it is natural to have a menopause at all (given the fact that, until recently, most women did not live long after their childbearing years), or whether it should be treated. If we sample countries around the world, we see vast differences in attitudes toward menopause and in the types of menopausal symptoms women experience. Some studies found hot flashes occurred in only 24 percent of women polled; in other studies, up to 93 percent of the women experienced them. Women of many countries report menopause as symptom-free, or as only a minor event. Hot flashes are rarely reported by Japanese women living in their native country—in fact, there is no word for hot flash in their language. In most Asian and many African countries, menopausal symptoms are few, none, or mild. And even in the United States and Europe there is wide variation: a summary of studies revealed that 16 percent of women polled remained symptom-free.

Furthermore, it's hard to disentangle the effects of fluctuating hormones from other changes in women's lives. Fluctuating hormones tend to go hand in hand with other major changes such as childbirth, nursing, surgery, aging, and various reproductive abnormalities, which can lead to stress, sleeplessness, poor eating habits, and nutritional deficiencies. Plus, there is no single female medical specialty best suited to diagnose and treat hormone-related issues—neither gynecology, endocrinology, psychology, nor neurology. Ever since Freud made his mark, women's complaints generally have been dismissed as psychosomatic—it's all in our heads.

Women have had to cope with the stigma of women's problems as being evidence that we are the "weaker sex" not only physically but mentally—delicate muscle coupled with a delicate brain. It has only recently become acceptable to acknowledge and objectively study uniquely female phenomena such as PMS and menopause, and to accept that although many aspects of these moments are subtle and difficult to measure and define, they are real. We are great accommodators and always have been. We would rather forget about forgetting than be labeled as having something wrong with us. And it's been all too easy to attribute a slipping mind to aging, rather than to a particular biochemical imbalance that may be a part of aging, but that may be influenced by various factors including medical treatments.

Unnatural Menopause

When talking about menopause, we usually mean the "natural" menopause that affects women in middle age. In these cases, mental changes usually come on gradually. In contrast to this natural and gradual menopause, some women undergo a sudden and "unnatural" menopause. In these women, memory loss is even more profoundly experienced. For example, women who undergo hysterectomy because of cancer, fibroids, endometriosis, or other conditions find themselves in instant "surgical menopause." The estrogen-producing ovaries and uterus are removed, and, bam!—they are estrogen-less overnight. These women undergo a double whammy: the sudden cessation of brain-feeding estrogen and the stress-provoking surgical experience itself. Women who have hysterectomies are generally unprepared for the consequences of surgery, be they hot flashes or mental fog.

Lisa had a total hysterectomy at the age of thirty-four. She says she noticed problems with thinking and memory shortly after the surgery. "I'm not talking about the aftereffects of the anesthesia or the shock you have with any surgery. I went into total surgical menopause immediately," she recalls. "They told me about the hot flashes and night sweats, which I started to have the next day. In a way, I was lucky: my mother also had surgical menopause early and she warned me about the tearfulness that you can also get. I can break down and weep, and I don't always know why. But no one warned me about memory loss as a side effect."

Lisa still has problems with long- and short-term memory, concentration, and speaking complete sentences. "I also sometimes get a vertigo feeling, as if the ground were coming up at me." She frequently gets disoriented and loses her way. "If there's a detour and I need to get home from work a new way, I will get lost, to be sure. Thank God I have a cell phone so I can call my husband up and ask him how to get home." She continues, "I can get lost just walking back from the shops to my office. If I take the wrong street, I get quite panicky sometimes; I just can't make out where I am. And sometimes I actually turn around and backtrack until I recognize where I am, and then start again. It's times like these when I'm afraid that I'm actually losing my mind."

An increasing number of women, particularly young women, are experiencing "chemical menopause" when they take drugs that are estrogen antagonists. These drugs prevent the estrogen receptor from taking up estrogen, so although the estrogen is present, the body cannot use it. Such drugs are used in conditions where estrogen worsens the symptoms, such as endometriosis, or breast and reproductive cancers in which estrogen stimulates the growth of cancer cells. The endometriosis drug Lupron is becoming well-known for causing memory and thinking problems as well as clumsiness and lack of coordination that can persist long after the drug has been stopped.

Angela, who is only twenty-eight, despairs of the future. Her endometriosis is so excruciating that she cannot drive out of fear of a pain attack. What makes her life even worse is the severe memory loss she suffered as a result of taking the drug Lupron. "I was only on it for two months," she says, "but the memory problems have persisted for six months now. It's very scary." Angela always had a great memory: "My high school yearbook quotes me as saying one of my ambitions is to 'never forget.' Now I have a hard time remembering anything—I have a hard time finding words . . . I just feel stupid. I used to say the endo pain was like someone had a voodoo doll of me and was stabbing it with pins in the pelvic area. Now I have to add the pins stuck into the head."

Other anti-estrogen drugs take their toll, such as tamoxifen, which is widely prescribed for women with breast cancer and has been touted as a preventive for women at higher than normal risk for the disease. Although its side effects are relatively mild compared with cell-killing chemotherapy drugs, many women complain about mental fogginess, and my co-author knows of one woman who stopped taking the drug because "it made her so stupid" that she could not continue her work as a textbook editor. My co-author, Nancy, had breast cancer at the age of thirty-one and did not take tamoxifen, but she did undergo conventional chemotherapy. In her book *Coping with Chemotherapy,* she wrote about the "chemo brain" she experienced and women still commiserate with her about this distressing side effect. But many doctors do not acknowledge these concerns, or will chalk it up to the stress of the disease and its treatment, or to aging. Worse still, many women find that the effects linger after chemo is over, and one breast cancer survivor even gave the problem an official-sounding acronym: CRS (which stands for "can't remember s—t"). Several studies have confirmed that the cognitive impairment—of mental flexibility, processing speed, memory, motor function, and thinking in general—can persist for at least two years after chemo is over. Dr. Ian F. Tannock, a medical oncologist at the University of Toronto, and one of the researchers says, "We would not want to discourage people from getting treatment, but we would want them to know about the potential cognitive losses, so that they are prepared for the possible need to adjust their lifestyles accordingly." According to many women, they never regain their cognitive abilities completely, meaning a permanent change in their quality of life.

Unlike tamoxifen, chemotherapy does not directly block the utilization of estrogen. Rather, chemotherapy throws women into chemical menopause because it "fries the ovaries" and hampers estrogen production. Hampered estrogen production is what causes women to go into menopause and is likely one reason it causes brain fog. But these drugs are toxic and may also affect the brain directly, as is suggested by studies involving both men and women on chemotherapy.

No Single Reason

I hope this chapter helps you get the idea that there is rarely, if ever, a single reason that women lose their memories, and therefore there is rarely a single solution for any particular woman. You may want the ease of taking a pill such as estrogen or Ginkgo biloba, but chances are you will also need to diagnose the underlying factors before you can find a complete treatment. In my practice, it's often necessary to keep on digging, trying various therapies and combinations of therapies before hitting upon the right approach. The experience of Sybil, one of my patients, is extreme, but it is also informative in that it shows that you need to be persistent in your search for treatment. She says

> It all began when I had my hysterectomy. I experienced a sudden drop in memory and many cognitive problems, and was told for many years that my problem was hormonal. I took hormone replacement therapy, which helped. I could at least form whole sentences again, but I still had problems with my memory. I went to several doctors but no one found anything. Finally, I went out of state and got an MRI, which showed that during the surgery, the blood sup-

ply to my brain had been cut off. So, I basically had brain damage similar to what you would find after a stroke. Then my story twists again: it was discovered that I had severe B_{12} deficiency anemia. They can't do anything to restore the brain damage, but vitamin therapy to correct the B_{12} deficiency has really helped me.

Clearly, many hormonal changes—the ups and downs and the imbalances between the two female hormones estrogen and progesterone—are not fully understood. Blaming forgetfulness on aging or menopause may lead you down the path of medication, which at best may help partially, but at worst may cover up the problem and bring on unpleasant side effects. The role of estrogen in any individual woman is still uncertain, which is why I discuss natural alternatives to estrogen therapy in chapter 11. Women are complex creatures, and our general health and lifestyle habits must be addressed as part of the effort to restore the mind. In my seventeen years of practice, I have come to understand that there are no "magic bullets," and since the cause of memory loss or cognitive impairment is multi-faceted, a comprehensive program like mine is most effective. For women of all ages who are experiencing mental glitches, a more active, positive, and holistic approach is to take a good hard look at our lifestyle choices, learn how they contribute to our memory problems, and then change to a healthier, brain-building way of life. The bonus is that the healthier lifestyle choices I'll discuss have many additional benefits besides a healthier brain.

CHAPTER 3

The Effects of Stress on the Female Mind

One afternoon at work, I was talking on the telephone with my headset on. I was synching my Palm Pilot, and the fax machine was screaming for more paper. My printer was humming away on a big job. Someone knocked on my door and asked me to attend to something or other on the spot. Meanwhile, I had to pee! I probably had needed to run to the ladies' room for over an hour, but I was so caught up in what I was doing, the demands of the moment, that I just ignored my uncomfortably full bladder. It had never entered my mind that I could have ignored the people and machines vying for my attention. So what if the fax machine was unhappy? I could have said to the person I was talking to on the telephone, "I'll call you back later." At that moment nothing was more important than the simple fact that I had to go to the bathroom. But I didn't get it.

*A*s Leah's story so forcefully shows, many women—intelligent, capable women—feel that their lives are out of control. She has hit upon one of the least recognized, least acknowledged factors in memory problems—a feeling of being overloaded and overwhelmed. Believe it or not, Leah, a Ph.D., is better off now than she was in the past. "Prior to my current job I moved eight times in thirteen years. I, a Californian, did my graduate work in New England. After that, the dismal job market required that I take a series of short-term positions. This is a common experience for academics," she says. "Moving from state to state wiped me out. I am more like an oak tree than a wandering Jew. I put down roots in one place, and I'm extremely unhappy being transplanted."

Today, Leah is forty-four and has a high-powered job at a major university to which she commutes up to four hours every day. In part, she blames her stressful job for her short-term memory problems, concentration problems, and occasional inability to think of words or finish sentences. "For someone in my position and with my visibility, this is devastating," she admits. "I used to regard myself as the least ditzy person on earth. I've always been able to balance a dozen different ideas along with the marketing list and the weekend's errands on the head of a pin. Now I often seem to be inattentive and forgetful. I really don't recognize myself." She feels she is driven by technology, overwhelmed by too many demands on her time, too few hours in the day, and an impossible commute to work to the point where sometimes she doesn't even take time to satisfy basic needs, like going to the bathroom. Yet she is reluctant to quit. "What can women like me do? It has taken me more than a decade to finally earn professional recognition and a salary that is commensurate with my training and talents. So I endure my commute and a contentious work environment."

The sheer exhaustion that often accompanies a stressed-out life can cause the mind to do strange things beyond forgetting keys and appointments. Claire, who had taken on extra family responsibilities while trying to keep up her income, says, "I was exhausted after teaching a night class at the local community college where I had shared a lot of information with my students—what I call a "brain dump." When I got into my car after class, I switched on the ignition, and drove out of the parking lot onto the road—and could not remember what side of the road I was supposed to be driving on! I had absolutely no clue. I went into a terrible panic. I never did actually remember—fortunately, I saw a car coming toward me and figured out that I was supposed to be on the opposite side. There was just no connection going on in my brain."

Our lives have become too full, too complicated, too stressful. We find ourselves juggling pressures that come from all directions: career, finances, family, relationships, chores, obligations, and responsibilities. Our society values hard work and achievement, an appreciation that can compel us to overachieve and overload our systems. Our lives are bursting with endless details and deadlines and sometimes conflicting priorities. Layer upon layer, the stresses build up. Eventually our neurological circuits get fried, and brain burnout results. Is it any wonder we are forgetting where we left our briefcases and our babies?

Having It All or Doing It All?

Despite the so-called equality that women have achieved over the last twenty years, in many instances we are still the servers, the housekeepers, the homemakers. It boggles the mind why more women don't say, "Okay, I'm working full-time and we both hate housework, so let's hire someone to do the laundry, cleaning, and perhaps the cooking." This phenomenon was first publicized in a book called *The Second Shift,* in which the author, Arlie Hochschild, described a generation of liberated women coming home at night from a full-time job to work a second full-time job. This struck such a chord that the book became a bestseller and generated a number of Second Shift support groups that meet regularly. Being both breadwinner and bread baker can be a source of constant stress and pressure, and can affect your quality of life at home and your productivity at work. As smart as we are, we can't figure out why things are so hard and so screwed up. One working mother wryly observed that she thought nothing of interrupting her own work to take care of home and family issues, until it dawned on her that, in contrast, her husband would go to the office and just do his work.

Women are not only stressed in different ways than men, but women, and society in general, react differently to women's memory loss. As a result, women may find that memory loss itself is quite stressful. Men are more likely to ignore or take this type of failing in stride, which they can do because of their position in society and the workplace. For example, men often have support staff to take up the slack of age-related mental decline. They are considered "big thinkers" who don't have to concern themselves about the little details.

Men can even use a memory lapse as a ready excuse for poor behavior. What was actor Steve Martin's response when the Internal Revenue Service found he was not paying his income taxes? He assumed a big grin, shrugged his shoulders, feigned a belly laugh, and replied, "I forgot!" Charming. Hilarious. We didn't think any worse of him for it; in fact, we admired him. In men, memory deficiency and befuddledness are often considered a sign of genius. The stereotypical absentminded professor is always portrayed as a man, too focused on great thoughts to be bothered with such small fry as remembering where he put his keys, or to pick up the kids from daycare.

When a woman's mental capacity starts slipping, many of us take it as a personal failing; we fear being viewed as the incapable, empty-headed ditz. We're supposed to drag ourselves out of bed at 5:00 A.M. after five hours of sleep, get breakfast ready, take the kids to daycare, get to the office on time and work a full day, figure out what to do when a child gets sick at school, shop for groceries, pick up the dry cleaning, cook a gourmet dinner, balance the checkbook, and hop into bed looking and feeling young and sexy? No problem.

Barbie Never Forgets

While visible aging may be ignored or accepted by some women, many women despair at the signs of age, and feel they must maintain a dewy complexion and girlish figure. Conversely, a mature look is often considered attractive in men. Laugh lines on a man's face are valued as a sign of character and experience; gray sideburns make him look more distinguished and authoritative; added weight gives him heft and presence. Even today, when women have never been so independent and equal, we feel pressure to be physically perfect and have buns of steel. Not to mention that as we get older, we find it takes greater effort to look good, to keep up our figures, our faces, our hair, our teeth—and this maintenance is a chore in itself. If Ivana Trump has three personal trainers who arrive at 7:00 A.M. to keep her body in shape, what hope is there for the average woman?

Recently, I took a look at some of the women in my health club. I thought about the difference between them and the women of my generation, who were raised to sew and cook, clean and crochet. When I was growing up, a woman got married, had two children, and lived happily ever after in a modest house. Today, everything is much harder on women. Our roles are much less well defined and much more complex and demanding. Modern women have an entirely different way of engaging with the world. Many think nothing of availing themselves of breast implants, face lifts, the latest cosmetic products. A woman today is expected not only to be a technological wizard and big money earner, but also a walking Barbie Doll.

Today, the old adage "a woman's work is never done" is truer than ever. Yes, we have gained some ground in the area of equal rights and r-e-s-p-e-c-t. But one of the downsides of feminism is that the option to have it all has somehow become a mandate to do it all. Because we have the opportunity to do anything and be anything, we feel we must do everything and be everything. The new freedoms and options have created a new kind of prison and pressure. Women are supposed to be great mothers and sex goddesses—and have killer careers.

Traveling at Warp Speed

Leah, the harried university employee, wonders how much of her memory loss and irritability is due to physical and mental exhaustion, and how much of it is due to "what we are all experiencing in this historical moment of rampant transformation, where the ground beneath our feet is in constant motion." Good question.

Many women, especially those in the workplace, are

suffering from information, technology, and task over-load. The ever-changing technology is part and parcel of our accelerated pace of life; the pressures to partake in this stunning age of invention and affluence competes relent-lessly for our time, attention, and energy, and eventually wears us down, body, mind, and soul.

It's no secret that everything has become faster—the main selling point of the new technology is that it is faster. It began with the fax machine invading every home and office. The simple act of instant transmission implied instant response. Now E-mail and instant mes-sages have pumped up the volume of communications. We expect men to be the techno-geeks, but few women escape the pressure to conform to all the technological advances, either. As Leah observes, it can all be very over-whelming. "Look at all the places that people can leave a message for me," she says. "My answering machine at home, my office voice mail, the fax, my cell phone, E-mail, my pager. Sometimes I just want to be left alone."

Every day there's a new thing to learn, a new thing to learn to use. With each new model, everything gets more complicated. Once you master one thing and feel fairly confident and comfortable with it, it's already outmoded. This is true whether it's a car, a computer, or a particular program. I finally mastered America Online, and then they came out with a newer version. You get a new bank card and need to memorize a new PIN code and read all about the great extra services the card provides, most of which you don't want anyway. Your bank statement and phone bill are indecipherable—there are a million and one services and options, a million and one ways to confuse your money.

Have you tried buying a TV lately? There's a connection for this, a connection for that, a stereo for all-around sound, a flat screen, a rounded screen. I've just finally become comfortable with my VCR, and now I'm supposed to choose among TVs that are DVD-ready. Refrigerators have so many little gadgets these days. I get nauseous just going to the store to look for these things. We do have expanding brain capacity, but sometimes all these knickknacks are really too much. I just bought a new house and I love it. But it was previously owned by a technical engineer and I can't even figure out how to turn on the thermostat or the stove—I need to study manuals as big as a phone book to understand how to do the simplest things.

Nothing is standardized these days, and all of this information is abstract, virtual. We were not really designed to remember this type of data. Our generation is accustomed to more concrete information. Middle-aged people in particular have trouble keeping up with these sorts of technological changes. We are simply not acculturated—we were not raised as techno-babies, we didn't cut our teeth on the computer. We need to adapt our perceptions and our way of thinking and learning and remembering. And it takes an extra effort to think and remember in this new way.

Even without the new technology, the amount of information and stimulation is staggering. A single issue of the *New York Times* contains more information than a person living in the Middle Ages was exposed to in his or her entire lifetime. And according to Dharma Singh Khalsa, author of *Brain Longevity,* the typical American sees an average of 16,000 advertisements each day, if you count the logos and labels. As Dr. Barry Gordon, director of the memory clinic at the Johns Hopkins School of Medicine, says, "There's just so much out there. We were never really designed to remember that much."

Of course this pace of development and replacement drives the marketplace and the economy. But amidst this easy, marvelous, rich, and luxurious life, both our brain and nervous system are overloaded. You feel inadequate if you haven't kept up. This is especially so in a woman who is aging and who likely feels devalued by society, and inadequate anyway. Today we are all running on a treadmill, but the treadmill is permanently set on uphill mode. There is no flat ground, no rest, and if we slip now, we'll never catch up. But who can keep up with it, really?

Major Life Events

Everyday stress is bad enough. What happens to your brain when in addition to the ordinary pressure of life, you're hit with the extraordinary stress of a major life event? Any of the major life stressors (see box on page 51) is not necessarily overwhelming if our lives and psyches are basically sound. Most of us ultimately have the inner resources to integrate the experience, deal with it, and move on. However, midlife women often have more than their share to deal with at any one time. Sometimes stress-

STRESS INDEX

It has long been acknowledged that major life events are stressful, and psychologists have come up with many "stress indicator" indexes. One of the research surprises is that even happy events, such as a new job, a new baby, or a new husband, can be quite stressful. Everyone reacts to major stressors differently, but in general the major life stressors include the following:

- Death of a spouse or other close family member
- Divorce
- Death of a close friend
- Change in residence
- Loss of job
- New marriage
- Scheduled surgery
- A new baby in the family
- A life-threatening illness
- Illness in your immediate family

ful events come so fast and furious, one after the other, that there is no time to cope or recuperate. For example, today's midlife woman may have a serious medical condition for which she's undergone surgery; at the same time, she may be faced with unruly children or grandchildren, or parents who are seriously ill, dying, or recently deceased; she or her aging husband may be worried about losing their jobs, or may have been downsized; she may need to relocate far away from friends and familiarity. This is a full plate indeed, and the cherry on top may be the fact that she is menopausal, which can be stressful itself.

My co-author, Nancy, recently experienced nearly every major life stressor, at a time when she was also peri-menopausal. She separated from her husband of twelve years and immediately took on a stressful work project that had "too many cooks in the kitchen," suffered from a low budget, and dragged on forever. "I eventually had to leave the project," she says, "something I had never done before, and which made me feel like a bit of a failure. I rushed right into my next project—a book about menopause—all the while living it, having hot flashes, night sweats, and insomnia. I began noticing some diffi-culty concentrating."

Nancy delivered the book only slightly late, and was trying to catch her breath when she experienced two more big blows on the personal front. A good friend died of breast cancer, and then Nancy's cat died. "I know it sounds silly to talk about my friend and my cat in the same breath, but my cat was with me through so much already—we'd lived together for fourteen years, longer than my marriage! And now she was gone, too." The task of coordinating and leading her friend's memorial fell primarily on Nancy's shoulders, and was something she'd never done before. Soon after that, her new and troubled romantic relationship ended. "This further devastated me, but it was also a relief. It was one less thing I had to juggle."

As mentioned, sometimes good things can be as stressful as bad; they can come one after the other, leaving us spinning with sometimes contradictory emotions. For example, while Nancy was going through all this turmoil, she also embarked upon a long-wished-for project: to find her two half sisters from her father's previous marriage.

As an only child with not much of a family, losing my husband and his warm, raucous relatives left a hole in my life. Little did I know that the hole would get bigger before it got smaller: soon after, my mother died quite suddenly. Two months after that, I was on a plane to Holland, where I found Barbara, one of my sisters. I was so happy, I cried. Then I cried some more, for another reason—Barbara told me that our other sister had died of breast cancer before I even got a chance to meet her. Imagine: I lost my sister Willie the very instant I found her. I was getting very, very tired of death by this time. How much more could a person lose? Between the jet lag and the incredible amount of experiences and information I was trying to absorb, my mind became a murky soup. I find it hard, today, to remember many details of this momentous event. I have this whole new family, but I can't remember all their names. It's all rather a blur. Fortunately, I took pictures and notes. But it's a wonder I made it home in one piece, and that I even remembered where home was.

Fortunately, Nancy had a network of very supportive friends at this time, and a lovely new man had entered her life to help her weather the storm. She's basically healthy, eats well, takes supplements, adores her work, meditates, and exercises regularly—all excellent tension-tamers, as I discuss in chapter 12. Things were quiet for about three months, and Nancy had begun to assimilate to the traumatic events, make plans for the future, and take on a new work project. But then a fire broke out in her building. At 3:00 A.M., she was evacuated, bleary-eyed in the smoky, unlit darkness, with nothing but her pajamas, coat, purse, and mewling new kitten in her arms.

Forgetfulness under stress and strain is not just about misplacing keys and forgetting appointments. It is about forgetting how to think clearly, and make good judgments, as Nancy discovered firsthand. "During the fire, I *completely forgot* that I had a fire escape. I *completely forgot* all the things they tell you to do during a fire: feel the door before you open it to make sure it is not hot, and that you are not going to walk into a wall of flames; cover your nose and mouth with a wet handkerchief to protect your lungs from smoke. I did none of these things. I am lucky to be alive and breathing today."

Nancy found herself making more bad judgment calls after the fire. "In spite of my sudden homelessness, I decided to go ahead with a scheduled surgery. I wanted to replace my silicone breast implant with a safer saline implant. I know I should have waited, but I was nervous about the state of this eighteen-year-old bag of gel that I had implanted after my mastectomy. These things are known to rupture after about ten years or so. I guess I just wanted one less thing to think about." The surgery was supposed to be a snap, but it was more extensive than expected because the implant had indeed ruptured—in

Nancy's rush to have the implant removed, she neglected to get an MRI, which would have detected the rupture.

Nancy's mind felt the strain:

> The fire reminded me how fragile my existence truly was—I was essentially homeless and officeless. My identity, my life, was my apartment. Everything was bearable, as long as I had a place to call my own. But now my rock, my anchor was gone. My friends were all amazed that I was even able to stand up and tie my own shoelaces. I'm such a trouper, always "coping," always "fine." But as I moved around from place to place, I felt groundless, and my mind got murkier. I had an ever-changing series of phone numbers and addresses—too many numbers floating around in my head, many of which I had to constantly look up. At one point, I was trying to get approval for a check to buy a new laptop computer so I could continue to work no matter where I was. And I completely blanked out on my Social Security number . . . a number I had said from memory about fifty million times was just not there. That was a moment of reckoning for me. Of course, I ignored it.

Parenting with a Twist

Horrible and plentiful as they were, Nancy's stressful events were of the kind that eventually gets resolved. But what if your parent is diagnosed with Alzheimer's disease, which has a genetic component? What if circumstances are such that you need to live with and take care of a parent who is losing it before your very eyes, and who is a living portrait of what you may become?

Claire, a freelance designer in her forties, has been dealing with her mother's growing dementia since the mid-1990s. By the time her father died, "small and shrunken" of cancer, Claire's mother had already begun to pull stunts like baking cookies without flour, bathing with all her clothes on, hiding her jewelry under the sofa cushions, and declaring she was going to "tomato the day." After Claire's father's death, her mother came to live with her. Claire says she loves her mother, but at that moment her world began to "unravel."

"My mother had become very frail and clumsy, and fell many times. She paced and paced all night, and I had to pile boxes in front of the upstairs staircase so she wouldn't take a tumble," she says. Claire's freelance life and social commitments had always enjoyed a precarious balance, one which she successfully juggled with her fierce intelligence, determination, and stamina. But one by one the juggling pins hit the ground. "I missed meetings, cancelled projects, and, of course, I lost clients. I hired and lost twenty home care professionals within the space of two months. I lost patience, and I lost weight."

Claire eventually found a care facility for her mother. Her business and social life are back to their pre-Alzheimer's selves. But the Alzheimer's itself will not go away, in her mother, or in Claire's mind. She says:

> When my mother was diagnosed [with Alzheimer's], I became aware of [the disease] and that it could really happen to people. I started noticing little

things in myself. Before, I had chalked these lapses up to nothing. For example, I usually say a little blessing before a meal, and one morning I was having breakfast and could not remember the words—they were just gone. As I tried to remember them, what came into my mind instead was a blessing I used to say when I was a little girl. And they say in Alzheimer's you go back to those earlier memories. It struck me, very painfully, that, oh my goodness, this is what happens to people who have that problem. I'm not saying that I have Alzheimer's, but I'm aware of the possibility.

Claire's brain fog incidents have seeped into her dealings with the physical world as well. She recalls another disturbing incident:

One day I drove to the train station to pick up my husband, who was returning from a business trip. I was in the BMW, which had an automatic door lock system, and the doors were all locked. I just couldn't remember how to unlock them. I had no idea what to do. And I just sat there, thinking, "how do I get out of here?" Then I started to panic—and this is the worst feeling—when you know you have forgotten something that is very, very simple and that you should remember. And then I got almost hysterical, I felt I was trapped in the car, and the train was coming and my husband would find me crying, locked in the car. To this day, I can't even remember what happened next. Did he show me how to get out, or did I remember how to pull that little button up?

"These may not be signs that I am losing my memory, but the fear makes me think they are," Claire adds. Such incidents can be psychologically and physically exhausting. "This might be part of the reason that people whose parents have Alzheimer's start to forget themselves," she theorizes.

Alzheimer's in a parent may be the worst thing a child has to face. But caring for aging, ailing parents always takes its toll. We are at the age where this is becoming the norm, and it's usually the daughter who dons the mantle of responsibility. In addition, many of us have delayed childbearing into our late thirties and forties, and thus are caught between caring for the older and younger members of our families. Sociologists call this the "Sandwich Generation." We find ourselves torn between caring for young children at home and racing to the home of our parents. In today's world, where parents often live hundreds and even thousands of miles away from their middle-aged children, this can prove emotionally and physically draining.

The Mind-Body-Mind Connection

By now we've all heard about chronic stress as a factor in illness. Few doubt that the mind and body are related, or that our thoughts, feelings, and emotions can affect body processes—everything from digestion to hormone secretion. There's even a new scientific field of study called psychoneuroimmunology, or mind-body medicine. But we also know that there are ways in which stress can loop back again to the mind: stress affects us mentally, which affects us physically, which in turn comes back to affect us mentally. In other words, there's a mind-body-mind connection.

This connection is why you find it difficult to retrieve a memory under stressful conditions. Blame it on adrenaline and cortisol, the stress hormones. Chronic stress overstimulates your adrenal glands to continuously release stress hormones. Adrenaline increases your metabolism, and, in excess, it uses up nutrients needed to maintain important body functions, including those of the brain. Adrenaline also causes digestion to slow down, which impairs your ability to absorb nutrients from food or supplements. Cortisol inhibits the utilization of blood sugar by the hippocampus, the main memory center, making it difficult to lay down new memories as well as access those that are already there. It also interferes with the function of your neurotransmitters, further interfering with your ability to access memories. Finally, the constant bath of cortisol can eventually damage the structure and function of your brain cells.

Stress stimulates your body to create free radicals, which are harmful to neurons. Free radicals assault the cell membranes, and cause the dendrites to shrivel up, thereby ruining the connection between neurons and making communication between cells difficult. Studies suggest that chronic stress actually causes the hippocampus to shrink in size. One neuroscientist has compared the stress-related death of neurons to the cell death caused by stroke.

The Stress Cascade

Stress is the psychological and emotional trigger for a complex physiological process. When you perceive something to be stressful, an internal alarm goes off. This in turn triggers a cascade of physiological changes: stress hormones adrenaline and cortisol flood your bloodstream. Your heart beats faster, digestion stops, your muscles get tense, your blood pressure shoots up, and your brain and senses become hyperalert. This is called the "fight or flight response," and for good reason: it heightens the senses and gives us a burst of energy that enables us, in critical situations, to fight for our life or run away from danger. Stress can be short-lived (acute) or prolonged (chronic). The response to short-lived or acute stress is also short-lived: once we fight or run, and the danger is gone, all body processes go back to normal. Short-lived stress is a marvelous tool of self-protection and survival.

Unfortunately, much of the stress we face is prolonged. You can't simply fight or flee from job insecurity or traffic jams or a computer that is out to get you. Unlike acute stress, we are not designed to handle such prolonged stress, and ultimately it wreaks havoc on all parts of the body. Chronic stress has been linked with fatigue, hypertension, diabetes, ulcers, loss of libido, reduced immunity to disease, and hormone irregularities that can lead to worsened menopause symptoms. It can also make it difficult to think clearly, remember, and learn.

In addition, consider the fact that chronic stress wears out your adrenal glands, and this in turn affects your estrogen supply. During your reproductive years, your ovaries are the main source of estrogen. Once in menopause, your ovaries may produce only 25 percent of their previous amount of estrogen. At this point, your adrenals take center stage and become your main source of natural estrogen. This is why I believe that it is so important to do everything you can to keep your adrenals healthy, especially in the years leading up to menopause. But, as we have seen, so many things in our lives conspire to deplete our adrenals—our lives are full of physical and psychological stress. After years of overstimulation, your adrenals can become utterly exhausted. They no longer produce the needed hormones, including post-menopause estrogen. Once the adrenals are depleted, there is less estrogen in the body generally, including the brain. If your adrenals are depleted, you will have a more difficult menopause, a more difficult transition, and perhaps your experience of memory loss and mental decline will be more obvious.

Stress and excess busy-ness can interfere with your efforts to eat better and exercise. It can lead to depression and loss of sleep, further compromising your brainpower. We don't know if, over time, these changes are permanent. Many researchers believe that stress can contribute to the development of Alzheimer's. Stress-related memory loss is likely to be a red flag that you should heed. Fortunately, studies show that the dendrites of animals who were exposed to excess stress hormones for a few weeks grew back after the hormones were returned to normal. Theoretically, reducing and managing stress should do the same for you.

CHAPTER 4

Nutrition and Lifestyle

Linda gets up before dawn to get her two preschool daughters to daycare before she begins her busy day. As a single parent, she runs around town, cobbling together a precarious living from a variety of jobs, with barely enough time to gulp black coffee for breakfast and wolf down pizza for lunch. She's on the go all day, and doesn't have a minute to care for herself. By bedtime, she's still so wound up that she needs to take sleeping pills to relax. She's also beginning to forget doctors' appointments, misplace her daughters' toys, and forget clients' addresses.

Amanda, a busy big-city editor, frequently eats large and lavish business lunches and dinners, but on many days she just skips lunch altogether. She means to quit smoking, but, she says, "those puffs keep me going during tough negotiations." She sits at her desk all day, and relaxes with wine at night. Amanda catches herself calling agents more than once to discuss terms they have already negotiated, has trouble concentrating when reading manuscripts, and wastes a lot of time looking for papers and important notes that she has misplaced or absentmindedly misfiled.

What's wrong with these pictures?

Linda and Amanda are vibrant, energetic women but they are not taking care of themselves. And, like most women, they may know that they are increasing their risk for serious physical diseases such as heart disease, diabetes, and cancer, but they don't connect lifestyle choices with their fading mental abilities. Alice, like many older women in their late forties or fifties, might blame poor memory on aging or menopause—but at best she's probably only partly right. While hormonal changes and the passing of time may be associated with failing memory, they do not necessarily cause it. They don't explain why younger women are experiencing lapses in memory and thinking; nor do they explain why some older women remain sharp throughout their lives. The fact is that poor memory, aging, and menopause symptoms can be accelerated and worsened by many of the same factors—they are all byproducts of the same constellation of bad habits and lifestyle choices.

In this chapter I point out unhealthy habits that affect mental power, such as smoking, excess alcohol or caffeine, and ignoring your biological cycle, and encourage you to change them. I also talk about exposure to environmental pollution, a frequently unacknowledged con-

FREE-RADICAL DAMAGE

Free radicals are good news/bad news items. We need some free radicals to maintain normal metabolism, but they are also a major source of damage to our neurons. Free radicals form when fats and other substances combine with oxygen in the body. The resulting molecules are missing an electron, and they attempt to remedy the situation by stealing an electron from a neighboring molecule. The newly robbed molecule then tries to steal an electron from its neighbor, and so on, creating a chain reaction of stolen electrons and damaged molecules in its wake. *Free-radical damage*, also called oxidation, is what causes metal to rust, rubber to turn brittle, butter to turn rancid, and paintings to deteriorate. When the victim molecules are components of cells such as neurons, the cells themselves are damaged by this process.

Free-radical damage has been linked with many diseases and conditions, including cancer, heart disease, and arthritis, and is also responsible for such signs of aging as wrinkled skin,

tributing factor, but one that is getting more attention. Many women are also taking one of the prescription or nonprescription medications that affect mental acuity. These are not the only contributors to memory loss; as you'll see, I devote individual chapters to the other major lifestyle factors that form the core of my program: stress, nutrition, and exercise. Until recently, these elements have been overlooked as contributors to memory problems.

As we discover what is assaulting our brains, we are

age spots, failing eyesight—and weak memory and decreased concentration. Fortunately, our bodies have natural mechanisms that control these unstable molecules so they don't run rampant. The controls include *antioxidants*: enzymes your body produces, or nutrients you pick up from food (particularly fresh fruits and vegetables) or supplements. Antioxidants quench free radicals' thirst for electrons by donating electrons of their own, thereby preventing the destructive chain reaction.

But despite this system, free radicals can overwhelm the body. We are being constantly bombarded by free-radical producing environmental pollution such as smog, cigarette smoke, radiation, stress, pesticides, chemicals in our food and water, alcohol, drugs, and electromagnetic frequency (EMF). My program helps you avoid excess free-radical exposure; it also maximizes your intake of antioxidant nutrients such as vitamins C and E, and other nutrients your body needs to produce antioxidant enzymes.

also finding out how they wreak mental havoc. For example, some causes of memory loss may damage the structure of your neurons through the actions of free radicals (see box on page 64). Or they may affect the electrochemical processes in the brain. They may interfere with the production and use of important neurochemicals that affect memory. These assaults on the brain cause memories to weaken, remain stubbornly hidden, or fail to form in the first place.

Alcohol

Alcohol is a socially accepted drug that has a relaxing effect, acts as a social lubricant, and enhances our enjoyment of food. So, what's the harm in a few drinks to help you relax at the end of a hectic day? Alcohol penetrates the blood-brain barrier minutes after you drink it. As a result, you feel relaxed, high. The bad news is that it also destroys cells in your central nervous system, including your brain. It slows your sensory ability and memory processes, and hampers reaction time and judgment. Experiences become hazy or nonexistent (as many a tattooed sailor can attest).

Excess alcohol depletes many B vitamins and minerals from your body that your brain needs for optimum function. It interferes with the way your body utilizes vitamins and metabolizes carbohydrates and can affect hormones. Excess alcohol shrinks brains over time, as shown in PET scans (a type of X ray). Memory gets worse with continued alcohol abuse. We don't know if the damage is permanent among regular imbibers. We do know, however, that older people who drink to excess have worse memories than those who don't, according to a 1997 study published in the professional journal *Neuropsychology.* And we also know that reducing or stopping alcohol consumption increases the likelihood of reversing any damage you have.

Alcohol in excess harms your health in many other ways. It can wreak havoc on your efforts to eat a healthier diet, since it weakens your resolve to stay away from junk food, increases your appetite, or may cause you to forget to eat at all! Too much alcohol can damage the liver, reducing its ability to metabolize toxic substances, which in turn can be toxic to your heart and nervous system. Alcohol has been shown to trigger hot flashes, accelerate aging of the skin, worsen premenstrual syndrome, contribute to the growth of fibroid tumors, and cause depression and sleep disturbances.

So, if you use alcohol at all, I recommend that you limit yourself to four ounces of wine, ten ounces of beer, or one ounce of hard liquor once or twice a week. Substitute light or nonalcoholic beverages such as wine coolers, nonalcoholic beer, iced tea drinks, and spritzers made with wine or fruit juice.

Caffeine, Coffee, and Cola

Caffeine, the active ingredient in coffee and cola drinks, is clearly America's favorite drug. It's also found in many other soft drinks, black and green tea, chocolate, and many prescription and nonprescription medications. We like it because it perks us up and helps us think more clearly and quickly. Coffee is such a part of our culture that the first thing many new patients say to me is, "I would have come in weeks ago, but I was so sure you would make me give up my morning coffee." Millions of people start their day with coffee, and many feel it helps them think and work better. Studies indicate that moderate caffeine consumption (about two cups of coffee per day) enhances cognitive performance, quickens reaction time, increases alertness and attention, and not only improves the ability to learn new information, but also improves reasoning. The problem with caffeine arises with overconsumption. If you drink coffee all day, caffeine will have a negative effect on your cognitive performance. That's because it stimulates the adrenals to overwork and produce stress hormones, which then take their toll on the area of the brain that affects learning and memory.

Additionally, in some people even moderate consumption of caffeine causes "coffee nerves," anxiety, heart palpitations, sleep disturbances, gastrointestinal problems, urinary tract inflammation, and breast tenderness. Because it acts as a diuretic, it pushes your kidneys into overdrive and depletes your body of many nutrients, including vitamin C, B complex, calcium, magnesium, and zinc.

If you are in relatively good health and enjoy coffee, I'm not going to take it away from you—just limit yourself to two cups per day. But if you have osteoporosis, high blood pressure, are pregnant, breastfeeding, or taking medications, you should probably avoid coffee and caffeine in general. Colas and other soft drinks are much worse than coffee. Besides depleting the body of calcium, they have residues of aluminum (from the cans).

Sugar and Aspartame

These sweeteners have their own detrimental effects. Too much sugar, for example, can cause hypoglycemia and, eventually, diabetes. If you think artificial sweeteners are a better alternative, think again. Aspartame (the active ingredient in Nutrasweet) may save calories, but it leads to formaldehyde accumulation in organs and tissue. Formaldehyde has been proven to cause gradual damage to the nervous system and the immune system, and cause irreversible genetic damage. "Aspartame syndrome" causes a number of toxic reactions, including memory loss, dizziness, confusion, irritability, depression, anxiety attacks, personality changes, and loss of blood sugar control.

Smoking

If you need another reason to quit smoking or avoid secondhand smoke, here it is: a recent study in London suggested that exposure to nicotine as you age puts you at greater risk of mental decline. Researchers studied 650 people for a year and found that the current smokers were about four times more likely to suffer mental decline than ex-smokers or those who never smoked. Previous studies showed that smokers were one-and-a-half times more likely to develop Alzheimer's than non-smokers were. It may be that smoking harms the brain via its damage to the blood vessels, which reduces the supply of oxygen to the brain. Fortunately, it appears that this damage is at least partially reversible once you stop smoking.

Other Social Drugs

Other recreational drugs seem to be bad for the brain in the long and short run. Ecstasy, a party drug thought by some to be harmless (wishful thinking), has been found to cause a long-term decrease in an important brain chemical involved with thinking and memory. A recent study conducted in Germany found that the drug, when used routinely and in conjunction with marijuana, leads to a decrease in a wide range of cognitive abilities, including short-term, immediate memory, logical thinking, complex tasks of attention, and learning. (Those who only smoked pot, by the way, did not perform any worse on the cognitive tests than the people who did not use any drugs.) This study looked at ecstasy use in twenty-year-olds; imagine what happens when it is used during midlife, when recuperative powers wane in general. Speed, or methamphetamine, has also been shown to damage the brain, and thus may have long-term consequences. In regard to both ecstasy and methamphetamine use, we don't know if the changes are permanent—but why take the chance?

Prescription Drugs

Medications can be lifesavers, and add immeasurably to our quality of life. But many prescription and over-the-counter drugs can have unintended effects on your brain. If you are taking any of the following, be aware that they can make you feel fuzzy-brained and make it harder to concentrate, especially when used in combination. Be careful not to overuse them and consider natural alternatives that do not have this side effect. (**Precaution:** Do not stop taking any medication without first consulting with your physician.)

- Sleeping pills and sedatives such as diazepam, Valium, Librium, flurazepam
- Barbiturates such as Amytal, Seconal, amobarbital
- Beta-blockers such as atenolol, Tenormin, Lopressor
- Digitalis
- Antidepressants such as Paxil, Zoloft, BuSpar
- Corticosteroids
- Antihistamines such as Allerest, Dimetapp, Actifed
- Painkillers such as Voltaren, codeine, meperidine, morphine

Being Out of Synch

The sun rises, the sun sets. The moon waxes, the moon wanes. These and many other natural processes happen with a cyclic regularity that is awe-inspiring in its dependability. The body has its regular cycles, too, which seem to be influenced by the phases of the moon and the location of the sun. One of the most obvious is a woman's monthly cycle. Today, we ignore the body's daily, monthly, and yearly cycles, and we do so at our peril. The one we mess with most is the daily rhythm, the twenty-four-hour cycle called the circadian cycle. We are still unraveling the body's rhythms, but we already know that many body processes (and possibly all of them) follow this daily cycle, which coincides with the position of the sun and earth. Digestion, blood pressure, pulse rate, body temperature, hormones, all rise and fall in concert at certain times of the day and night.

Circadian rhythms govern sleep and mental alertness as well, and many of my clients report getting too little sleep or poor quality, restless sleep. They jangle themselves awake with an alarm clock way before their minds and bodies are rested and ready to face the new day. They are often jet-lagged from business travel across time zones. Some of them have night shifts or rotating shifts at work. All of these things upset the body's circadian rhythms. We are designed to sleep at night and be alert and active during the day.

Leah admits her four-hour commute has greatly affected her sleep cycle. She says, "Partly because I vanpool, and am at the mercy of other people's schedules, my workday is extended and I may not get home until 9:00 P.M. When I finally do get home I'm too wired, I need to eat, I need to wind down. So, I'm chronically sleep deprived. I function optimally on nine hours of sleep, and I'm getting nowhere near that. Right now, I'm absolutely exhausted." For the moment, Leah is hanging in there, using the weekends to "sleep and sleep." For this, she says, she needs "a special medication cocktail" prescribed by her neurologist.

Although we don't completely understand the reasons, people who are chronically sleep deprived become mentally dull; they have difficulty remembering, learning, and concentrating. They are less creative and unable to solve problems quickly. People who are jet-lagged and disrupt their normal sleep-wake cycle feel lethargic and fuzzy-brained, and have problems with focus and concentration. They are fatigued and irritable, and have headaches and digestive problems. Disrupting your circadian rhythm is a source of stress, and can also be caused by stress and anxiety. Chapter 12 shows you ways to get your mind and body back into synch.

Environmental Pollution

Pollution comes in many forms: chemicals, heavy metals, and even energy waves. We don't know about all the possible toxic effects of these various forms of pollution. We don't know how much is dangerous, how they interact with each other in the body, or what happens when they accumulate over years and years of exposure. But there is growing scientific evidence that these everyday items can wreak havoc on your brain. We do know that many of the thousands of chemicals in the environment have been linked with loss of concentration, memory impairment, slow thinking, headache, fatigue, nausea, and sleep disturbances. We also know that it is best to try to avoid them. If you are sensitive to these chemicals now, you may be able to reverse the memory damage they've caused, or at least help prevent it from getting worse; if you are not currently sensitive, you can try to avoid becoming sensitive to these substances. For ways to reduce your exposure to toxic substances, see chapter 12. For more information about environmental pollution and its effects on health, refer to *Rachel's Environment and Health Weekly,* available on-line at www.rachel.org.

Chemicals

Just imagine: in 1995, 220 billion pounds of synthetic chemicals were produced worldwide, according to a 1997 *World Watch* article. Where do these chemicals end up? In our air, water, soil, and food. We encounter them as automobile exhaust, industrial waste, insecticides, weed killers, and household cleaners, as food preservatives and "enhancers." An estimated 75,000 new synthetic chemicals were introduced in the last half century. In the United States, 90 percent of new industrial and commercial chemicals are approved for production or use without any mandatory health testing, according to an article in *Amicus Journal*. If chemicals are tested for toxicity, researchers usually look for carcinogenic factors, but not for other, more subtle, health-harming effects, such as neurological damage. The Environmental Protection Agency (EPA) estimates that between 2,400 and 4,000 industrial chemicals now on the market are neurotoxic, and that nearly a billion pounds of known neurotoxins were released directly into the air and water in 1997.

Studies indicate that we spend 90 percent of our time indoors. Yet, indoor air can be up to ten times more polluted than outdoor air. Many furnishings are made of synthetic materials that "outgas," meaning they release toxic molecules into the air that we then inhale. Among the most notorious outgassers are soft plastics, such as shower curtains, plus carpets, glues, fabrics, oil-based paints, and detergents, and formaldehyde-containing products such as plywood and particleboard furniture.

Trapped indoors by energy-saving construction, these fumes become highly concentrated.

These so-called *xenobiotics* (substances foreign to the body) are now ubiquitous in our environment. I believe they are a key link in the brain impairment epidemic we see in industrialized countries. Your brain cells are extremely vulnerable to many toxins in the environment. These neurotoxins can attack the brain cells by the action of free radicals (see box on page 64). They can cause brain-disrupting inflammation. In some people, they cause allergies or brain sensitivity.

Neurotoxins affect everybody, including our children, both before birth and after. They may be one of the major factors in the skyrocketing incidence of behavioral and learning problems such as autism, attention deficit/hyperactivity disorder (ADHD), and dyslexia. In allowing these compounds in our lives, we not only harm ourselves, but may be dooming future generations to a diminished and troubled life. Another group of chemicals that is particularly suspect is called "endocrine disruptors." They can affect estrogen levels, perhaps worsening menopause symptoms, including forgetfulness.

Heavy Metals

Exposure to heavy metals such as arsenic, cadmium, lead, nickel, and mercury is another possible source of memory problems. When these chemicals penetrate the blood-brain barrier, they increase the permeability of neurons, causing the cells' vital nutrients to bleed through the cell

GETTING PAST THE BLOOD-BRAIN BARRIER

Your brain has a special structure composed of two layers of cells designed to protect neurons from harm. Called the *blood-brain barrier*, it stands guard against harmful substances that may have entered your blood through the ingestion of food or water, breathing of air, or absorption by the skin.

However, this barrier isn't perfect or foolproof, and sometimes harmful substances, such as heavy metals, can get through. When the barrier fails, your brain is more vulnerable to damage by free radicals, so it is crucial to protect the protector by minimizing your exposure to toxic substances and free radicals, and by supporting your brain tissue with protective antioxidant nutrients.

walls. As a result, everything gets thrown off balance in the cell and components and neurotransmitters do not get properly produced. Heavy metals also interfere with the body's ability to neutralize free radicals. Symptoms of heavy-metal toxicity include poor memory, problems with focus and concentration, low body temperature, and chronic constipation.

ALUMINUM

Aluminum is not a heavy metal, but it is toxic. It has been linked with Alzheimer's disease and has been found in large quantities in the neurons of autopsied Alzheimer's patients. We are exposed to aluminum compounds, which can pass through the blood-brain barrier, in cookware, foil, deodorants, baking powder, antacids, and toothpaste.

ARSENIC

Arsenic, a poisonous element, is found in pesticides, laundry soap, smog, tobacco smoke, and table salt, and is associated with headaches, drowsiness, and mental confusion.

MERCURY

Mercury is one of the most toxic metals and is present in soil, water, food, and pesticides, but most of the mercury we are exposed to is in dental fillings. The American Dental Association denies that mercury dental fillings can cause health problems. Yet many scientists disagree, pointing out that the World Health Organization has found that two to fifteen micrograms of mercury are released into your mouth each day. Mercury finds its way into your brain, where it blocks nutrients from entering the cells and prevents waste products from being carried out. Mercury in the brain has been found to cause arthritis, depression, muscle weakness, and memory loss. Studies have shown that the more fillings you have, the more mercury is in your neurons, including areas related to memory and learning such as the hippocampus. Other studies show that mercury is present in the brain to a greater degree in people with dementia and memory loss than in healthy people. Plus, many people with a wide range of health problems have improved after having their mercury fillings removed.

Electromagnetic Energy

Did you know that your electric blanket, heating pad, bedside alarm clock, radio, TV, microwave, cell phone, and computer monitor could be affecting your memory? These and other electrical appliances emit a type of energy wave called *electromagnetic fields* (EMFs).

Even exposure to low levels of EMFs can affect the body and has been linked to a variety of ills, including memory loss and dementia. Because they emit energy waves at a rate that differs from the rate waves are emitted by natural sources—such as the sun, moon, plants, and our own bodies—they may interfere with the body's and brain's own electrical energy. As we know, thinking and memory depend on our cells' bioelectric energy impulses. Animal research shows that exposure to low-level EMFs decreases the activity of the neurotransmitter acetylcholine in the hippocampus, injures DNA, and weakens learning ability.

Although evidence is conflicting, why take chances? I recommend that you keep your distance from sources of EMFs, and use EMF-emitting objects as infrequently as possible. If you use a cell phone, use an earpiece and microphone that keeps the body of the phone away from your head. For more information, contact *Microwave News,* P.O. Box 1799, Grand Central Station, New York, NY 10163.

As you have seen, these lifestyle factors and those dealt with in other chapters, such as nutrition, stress, and lack of exercise, can exert subtle and sometimes not so subtle effects on our minds. They often work in combination, as JoAnn discovered. She's had problems with memory and concentration ever since childhood, and she believes it runs in her family. Since she has always had allergies and sensitivities to foods and chemicals in her environment, she has spent twenty years altering her diet, "trying supplements and experimenting with different healing modalities to try to avoid allergic responses to food, medicines, and environmental substances," she says. "I'm also very sensitive to dental materials and I think this is an important and underdiagnosed problem. Nearly two years ago I had a root canal, and from day one, I suffered head pain and a permanent increase in brain fog and fatigue. I spent a year seeing many specialists, including acupuncturists, chiropractors, physical therapists, and homeopaths. However, it wasn't until I found a very good dentist who specializes in root canal and dental material problems that I found relief. I was sensitive to the root canal filling material and some of the metallic dental crown material used in the initial procedure. When the root canal was redone and different material used, the problems went away."

As JoAnn observed, it sometimes seems that poor memory and concentration can run in families. Certainly, genetics help shape the brain and its potential abilities, and can increase or decrease our risk of developing any condition or disease. But as a physician once pointed out, our genes are not dictators that give orders—they are committees that make suggestions. What we eat and the way we live our lives can help override genetic tendencies or encourage them. It is theorized that even the risk of Alzheimer's, which is associated with identified abnormalities in certain chromosomes, is primarily due to other factors such as infection with a slow virus, environmental toxins, or chemical imbalances due to diet and lifestyle. Clearly, the health of your memory is usually a reflection of your overall health; in the next chapter, I explore this further by taking a look at the chronic medical conditions that influence the mind.

CHAPTER 5

Other Factors in Memory Loss

*T*here are many medical conditions that can contribute to memory loss, fuzzy thinking, and poor concentration. These are often overlooked. Several, such as depression, chronic fatigue syndrome, and underactive thyroid, affect women more often than men; as we get older, the risk of experiencing one or more of these conditions increases. Other frequent culprits are arteriosclerosis, poor circulation, and low blood sugar (manageable with diet and nutritional supplements), fibromyalgia, allergies, and the yeast infection known as candida. When left untreated, these conditions can be stressful, and the stress itself can worsen memory problems. However, if you diagnose and treat these conditions, you can stop and even reverse the memory loss they cause. Fortunately, many of these conditions respond beautifully to a holistic approach and to the specific measures that are included in my program.

Depression

Depression is an illness that affects your mind, body, and spirit. It can affect your whole life. It is also a major cause of forgetfulness, confusion, poor concentration, and brain fog—in fact, this set of symptoms is one of the criteria for diagnosing depression. Depression is a medical disease that seems to be caused by an imbalance of neurotransmitters related to mood and behavior. One study found that people born during the 1950s are twenty times more likely to experience depression than the previous generation, so baby boomers take note. And, according to the *Diagnostic and Statistical Manual of Mental Disorders,* or *DSM-IV,* women are two to three times more likely than men to develop depression. But only about one-fifth of these women get the treatment they need. Depression has genetic, environmental, and psychological factors, and of course stress also plays a huge role (see chapter 3).

According to Patrick Mathiasen in his book *Late Life Depression,* the following are risk factors for depression late in life:

- Having a personal or family history of depression
- Being female
- Having a chronic illness, such as heart disease; or

> chronic conditions, such as arthritis; or caring for someone who does
> - Suffering the loss of a spouse
> - Lack of a social support system
> - Abuse of alcohol or drugs

Sometimes menopause, aging, or surgery such as a hysterectomy can trigger depression, which worsens their own effects on memory and thinking. For example, Lynn had a hysterectomy for her fibroids and started experiencing memory problems immediately after surgery. But she also experienced "some pretty severe depression," which she feels worsened her memory problems and mental confusion. "As a lesbian, I'm not depressed so much because I lost my 'womanhood,' but because I hadn't decided whether I wanted to have kids. Having that choice taken away from me was really upsetting. I also think it was a hard thing to be under general anesthesia and to recover from having yourself torn open," she says.

Studies show that prolonged depression leads to elevated levels of the stress hormone cortisone. This wears down and shrinks the hippocampus, the main memory center of the brain. While there are many natural approaches that help depression—herbs such as St. John's Wort, exercise, and homeopathy—treating clinical depression is beyond the scope of this book. If you think you might be suffering from depression, ask your physician for a referral to a reputable therapist for diagnosis and treatment. However, research shows that when you treat depression, memory and cognitive function improve.

Poor Circulation

Your brain cells need oxygen, nutrients, and glucose to form energy. In fact, your brain uses 20 percent of your body's oxygen and 25 percent of the glucose to fuel its metabolism, even though your brain accounts for only 2 percent of your body weight. The oxygen and glucose are supplied by blood. Cells also need to have the toxic byproducts of metabolism carried away—another job for your blood. All the cells of your body have these requirements, but unlike other cells, brain cells are not able to store the energy they create during metabolism. This is why it is crucial to keep your brain cells continually bathed in the oxygen, sugar, and other nutrients they need. If the blood supply to your brain becomes blocked, your neurons will have a hard time processing thoughts and memory. Poor circulation can also eventually damage neurons permanently and lead to their death.

If your blood vessels are narrowed by fatty deposits, a condition known as *arteriosclerosis,* you are literally starving your brain of the oxygen, glucose, and nutrients it needs to keep your memory and thought processes sharp. This leads to a condition that is called vascular dementia, which is the second most common form of dementia after Alzheimer's disease. Brain scans of arteriosclerosis sufferers often reveal that small strokes have destroyed parts of the brain, causing cognitive impairment. This is why it is absolutely crucial that you maintain a healthy circulatory system. Both the carotid artery, which is the neck artery that goes to your brain, and the tiny blood vessels of the brain need to be clear and healthy. Many people take the herb Ginkgo biloba because it has been found to improve circulation. But Ginkbo biloba alone rarely does the trick. My program includes other factors that maintain and improve your circulation, such as vitamin E, heart-healthy eating patterns, and exercise.

Low Blood Sugar

Low blood sugar, or *hypoglycemia,* is an often overlooked but important metabolic culprit in poor brain function. It can cause a wide range of mental symptoms, including mental fogginess, lack of concentration, short-term memory loss, mental fatigue, depression, mood swings, physical and mental exhaustion, and the inability to learn or comprehend new information. It is one of the first things I screen for in new patients, since it is often at the root of a wide variety of problems. Hypoglycemia is epidemic because of the sugary diets we eat today. Your brain needs glucose to form the energy that fuels its processes. It gets glucose from the food you eat—mainly carbohydrates, which the digestion process breaks down into sugar. Researchers have found that too little sugar in the form of glucose hampers memory and learning. But before you reach for that candy bar, you should know that too much sugar does the same thing. Hypoglycemia is one of the most undiagnosed conditions in America. Many people who suffer from it are totally unaware that they have this problem, and even their doctors confuse their symptoms with those of other conditions. Eating too much sugar and other simple carbohydrates is not a good idea for your overall health, but it is especially bad for memory. Sugar overload can cause hypoglycemia or "insulin resistance," in which your cells do not recognize insulin and thus sugar cannot enter them. According to the *Merck Manual of Medical Information,* prolonged hypoglycemia can permanently damage your brain cells.

Because the brain runs on energy derived mostly from carbohydrates, it is important to have the right kind of fuel available to promote optimum brain functioning. My program helps you replace simple carbohydrates with healthy complex carbohydrates, such as vegetables, fruits, and whole grains, which can bring about remarkable improvement in your thinking and overall health.

One of my older female patients came in with a host of health problems, but what bothered her most was that she had been fainting frequently, and, although she had been mentally sharp all her life, was now "losing it." She had been to many specialists and none of them could explain these symptoms. I found out she was addicted to sugar and often would have a piece of cake or a candy bar for breakfast. Her blood sugar would roller-coaster all day. When she switched her breakfast to oatmeal with a small amount of tofu or other protein food, not only did her cognition improve, but, much to the surprise of her physician, her fainting problem completely vanished.

Food Allergies

Food allergies or sensitivities can trigger brain fog and forgetfulness in a number of ways. A food particle may leak from the digestive system into the bloodstream without being fully digested, and the immune system sees this harmless food particle as a potential invader. White blood cells, blood vessels, and even distant organs, such as the adrenal glands, respond to the intrusion by releasing a torrent of biochemicals, including histamines, which produce allergic symptoms. An allergic reaction and its brain symptoms can occur within minutes or hours of eating the offending food, as the chemicals build up in the brain and cause inflammation. Allergies to foods can trigger a variety of other symptoms, such as headache, sinus congestion, runny nose, cramping, diarrhea, and skin eruptions. Lesser-known reactions include edema, sore throat, heart palpitations, anxiety, fatigue, mood swings, joint pain, irritable bowel syndrome, and migraine. Many people who have food allergies can eat the food to which they are allergic, but no more than once every three days—this is called a rotation diet.

Becoming bloated and gassy when consuming milk is a fairly typical reaction for people who are lactose intolerant, but I have also seen patients whose allergies or sensitivities manifest on a cerebral level. I can recall one patient who, after consuming any dairy products, became mentally lethargic and lost her mental clarity to the point of being almost sedated. This is called a "cerebral allergy," and is one of the more controversial areas of medicine because it is not your classic "allergic reaction" involving the usual immune system mechanisms with which mainstream allergists are familiar. Rather, there seems to be another mechanism at work. This type of allergy is also questioned because it can be triggered by food as well as "nonallergenic" chemicals such as formaldehyde, auto exhaust, or chlorine. When exposed, sensitized people report reactions that range from brain fog, to disorientation, depression, anxiety, poor reasoning powers, and memory loss.

Gretchen is a case in point. She was having a great time and feeling wonderful when she woke up in the "casa" she had rented in Puerto Vallarta, Mexico. She was served oatmeal for breakfast and immediately noticed that she became spacey and had trouble keeping track of conversation. When I muscle-tested her using applied kinesiology, I found that she was allergic not only to oatmeal, but to all gluten products. Just to be sure, the next day she ate oatmeal again, and she had an even stronger reaction bordering on disorientation.

In chapter 8 I help you detect the most common food allergies so you can avoid the triggering foods. If you decide to get tested professionally, remember that although a scratch test is effective for detecting allergies like pollen and ragweed, it is more beneficial to use blood testing when you suspect allergies to foods, spices, or herbs.

Thyroid Imbalance

You may know that an underactive thyroid can cause symptoms of low energy, dry skin, hair loss, depression, weight gain, and diminished libido. But did you know that brain fog can also be due to too little thyroid hormone? If you are forgetting your keys, forgetting where you parked your car, or forgetting where you are going, look to your thyroid as the potential culprit. This small, bow-tie-shaped gland located just below your Adam's apple produces an army of hormones that regulate metabolism and stimulate nearly every type of tissue in your body. Unfortunately, as we age, this spark plug can itself lose its spark and slow down like everything else. A thyroid imbalance can cause a malfunction in the signaling system that sends the brain regulatory messages, resulting in a delay in sending the messages, or in the messages being sent to the wrong place. We've known for quite some time that thyroxine (thyroid hormone) is needed for the development of the brain, but it now appears that it is needed to maintain the brain and its intellectual capacities. Studies also show that the condition of some people with dementia improves when they receive thyroxine. Thyroid failure can strike at any age, but the risk starts to increase when a woman reaches her mid-thirties. Experts estimate that 13 million Americans have thyroid problems—primarily hypothyroidism, or underactive thyroid. Eight times as many women have it as men, and at least one woman in ten has signs of a failing thyroid by age fifty. Thyroid testing obviates any confusion about whether symptoms are caused by hypothyroidism or menopause—the two are often misinterpreted in the midlife woman. Experts are beginning to recommend the thyroid test as part of a routine physical for women over the age of thirty-five.

Unfortunately, most thyroid problems remain undiagnosed. Physicians often use a test that measures just one thyroid hormone called T4. A better test measures T4 and

TSH (thyroid stimulating hormone) levels, but while the combination testing is more accurate and may be adequate for some women, many other women with an underactive thyroid still fall through the cracks. Their tests can come back normal for both hormones, but their hypothyroidism symptoms improve when they are given thyroid hormone therapy. (You can also perform a self-test at home: take your temperature first thing in the morning, while you are still in bed. Do this for three days in a row. If your temperature is consistently below 98.6° Fahrenheit, you probably have an underactive thyroid and should consult your physician.)

Some physicians believe that the conventional treatment for hypothyroidism—medication consisting of 100 percent T4—is inadequate. Since the thyroid normally secretes small amounts of T3 hormone as well as T4, these physicians believe the treatment should consist of T4 and T3 in the same proportion in which the thyroid normally produces them (95 percent and 5 percent, respectively). In their experience, even though T4 is converted to T3 in the body, many midlife women get better results when they take both hormones. In my practice, I find that when a thyroid condition is mild, a woman may not need prescription thyroid medication. Sometimes kelp, L-tyrosine, or even raw thyroid extract will help regulate a sluggish thyroid, as will weight loss.

Often, a woman with low thyroid has overall hormone imbalance, as was the case with Carla. She showed up for her first office visit wearing too many layers of heavy clothing for a warm southern California day, complaining of multiple fibroid tumors, chronic fatigue, and memory loss. She told me her job was suffering not only due to the fatigue she compensated for by consuming enormous amounts of caffeine, but because of the loss of concentration and short-term memory that was now becoming apparent to her supervisor. She had taken various herbal "memory enhancers," to no avail. The clues that her thyroid might be the culprit came out in her case history: she had had a goiter as a child, and couldn't seem to get enough fish in her diet. I referred her to an endocrinologist who put her on thyroid hormone. Happily, even before her extra weight began to fall off, she noticed an improvement in memory and concentration.

Other Chronic Medical Conditions

Jessie, a retired social worker, had breast cancer treated with surgery and an anti-estrogen drug, which altered her sleep pattern. "Since I also have chronic sinusitis, brain allergies, and other allergies, brain fog is a given," she says. "I have chronic pain, chronic depression, chronic insomnia, fibromyalgia, and chronic fatigue, and these things also affect my ability to remember and to organize my thoughts." Jessie is right: there are many chronic conditions, such as chronic fatigue syndrome, fibromyalgia, and candida, that can affect the brain directly and indirectly. Irritable bowel syndrome, for example, affects brain power indirectly by interfering with your ability to absorb nutrients. People with chronic fatigue syndrome are invariably low in B_{12}, vitamin C, and magnesium, as the viruses that cause their disease destroy these nutrients.

The most common chronic infection I treat in my practice is candidiasis, caused by an overgrowth of the yeast-like *Candida albicans* organism. In any long-term illness the immune system continues to fight infection over time, although at a low level. This sends inflammatory chemicals throughout the body, including the brain. What's more, toxins from the invader can affect the entire nervous system. As a result, chronic-infection sufferers experience low-level flu-like symptoms such as fatigue, memory problems, mental fog, depression, and mood changes. These infections and conditions must be treated professionally and often require a combination of conventional and natural holistic approaches.

Whether everyday stress, poor nutrition, lack of exercise, or a chronic condition is eating away at your brainpower, or you suffer major life setbacks, my program can help. The healthy diet and supplements I recommend correct nutritional deficiencies and nutritional and hormonal imbalances, and help to heal chronic medical conditions. They support your body's innate ability to handle stress and replenish the vitamins and minerals that stress depletes. Herbs and behavioral changes further minimize the effects of stress, improve mood and sleep, and balance hormones. Exercise is a wonderful stress buster and appetite suppressant. But before you begin my program and learn to manage your life, you need to define your problem using the self-assessments in chapter 6.

Identify Your Needs

My program works best when tailored to an individual's needs. In order to do this, you need to narrow down your own particular problem and the likely causes, so you can pick and choose the types of therapies that are most likely to help you.

This chapter is essentially a two-part self-assessment. The first part is designed to help you determine the kind of memory loss you have, and how frequent and severe it is. The second part evaluates hormonal, nutritional, lifestyle, and medical factors to assist you in pinpointing gaps and flaws in your current way of living. The assessment also gives your physician key information, and allows you to more accurately monitor yourself while on the program.

Make several photocopies of the assessment so you can take it again every two months to monitor your progress. Be sure to write the date you take the test on each copy. To take the test, set aside a time when you will not have any interruptions or distractions. Think carefully before answering each question, and answer as honestly as possible. To help you answer these questions, I suggest keeping a journal for a month that is a record of the topics covered in the questionnaire before completing the questionnaire.

Part One: Type and Severity of Memory Loss

If you have mild to moderate memory problems, my program alone may be sufficient. If you have moderate to severe problems, you should seek professional medical care to rule out Alzheimer's or other forms of senile dementia (see box on page 98). However, even if you do have a more serious memory problem, following my program in addition to your medical care may benefit your brain.

SHORT-TERM MEMORY LOSS SELF-TEST

1. Do you walk into a room and forget why you are there?
2. Do you misplace your glasses, keys, pen, etc.?
3. Do you occasionally have trouble remembering where you parked your car?
4. Do you do things like turn off the house lights, lock the door, or unplug the iron and then have

difficulty recalling if you did it so must go back and check?

5. Do you arrive at a specific destination, like the gym, only to discover you've forgotten an essential item, such as your gym bag, workout shoes, or swimsuit?

6. Do you have trouble remembering what you ate for dinner last night or what you did last weekend?

7. Do you forget a phone number too soon to dial it after hearing it or looking it up?

8. Do you dial a phone number and forget whom you are calling?

9. Do you forget appointments?

10. Do you answer call waiting and tell people you'll call them back, then forget to do so?

Scoring:

If you have answered yes to

3–5 of these questions, you have mild short-term memory problems

6–8 of these questions, you have moderate short-term memory problems

9–10 of these questions, you have significant short-term memory problems

LONG-TERM MEMORY LOSS SELF-TEST

1. Do you forget the birthdays of people close to you?

2. Do you forget anniversaries that you used to remember?

3. Do you momentarily forget how to turn on your

computer or perform a function you have known how to do for some time?

4. Do you momentarily forget how to start your car or turn on the headlights or turn signals?

5. Do you forget things that have happened long ago in childhood?

6. Do you forget things that people have told you in years past, or blank out entire conversations?

Scoring:

If you have answered yes to

1–2 of these questions, you have mild long-term memory problems

3–4 of these questions, you have moderate long-term memory problems

5–6 of these questions, you have significant long-term memory problems

BRAIN FOG AND MENTAL CONFUSION SELF-TEST

1. Do you sometimes not know where you are?

2. Do you say one word when you mean another?

3. Do you have trouble completing sentences?

4. Do you lose your train of thought?

5. Do you have trouble spelling familiar words?

6. Do you sometimes not know the name of an object?

7. Are you becoming more disorganized and less efficient?

8. Do you spend a lot of time going through papers looking for something?

Scoring:

If you have answered yes to

2–3 of these questions, you have mild brain fog

4–6 of these questions, you have moderate brain fog

7–8 of these questions, you have significant brain fog

LEARNING AND CONCENTRATION PROBLEMS SELF-TEST

1. Do you need to read sentences and paragraphs several times to get the meaning?
2. Do you have trouble concentrating if there is background noise and activity?
3. Are you less able to do more than one thing at once?
4. Do you have trouble learning how to do something new, such as using a new application on your computer?
5. Do you have difficulty learning to operate a new appliance or device at home or work?
6. Do you get lost when driving to a new destination?
7. Are you less coordinated while driving, or, in general?
8. Do you find yourself momentarily "tuning out" what people are saying or doing?

Scoring:

If you have answered yes to

2–3 of these questions, you have mild learning and concentration problems

4–6 of these questions, you have moderate learning and concentration problems

7–8 of these questions, you have significant learning and concentration problems

IS IT ALZHEIMER'S?

Four million Americans have Alzheimer's, and experts project that 14 million will have it by the year 2050. Today, one out of every ten people over age sixty-five have it, and half of those over eighty-five. You may be surprised to learn that Alzheimer's can occur in people as young as their thirties, forties, and fifties. However, this early onset form of the disease accounts for less than 10 percent of all cases. Below is the Alzheimer's Association's list of warning signs of the disease (some of the common Alzheimer's symptoms also apply to other dementias). The list will help you distinguish between "normal" memory problems and this more serious disease. If you exhibit several of these symptoms, you should see a physician for a complete examination.

1. *Memory loss that affects job skills.* It's normal to occasionally forget an assignment, deadline, or colleague's name, but frequent forgetfulness or inexplicable confusion in the workplace (or at home) may signal that something's wrong.

2. *Difficulty performing familiar tasks.* Busy people get distracted from time to time. For example, you might leave something on the stove too long or not remember to serve part of a meal. People with Alzheimer's might prepare a meal and not only forget to serve it, but also forget they made it.

3. *Problems with language.* Everyone has trouble finding the right word sometimes, but a person with Alzheimer's disease may forget simple words or substitute inappropriate words, making his or her sentences difficult to understand.

4. *Disorientation to time and place.* It's normal to momentarily

forget the day of the week or what you need from the store. But people with Alzheimer's disease can become lost on their own street, not knowing where they are, how they got there, or how to get back home.

5. *Poor or decreased judgment.* Choosing not to bring a sweater or coat along on a chilly night is a common mistake. A person with Alzheimer's, however, may dress inappropriately in more noticeable ways, wearing a bathrobe to the store or several blouses on a hot day.

6. *Problems with abstract thinking.* Balancing a checkbook can be challenging for many people, but for someone with Alzheimer's, recognizing numbers or performing basic calculations may be impossible.

7. *Misplacing things.* Everyone temporarily misplaces a wallet or keys from time to time. A person with Alzheimer's disease may put these and other items in inappropriate places—such as an iron in the freezer or a wristwatch in the sugar bowl—then not recall how they got there.

8. *Changes in mood or behavior.* Everyone experiences a broad range of emotions—it's part of being human. People with Alzheimer's tend to exhibit more rapid mood swings for no apparent reason.

9. *Changes in personality.* People's personalities may change somewhat as they age. But a person with Alzheimer's

(continued)

(continued)

can change dramatically, either suddenly or over a period of time. Someone who is generally easygoing may become angry, suspicious, or fearful.

10. *Loss of initiative.* It's normal to tire of housework, business activities, or social obligations, but most people retain or eventually regain their interest. A person with Alzheimer's disease may remain uninterested and uninvolved in many or all of his usual pursuits.

Part Two: What Are the Possible Causes of Your Memory Loss?

Once you have ruled out chronic medical conditions as the cause of your memory problems, this assessment will help point the way to the steps in my program that are most likely to help you restore your memory or at least slow its loss.

Chronic Medical Conditions

Chronic medical conditions are often either undiagnosed or overlooked as a source of memory problems. The most common conditions associated with memory loss include depression, arteriosclerosis, blood sugar problems, chronic fatigue syndrome, fibromyalgia, thyroid imbalance, allergies, or an infection such as candida. If you have already been diagnosed with any of these conditions and are experiencing memory problems, consult with your physician to confirm that you are receiving the appropriate medical treatment. If you have not been diagnosed with any of these problems, the answers to the following questions may suggest a medical examination to diagnose them or rule them out. Even if you do have a chronic medical condition, you can often integrate the natural therapies in my program along with conventional medical treatment for improved results. For example, changing your diet to include fewer sugary foods will help control low blood sugar, and exercising will help ease depression and improve circulation.

Poor Circulation Self-Test

1. Do you have a family history of premature heart disease (before age fifty-five in male relatives; before age sixty-five in females)?
2. Do you have high blood pressure?
3. Do you have diabetes?
4. Is your HDL (or good) cholesterol under 35 mg/dl?
5. Is your total cholesterol equal to or over 200?
6. Are you overweight?
7. Do you get very little exercise or have a sit-down job?
8. Do you feel the cold more than other people?
9. Do your hands and fingers get cold easily?

Scoring: If you have answered yes to 4 or more of these questions, poor circulation may be contributing to your memory problems.

ALLERGIES AND SENSITIVITIES SELF-TEST

1. Do you eat the same foods pretty consistently?
2. Do you have food cravings?
3. Do you ever get brain fog or notice thinking problems after eating certain foods?
4. Do you have any of the following symptoms after eating certain foods? Burping, bloating, flatulence, skin reaction, difficulty swallowing, headache, anxiety, fatigue, mood swings, joint pain, wheezing, or asthma.

Scoring: If you have answered yes to any of these questions, allergies may be contributing to your memory problems.

LOW BLOOD SUGAR SELF-TEST

1. Do you get irritable or shaky if your mealtime is delayed?
2. Do you crave sweets and do you eat a lot of them?
3. Does your brain feel sluggish and foggy and then improve after you have eaten?
4. Do you get tired during the day if you don't eat regularly?

Scoring: If you have answered yes to any of these questions, low blood sugar may be contributing to your memory problems.

DEPRESSION SELF-TEST

1. Are you frequently tired and irritable?
2. Have you lost interest or pleasure in your usual activities, including sex?

3. Do you suffer from lack of appetite and weight loss, or increased appetite and weight gain?
4. Do you get too much or too little sleep (much more or less than eight hours a night)?
5. Do you exercise too much or too little (much more or less than one hour three to five times a week)?
6. Are you frequently fatigued or lacking in energy?
7. Do you feel worthless, or are you overly self-critical, or do you suffer from excessive guilt?
8. Do you frequently entertain thoughts of suicide?

Scoring: If you have answered yes to 4 or more of these questions, depression may be contributing to your memory problems.

STRESS SELF-TEST

1. Do you feel as if you are on a treadmill and can't get off?
2. Are you feeling stressed out or overwhelmed?
3. Do little, inconsequential things bother you disproportionately?
4. Are you irritable and short tempered?
5. Do you feel there is never enough time—are you always in a rush?
6. Do you try to do too many things at once?
7. Do you feel that you do not have a balance between your work, your social life, and your family life?
8. Have you experienced major traumatic events recently?

Scoring: If you have answered yes to 3 or more of

these questions, stress may be contributing to your memory problems.

POOR NUTRITION SELF-TEST

1. Do you frequently skip meals?
2. Do you eat fewer than five servings of fresh vegetables and fruits everyday?
3. Do you diet to control your weight?
4. Do you frequently overeat?
5. Do you frequently eat processed foods, such as cookies, pastries, chips, and candy?
6. Do you regularly eat fatty foods such as pizza, hamburgers, french fries, cheese, and ice cream?
7. Are you over fifty-five years of age, or do you have a medical condition such as Crohn's disease that might interfere with your absorption and utilization of nutrients?
8. Do you have frequent loose bowel movements or are you constipated?
9. Do you drink a lot of carbonated beverages or distilled water?
10. Are you anemic no matter how well you eat?

Scoring: If you have answered yes to 3 or more of these questions, poor nutrition may be contributing to your memory problems.

HORMONE IMBALANCE SELF-TEST

Do you have any of the following?

1. Hot flashes or night sweats
2. Trouble sleeping

3. A personal or family history of PMS or menopause symptoms
4. Lowered libido
5. Vaginal dryness
6. Feelings of panic
7. Increased hypoglycemia reactions
8. Unexplained mental and physical exhaustion
9. Water retention
10. Proneness to accidents

Scoring: If you are menopausal or peri-menopausal, either naturally or medically, or if you are postpartum or have PMS or fibroids, and have answered yes to any of these questions, you are likely to have a hormone imbalance that may be contributing to your memory problems.

Lifestyle Factors

Lifestyle factors include lack of exercise, habits such as smoking and consuming excess alcohol or caffeine, and patterns that disrupt your body's rhythms of activity and rest. These often accompany and are interrelated with stress and depression.

EXERCISE

1. Do you avoid exercise?
2. Do you have a sedentary job?
3. Are you overweight or underweight?
4. Do you drive everywhere rather than walk or bicycle?
5. Do you sit for hours without taking breaks for walking and stretching?

HABITS

1. Do you smoke?
2. Do you drink more than two alcoholic drinks per day?
3. Do you drink more than two cups of coffee, or four cups of tea, or two caffeine-containing beverages every day?
4. Do you use other nonprescription or prescription drugs regularly?

BODY RHYTHMS

1. Do you need an alarm clock to wake up?
2. Are you tired during the day?
3. Do you sometimes find yourself dozing off while driving or working?
4. Does your work require you to change shifts, or do you work night shifts?
5. Do you fly frequently and experience jet lag?
6. Is your memory worse by the end of the day?
7. Do you override your body's need for rest by staying up late or substituting caffeine for a nap?
8. Are you constipated or do you ignore the urge to have a bowel movement until it is convenient?

EXPOSURE TO TOXIC SUBSTANCES

1. Do you live in a big city or industrial area?
2. Do you live near a dry cleaner or have your clothes dry-cleaned?
3. Do you have new furniture or carpeting, or have you recently painted your home or office, or

made other home changes without checking on the toxicity of the products used?

4. Are you exposed to pesticides at home, work, or play (such as on a golf course)?
5. Do you have a history of surgery and anesthesia, or do you take medication?
6. Do you spend many hours near a computer or other electromagnetic-emitting appliance?

Scoring: If you have answered yes to at least 5 out of the 23 lifestyle questions, lifestyle factors may be contributing to your memory problems.

Most "normal" cognitive problems are due to life changes and pressures such as stress, poor nutrition, lack of exercise, hormone imbalance, and unhealthy habits. Most women who take this quiz should be reassured that they have "normal" mild to moderate memory loss, and should feel motivated to do something about it.

Now you understand the way memory works, and the factors that may be contributing to memory loss. You've learned to identify your individual needs and problem areas. The second half of this book will outline my Six-Step Program of nutrition, supplements, herbs, hormone balancing, exercise, and stress management. Before you begin, learn how to individualize the program and tailor each component to target your specific needs, as I explain in the following chapter.

Dr. Lottor's
Six-Step Program

CHAPTER 7

Your Individualized
Brain-Boosting Program

*F*ew things in life seem as elusive and immaterial as our thoughts and feelings. Yet all knowledge and memory exist as a physical entity—in the biochemical structures of our nerve cells, in changes in our genetic codes, and in bioelectric currents of pure energy. Because these things are physical—or at least have physical counterparts—they can be affected by physical forces. The first part of this book helped you determine which physical forces are working against you—poor nutrition, alcohol, drugs, stress, toxins, and inadequate mental exercise and rest. In this chapter you'll see how to use beneficial physical forces—the six steps in my program—to work for you.

The six steps are straightforward changes you can accomplish on your own:

1. Maximize nourishing foods and minimize anti-nutrients
2. Take nutritional supplements
3. Take herbs and other botanicals
4. Balance your hormones
5. Exercise your body and brain
6. De-stress and streamline your life

This program is designed to help you protect your brain from damage, build it up, and restore your memory and ability to concentrate. All six steps contribute to improving memory by dealing with the underlying causes of memory loss, and do so without depending on estrogen replacement therapy. The program is tailored to the special needs of women both as a group and as individuals, and emphasizes the importance of supplying the brain with the natural substances needed to help it heal itself. I hope to encourage your body to optimally produce and use neurotransmitters, protect the structure of neurons, and increase neuron growth. Overall, this book aims to diminish the sense of powerlessness, hopelessness, helplessness, anxiety, and isolation that so many people with memory loss feel.

Getting Started

To begin, get acquainted with the program by reading through the following chapters. Based on your self-assessment in chapter 6, identify the approaches most likely to improve your memory, and then gradually start to make changes. Although you may be highly motivated and want to change everything at once, I recommend that you introduce only one or two changes at a time. Be sure to take into consideration not only what the self-assessment suggests, but also your financial situation and what you can spare of your time and energy. Remember, too, that the natural approaches in my program generally take time to have an effect. So, once you have introduced a change into your life, hold to it consistently for at least two weeks and preferably for one month, then reevaluate your memory using the self-assessment. You may also want to take a few minutes at the end of each day to record your mental symptoms. Since memory is the problem, a daily diary may be the only way you can accurately keep track of what's going on. Once you notice positive changes in your mind and memory, decide if you want to try improving further by adding one or two more changes. Or you may want to increase the intensity of the changes you have already made, for example, by increasing the dosage of a supplement or botanical, or by exercising six days a week instead of three. Before beginning the program, make yourself a promise to be realistic, and be kind and good to yourself. Chances are you've got plenty on your plate already—the idea is not to give you so much more that you stress out over it! Ask yourself some questions: What am I ready to change now? What am I most likely to keep up? Pick and choose those approaches that are most likely to be effective in your individual case.

For example, in your self-assessment you may have answered "yes" to seven questions about poor nutrition, five questions about stress, and three questions about lifestyle. Nutrition would be your highest priority, so begin by making changes in your diet as recommended in chapter 8. Make sure you eat more fish such as salmon and tuna, because they contain the protein and essential fatty acids your brain needs to produce neurotransmitters and keep neurons healthy and functioning. Keep tabs on your intake of fresh vegetables and fruits, because they are rich in brain-cell protecting antioxidants such as vitamin C and beta-carotene.

Nutritional changes may be all you wish to focus on at first. However, if, after giving dietary changes a chance, you are not satisfied with the results, you will need to add another component, such as the nutritional supplements described in chapter 9. Although many people with nutritional problems will improve just by making dietary changes alone, it's hard to get adequate amounts of most brain-supporting vitamins and minerals from food— especially the B vitamins and protective antioxidants. Taking a multivitamin formula fills the gap. Perhaps you will also want to add some amino acid supplements such as phenylalanine and acetylcholine, which are the building blocks for neurotransmitters.

After you have implemented supplements, reassess yourself again in two to four weeks. If you want to see more improvement, add a third approach, such as a stress-reduction technique from chapter 13. I have seen many women improve their brainpower dramatically once they start calming and clearing their minds with meditation. Meditation has been shown to enhance the type of brain waves related to an improved ability to think and learn.

If you have a diagnosed medical condition that may be contributing to your memory problems, my program is a helpful complement to medical treatment. For example, if you have low blood sugar and trouble concentrating, you need to follow a primarily dietary approach with perhaps a few supplements and herbs to help regulate glucose. If you have poor circulation, you will benefit from an artery-unclogging diet, supplements that reduce the risk of heart disease, and an appropriate amount of exercise.

My Program in Action

My program combines a number of different components, and it works. Take, for example, the story of Alice, an actress. When menopause hit she began to notice that she was having trouble remembering her lines. She was already following a rather healthy lifestyle, but she needed to pay more attention to her program and fine-tune it. As an actress Alice had to stay on top of things and look good for her work, so she was willing to change her diet (she actually needed to add some whole grains and other healthy carbohydrates) and improve her exercise regimen by taking long walks near her home in the Los Angeles hills. Alice now takes estrogen replacement therapy, a "high-end" multi-nutrient formula that includes vitamins, minerals, several herbs, and other botanicals, and Coenzyme Q-10. She also takes a separate supplement of the herb Ginkgo biloba, a plant-based medicine called vinpocetine, a growth-hormone supplement, and the smart drug Deprenyl. Alice has definitely noticed an improvement in her ability to remember her lines, and has the confidence to go after—and get—significant parts in major movies.

Working with Your Doctor

In deciding whether to seek a medical evaluation, consider three things: the frequency, the intensity, and the duration of your mental lapses. In other words, how often do they occur and are they occurring more frequently than usual? Are they intense enough to affect your life or are they a danger to yourself or others? How long do they last—do you miss a moment or are you losing entire days? Are you having noticeable problems fulfilling your job responsibilities? Are your lapses on the level of, "Oh, I forgot to buy mayonnaise!" or "Ohmigod, I left the oven on"? Do you forget the keys to your home or do you forget where your home is?

If you suspect that a more serious problem exists, I cannot emphasize strongly enough the importance of obtaining a medical evaluation and establishing a good working relationship with a knowledgeable physician or healthcare provider. Memory loss can be a marker for serious medical conditions and these would need to be ruled out, or treated, before beginning my program.

You may see your primary care physician, gynecologist, or an endocrinologist or neurologist trained in memory loss. There are several well-understood and recognized causes of memory loss, including overt nutritional deficiency, alcohol and drug abuse, cardiac insufficiency, and tumors. Cardiovascular disease, high blood sugar, diabetes, and thyroid dysfunction can also contribute to memory problems, so you should get a thorough physical examination and follow up with lab tests if your doctor suspects any of these conditions. You also should assess any medications you are taking to see if they may be culprits (see list in chapter 4). A PET scan and other tests can show if your brain is getting enough blood, and whether glucose is being used properly in your brain. There are blood and urine tests to see if you are producing enough neurotransmitters, and to determine your hormone levels.

I must warn you that many doctors will prescribe estrogen or antidepressants or sedatives because these are the kinds of medications they are familiar with. But these medicines do not treat all the underlying causes of memory loss, and can trigger annoying or serious side effects now, or down the road. It may be more convenient for everybody if you just pop a pill; even if depression, anxiety stress and insomnia, and low estrogen are contributing causes, however, there are natural remedies for these ailments that are safer and more effective in the long run.

Unfortunately, under the current health insurance system, you may not have much choice. You may have access only to doctors who are under such pressure to see so many patients in a day that they can only spare a few minutes of attention per patient, enough time to scribble out a prescription. Fortunately, natural medicines are becoming more credible, accepted, and available. Yet they are still not cheap or commonly covered by insurance plans. Someday this will change, as more people, including mainstream medical-care providers, realize that many natural medicines are both effective and cost-effective in the long run. What's more, instead of harmful side effects, natural medicines have beneficial effects on health in general, such as lowered risk of heart disease, cancer, osteoporosis, overweight, and diabetes.

Interestingly, many women liken certain aspects of their cognitive problems—such as inability to concentrate or easy distractability—to an attention deficit disorder (coupled with hyperactivity, or ADHD). Many experts who treat ADD naturally recommend a program that is similar to this one—supporting a commonality of symptoms, and suggesting a common underlying cause or causes.

Why You Should Act Now

Why wait to try to turn things around? Each moment that you are bothered by forgetfulness reduces your quality of life. And while scientists can't say for sure that any person who has memory lapses, or age-related cognitive decline, or even mild cognitive impairment will be on the road to developing Alzheimer's, why take the chance? Why sit back and wait to see if you are one of the unlucky ones who progresses beyond mild forgetfulness? Educator and consultant Parris Kidd, Ph.D., has written in the *Alternative Medicine Review,* "A workable approach to curbing this virtual epidemic of dementia hinges on the development of a strategy for halting (or at least slowing) cognitive decline before it crosses the threshold to dementia. Research is progressing towards the definition of a 'window of opportunity' for effective intervention to halt the progression to dementia." This window of opportunity, according to Kidd, "probably is closed when so many circuits cannot sufficiently adapt to maintain an acceptable level of learning, recollection, or concentration." There's no question: early intervention is your best bet. By beginning my program now, you may be able to slow the breakdown of the functioning of your brain cells and memory circuits.

Your brain is an organ. As with your other organs, you can take measures to strengthen it just like you strengthen your body. The steps in my brain-boosting program are ultimately quite compatible with other health-building or anti-aging measures you may already take. Many of us spend a lot of time, effort, and money taking care of our bodies—we stretch and lift weights and run to remain flexible, build muscle, and become physically fit—but we ignore the most important organ, the seat of the conscious mind, and of the soul. When you start my program, you start to pay attention to the most important organ of the most important person in your life—you.

CHAPTER 8

Step One

Food *for* Thought

Dear Dr. Lottor:

I just wanted to let you know how wonderful I feel after making the changes you suggested. I find I have more sustained energy throughout the day, my moods are more even (my husband noticed that), and best of all, I wake up refreshed, clear-headed, and ready to take on the day. How can it be that my whole mental outlook and even my memory has improved, just because I changed my diet?

M.W., Malibu, California

*T*his is just one of the many letters I receive from my patients that prove to me how, time and again, food can make a huge difference in the way my patients feel, think, and remember. Food is the cornerstone of my program because food is the soil that nourishes the plant. You need to be adequately nourished for your brain and body to work properly. This is the place to start your program if the self-assessment in chapter 6 shows that your eating habits could be contributing to your memory problems. Even if you eat a basically healthy diet already, chances are that you can still fine-tune your meals so they emphasize "brain foods." These include foods that supply the nutrients needed to form neurotransmitters and other components of the brain, protect brain cells from aging and harmful chemicals, and improve or help prevent such brain-draining chronic conditions as low blood sugar or circulatory problems. In addition, the supplements, herbs, botanicals, and other aspects of my program work best if you first supply the raw materials for them to use. These raw materials come from the foods you eat.

You've probably heard the expression that fish is brain food, but did you ever wonder why? Did you realize that sugar, complex carbohydrates, protein, and fats all affect brain metabolism? Did you know that you need to eat foods high in B vitamins and antioxidants every day to maintain optimum brain function and slow the aging process? When eating a low-fat diet, do you distinguish between good and bad fats? Do you know which foods are linked with cardiovascular disease and poor circulation, both of which lead to poor brain function? Do you regularly eat foods containing chemicals that can damage brain cells? By the time you finish reading this chapter, you will know the answers to these questions and how to apply them to your own life. In addition, I will supply you with several delicious recipes to start you on the road to eating the kinds of foods that help, not hurt, your brain.

Although I do not advocate being overweight by any means, I do object to the be-thin-at-any-cost mentality that is running rampant in this country. If you go to extremes—by skipping meals or following an unbalanced fad diet—to achieve a certain body image, you are short-changing your brain of nutrients. If you are fat-phobic and keeping your percentage of body fat too low, you may be making it impossible for your body to produce the estrogen your brain needs. That having been said, many of my patients—and American women in general—need to lose weight or at least watch their weight in order to achieve optimum body and brain health. This chapter shows you how to eat well without gaining weight and without starving your brain of essential nutrients.

Why My Food Plan Is Good for Your Brain

An overwhelming amount of evidence supports food as the first weapon against poor health and premature aging, but you can also use food to specifically boost brainpower and restore brain health in the face of physical and mental assaults. This way of eating not only aids memory directly by keeping your brain healthy—it also balances blood sugar and supplies foods that improve your health generally and may also decrease your risk of serious diseases such as heart disease and cancer.

My brain-supporting diet plan consists of a wide

PREVENTING ALZHEIMER'S

Food can affect the overall health and functioning of your body and brain. Recent studies indicate that what you eat may also protect you from Alzheimer's disease and other dementias. According to research presented at the World Alzheimer Congress 2000, eating large amounts of vegetables rich in vitamin E, beta-carotene, and vitamin C is associated with a decreased risk of dementia and Alzheimer's disease. According to another paper presented at the congress, a high-fat diet during early and mid-adulthood may also be associated with increased risk of developing Alzheimer's, especially in people with a specific genetic marker called the ApoE-e4 allele. In two other studies presented, individuals who were taking certain cholesterol-lowering medications called statins were about 70 percent less likely to have dementia than those who were not diagnosed with high cholesterol, or those taking other cholesterol-lowering medications. The next question to pose is whether it was the drugs themselves or the lowered cholesterol that reduced the incidence of dementia—and whether natural methods to lower cholesterol are as effective.

variety of foods and emphasizes an array of wholesome ingredients: fresh fruits, vegetables, and whole grains that are high in vitamins and minerals; a moderate amount of protein foods; and a modest amount of fat with the emphasis on the right kinds of fats. In following this pattern you will be eating a balanced whole-foods diet that includes sufficient amounts of protein and amino acids to support brain nutrition and provide the building blocks for neurotransmitter production. You will be eating foods high in B vitamins and antioxidants, which are needed for optimum brain function, protection against damage, and premature, accelerated aging. The plan emphasizes brain-cell nourishing essential fatty acids, and virtually eliminates the bad fats that slow down digestion and make important nutrients unavailable for up to three hours, thus affecting short-term memory. It also avoids foods containing chemicals that can damage brain cells.

There's No Such Thing As Too Many Fruits and Vegetables

All vitamins and minerals work together in the body to activate the chemical reactions we produce to stay alive. Breathing, blinking, reading, running, digesting, fighting viruses, and thinking and remembering—vitamins and minerals are used in everything we do. My eating plan emphasizes fresh fruits and vegetables and whole grains, which are naturally rich sources of vitamins. The vitamins and minerals most associated with brain functions are the B vitamins, found most abundantly in leafy green vegetables and whole, unprocessed grains. Some vitamins, such as vitamin E, beta-carotene, and vitamin C, are antioxidants. Antioxidants protect us from free radicals, the molecules that damage cells and tissues including brain cells. Antioxidants protect your blood vessels from free-radical damage and thus help prevent clogs in arteries, including those that supply the brain. It is often said that "what is good for the head is good for the heart," because of the benefits of clean, healthy arteries to both. Foods especially rich in antioxidants include the most colorful fruits and vegetables—the more colorful and the deeper the color, the better. Antioxidants are also found in many herbs, green tea, and garlic.

I believe vegetables are the carriers of the life force, and therefore one of the key elements necessary for longevity and good health. All foods, but vegetables in particular, are transmuted energy from the sun. This is not so much the case when we eat animal protein, however, since the chicken, for example, eats the corn, and we eat the chicken. But there's no middleman with fruits and vegetables. Because of this—and because they are so high in beta-carotene, cancer-preventing nutrients, and fiber—it is a good practice to consume both raw and cooked vegetables with most meals. When the weather is hot, salads are perfect. In the winter, put vegetables in soups and stews, and serve them baked and steamed as main courses or sides.

Many people actually like vegetables, but their lives are so busy that they don't have the time to eat right or prepare food. Leah, for example, says, "I love to eat greens—if only someone would prepare them for me! I have often spent four dollars for a beautiful bunch of organic broccoli—and let it sit in the refrigerator until it rotted. In spite of my best efforts to take time for meals, I often eat on the run. My partner and I rarely have dinner together. When we do, we usually haven't planned in advance and may end up eating take-out food." Although it's not an ideal situation, as a start, Leah and her equally harried partner could buy frozen vegetables rather than fresh, and bring home already washed and cut vegetables and salads from a salad bar.

To make the transition easier, start by emphasizing fruits and vegetables you already like. You are probably already eating potatoes, corn, peas, tomatoes, carrots, celery, zucchini, iceberg lettuce, apples, bananas, oranges, lemons, pears, and watermelon. Why not add color and variety to your diet by broadening your palate to include fruits and vegetables you have been eating less frequently or not at all? Consider broccoli, green beans, mushrooms, beets, spinach, cauliflower, peppers, cabbage, sweet potatoes, watercress, romaine lettuce, winter squash, asparagus, brussels sprouts, kale, collards, turnip greens, bok choy, artichokes, arugula, fennel, endive, sprouts, grapes, strawberries, cantaloupe, cherries, persimmons, pomegranates, prunes, peaches, raisins, pineapple, grapefruit, blueberries, avocado, rhubarb, apricots, blackberries, raspberries, limes, kiwi, tangerines, mango, papaya, plums, and dates.

Take a cue from one of my patients, who had a wonderful way of increasing her taste for vegetables. She brought home a different vegetable from the local farmers' market every week, and both she and her husband looked forward to the weekly culinary adventure. Eating seasonally and locally grown foods keeps appetites and anticipation sharp. If you make it a habit to purchase your produce weekly at your local farmers' market, you will begin to recognize the superior taste of fresh, locally grown fruits and vegetables as compared to the supermarket, frozen, or canned versions.

Not All Carbs Are Bad

Carbohydrates are needed to fuel the body and brain and create mental energy. The healthiest carbohydrates are complex carbohydrates found in whole grains, beans, nuts, fruits, and vegetables. The body digests these complex molecular structures slowly, making these foods more filling than simple sugars and providing a steadier supply of the glucose your brain needs for energy. These foods are also generally relatively high in the vitamins and minerals needed to support brain cell function and production and neurotransmitter production. In addition, complex carbohydrate foods contain more fiber than simple sugars and refined-carbohydrate foods, such as white bread. Fiber not only aids digestion: it prevents constipation and may help prevent colon cancer and breast cancer. By lowering cholesterol and blood sugar levels, fiber may also protect you from circulatory problems such as cerebral insufficiency, which can lead to memory and thinking problems, heart disease, and diabetes.

By way of contrast, foods high in simple carbohydrates like sugar are digested quickly, causing the rapid rise and fall of glucose levels in the blood. Americans eat an average of 150 pounds of sugar and other sweeteners every year. Our collective sweet tooth is a health problem for many reasons. Sugar contains no other nutrients than calories; if your body doesn't expend the calories as energy, they turn into fat. Furthermore, in the process of using sugar to create energy, or by converting the excess sugar into fat, the body depletes itself of its own stores of nutrients, including B vitamins and the minerals chromium, zinc, and copper. High sugar intake also increases the excretion of nutrients by the body such as calcium, magnesium, and chromium, and limits our ability to absorb calcium. Sugar eaten in excess can lead to blood sugar problems, which can lead to mental confusion, brain fog, and problems concentrating.

My eating plan will help you reduce the amount of sugar and refined carbohydrates you eat, and will keep you on a more even keel. But if you already have blood sugar problems, you will need to fine-tune this diet further by choosing foods with a low glycemic index. The glycemic index is a way of measuring the rate at which a food elevates blood sugar levels. The higher the index, the faster the effect. It's not surprising that refined white sugar has the highest glycemic index—100. What may surprise you is that most pastas and breads, and white rice and white potatoes, also have a high glycemic index of 70 or more, and thus should be minimized if you have a blood sugar problem. On the other hand, most fruits have a moderate or low glycemic index of 50 or less, even though they contain a lot of sugar in the form of fructose. As you might expect, most vegetables are low on the glycemic index. Certain vegetables, such as sweet potatoes and carrots, are sugary, but as is the case with fruit, they also contain a lot of fiber, which slows carbohydrate digestion.

I have seen firsthand how a high-sugar diet can contribute to a variety of mental emotional states, including mood swings, depression, anxiety, panic, paranoia, mental and physical fatigue, and a spaced-out feeling. The first time I met Sally, a patient of mine, she was addicted to sugar. Although she was having some problems at work that she felt were a direct result of eating too much sugar, she refused to give it up. As a result, she found she was irritable and short with co-workers. She was spacey and would often forget where she filed things, or would even put things in the wrong place, like a pen in the refrigerator. She would have no recollection of what she had done until she opened the refrigerator and found the pen by accident.

Her case was a challenge, as she wasn't really motivated to cook, make changes to her diet, or even to eat balanced meals. So we began slowly, with a change she was comfortable with. She was amenable to switching to energy bars instead of regular candy bars, and she did not feel deprived. In this way we took the first step on the road to healthful eating for mental alertness. On her next visit, Sally reported that she was feeling so much better, she was ready to include some fruits and vegetables as snacks.

To make the transition easier, try gradually substituting honey for sugar, whole grain flours for white bleached flour when baking, and whole wheat or corn tortillas for white bread and rolls. To wean yourself off of cookies and chips, don't keep them in the house; rather, keep whole natural foods like baby carrots or air-popped popcorn on hand for snacking. Or try one of these tasty alternatives: an apple and a handful of walnuts; a banana with some peanut butter spread on it; bean dip with cut-up raw vegetables like celery, carrots, and jicama; guacamole or tofu dip with baked chips. Use vegetarian cookbooks, which are a gold mine of ideas for ways to prepare and combine vegetables and other healthy ingredients.

Perfect Proteins

While fruits, vegetables, and whole grains are healthful, the body also requires protein. Protein is needed to repair and replace cells, and is the building block for biochemicals such as enzymes and brain chemicals. In the United States, however, too much, rather than too little, protein is the norm. Eating excess protein contributes to a host of health problems, including heart disease, colon cancer, osteoporosis, and constipation. Most of the protein we consume comes from animal products like beef, chicken, turkey, pork, fish, eggs, milk, and cheese, some of which are also high in saturated fat.

Because protein is so concentrated in animal products, cutting your intake of these foods is by far the best way to bring your protein down to a healthier level. Replacing some animal proteins with vegetable proteins is wise, too, because vegetable sources can contain more vitamins, minerals, carbohydrates, and fiber, and come packaged without the saturated fat found in animal products. Recently, several high-protein diets have become very popular. Against my advice, many of my patients gave up carbohydrates and ate only proteins and fats. At first they felt great, but in a few months they became depressed, slept poorly, became constipated, and craved sugar. So, extreme diets or diets that eliminate a complete food group can present problems in the long run. A balanced diet contains protein, fats, carbohydrates, vitamins, and minerals. Aim for a balanced amount of protein in each meal—about 15 percent of your total calories.

Despite most Americans' excess-protein problems, I've seen women who mistakenly skimp on protein: they eat a high-carbohydrate diet, or just don't eat enough—period. If you feel the need to eat all day or have a snack an hour after you've eaten, this indicates that your last meal did not meet your nutritional requirements, and that the snack you crave is meant to complete the deficiency. Such was the case with Pauline, a petite yoga teacher, who told me that she was a "grazer." In other words, she ate all day long, instead of having set meals. It was clear to me that an apple, some green pepper, a salad, a carrot, and popcorn do not constitute the elements of a balanced diet. Invariably, when people become more conscious of what they eat, they notice that making just small changes can have incredible results. When Pauline added some protein to her breakfast shake, and some beans to her salad, and ate a real dinner, her energy was more sustained, and her ability to concentrate during her meditation and yoga classes improved dramatically.

The timing, not just the amount, of protein consumption can have an impact on your ability to think. If you need to be more alert during the day, try to eat more protein and vegetables for breakfast and lunch because protein contains more dopamine, a neurotransmitter that keeps the brain "turned on." Reserve those higher carb meals of pasta and grains for nighttime, because they are serotonin precursors and will make you more physically and mentally relaxed.

To make the transition easier, if you are eating too much protein, think of protein more as a condiment than as the meal's star attraction. Emphasize the role of vegetables, and substitute "clean protein foods," such as fish, skinless chicken and turkey, beans, nuts, and cheese, for high-fat, high-salt foods like hot dogs, hamburgers, and red meats. If you don't have time for a full meal and are tempted to skip the protein, make a protein smoothie that you can drink on the run. They are great for a quick meal, warm weather snack, or when you are going to the gym and can't really eat, but want something fast and nutritious. Blend fresh fruit chunks, a nondairy milk, and protein powder. It's fine to use a bit of frozen fruit in a pinch, and it gives the drink more texture; my patients use frozen strawberries, pineapple, or blueberries. You can even make enough to leave in the refrigerator so you have a healthful snack when you get home from work. Or freeze the leftovers for a frosty dessert later on.

The Good Fats

If you believe the commercials and some extreme diet plans, all fat is bad, bad, bad. This is not true. All women need some fat in their diets—your body needs fats in order to absorb minerals and carry certain fat-soluble vitamins, such as A, D, E, and K, through the system. Fats are also a part of our cell membranes, including those of nerve cells, and are needed to produce hormones. Your brain is the fattiest organ in your body—it's composed of 40 percent fat. So, don't shortchange your brain by avoiding all fat, just limit your fat intake to 40 grams or less per day. If you want to lose weight, limit yourself to 30 grams or less.

My eating plan supplies you with the necessary *essential fatty acids,* or *EFAs,* which are by and large the "good" fats. Essential fatty acids are used in forming neurotransmitters needed for brain cells to communicate with each other. They are found in every cell of our bodies, including the brain's neurons, and bring fluidity to the cell membranes, which allows them to absorb nutrients and get rid of toxic waste products. In this country, we eat an excess of one type of EFA, called "omega-6," and consume too little of another type, "omega-3." (For more about omega-3 and the brain, see chapter 9.) Our ancestors' diets included roughly equal amounts of the two fatty acids, omega-3 and omega-6, and my eating plan helps restore the balance. Omega-3 fatty acids are found in varying amounts in seeds, nuts, and beans as well as the oils made from them, including flaxseed, hemp, canola, soy, and walnut oils; in dark green leafy vegetables; and in fatty fish such as herring, salmon, cod, and tuna. Food sources of the often overconsumed omega-6 fatty acids include vegetable oils like safflower, sunflower, corn, and peanut. Also, if your diet contains too many processed foods, which are high in hydrogenated fats, trans-fatty acids, and saturated fats, this tends to concentrate the omega-6s in your blood at the expense of the more desirable omega-3s.

I encourage the consumption of *mono-unsaturated fats* as well, because they seem to lower levels of *low-density lipoproteins,* or the "bad" LDL cholesterol, while raising levels of *high-density lipoproteins* or "good" HDL cholesterol, which lowers risk of cardiovascular disease. The best sources of mono-unsaturated fat are olive oil, peanut oil, avocados, and cashews.

Many women need to change both the amount and type of fats they are eating. Excess fat in itself seems to be unhealthy, but another downside is that the more we fill up on fatty calories, the less room we have for healthier foods such as fresh fruits and vegetables. As a nation, we consume far too much fat—the equivalent of six to eight tablespoons daily. All we really need is the equivalent of about one tablespoon of high-quality fats per day and this can be obtained from a whole-foods diet that contains small amounts of high-quality cooking oils, salad dressings made with appropriate oils, and fresh nuts.

I remember meeting Karen, a private trainer at my gym in Santa Monica. She had a truly perfect body. We would often sit near each other on the lifecycle and chat, and when she found out my line of work, she confided to me that not only was her hair falling out, but she had chronic fatigue syndrome and memory loss. Upon questioning her, I found out that because she needed to be lean for her work, her diet contained only 10 percent fat—women need about 25 to 30 percent. When she followed my suggestion to add two tablespoons of flaxseed oil to her diet per day, she immediately noticed that she was thinking much more clearly.

Although I recommend some fats, my eating plan is

low in *saturated fat,* because this type of fat tends to raise cholesterol and clog your arteries and your brain. Eating saturated fat may also raise your risk of Parkinson's disease and of breast, ovarian, and colon cancers. Animal products are the main source of saturated fats, but some vegetable oils such as palm and coconut oil also contain saturated fat. Hydrogenated vegetable oils have been chemically changed into saturated fats by adding hydrogen atoms, and they shrivel your brain cells, making it difficult for nutrients to get in and toxins to get out. They are used to increase shelf life in solid margarine and processed foods such as pastries and baked goods. The latest evidence shows hydrogenated oils are even worse for your circulatory health than butter, and thus also are bad for your brain.

My diet plan is also relatively low in *polyunsaturated fats.* Although they appear to lower cholesterol in the blood, and may be less promoting of heart disease than saturated fats, polyunsaturated fats cause inflammation and plaque formation in your arteries. Furthermore, they are implicated in many types of cancer, including those of the colon, breast, and uterus. This type of fat is particularly vulnerable to damage by free radicals, and heating or cooking with polyunsaturated fats also creates free radicals. Vegetable oils such as corn, sunflower, and sesame are high in polyunsaturated fats, and you should keep these to a minimum to protect your brainpower.

To make the transition easier, begin by avoiding all fried and deep-fried foods, if you eat them now. Sauté foods in a small amount of oil instead. Better yet, steam, bake, or broil foods, without added fat or using just a spray of olive oil. Steaming vegetables until tender yet still bright in color preserves their nutrients better than boiling or overcooking. Try dressing up steamed vegetables with a dollop of mild salsa or melted cheddar soy cheese. Although a staple in low-fat cooking, avoid using a microwave because there is evidence that microwaves break delicate chemical bonds in foods, and microwave ovens tend to leak electromagnetic radiation, which may be harmful.

Processed Foods

My plan avoids processed foods as much as possible, because they are low in mind-boosting nutrients and full

---

EATING ORGANIC

I feel the best brain food is also "clean" food that does not add to your body's burden. That's why I recommend food that is not only unprocessed and additive-free, but also organically grown. Although "clean" foods are often (but not always) more expensive and harder to find than conventionally grown foods, they are worth the time and investment. This is especially true since they are superior not just in health but in taste.

Your local health food store is a good place to start. Many chain supermarkets have also begun to carry extensive lines of organic produce and products. (If they don't, request that they do—that's how change happens.) With the advent of farmers' markets in most cities and towns, you can buy produce that is not only organic, but fresher because it is locally grown.

of sugar, hydrogenated fats, and additives. Here are some of the culprits: candy, cookies, pastries, muffins (which are just little cakes), pies, sodas, ice cream, snack foods such as potato and corn chips, and fatty fast foods such as burgers and fries. You should save these for special occasions, if you eat them at all. I also recommend that you limit coffee or other caffeinated beverages to no more than one to two cups per day, preferably in the morning. Despite all of its reputed anti-cholesterol attributes, alcohol is still a risk factor for breast cancer, so I recommend moderate alcohol consumption—one to two drinks per week. Many people's nightly glass of wine with dinner becomes three glasses before they know it. What is particularly interesting is that everyone has a different tolerance and metabolism of alcohol, so even a half of a cocktail or one beer for

---

If organic food is too costly or just hard to come by, consider switching to organic as a substitute for the worst offenders. According to the organization Mothers and Others for a Livable Planet, the ten most contaminated foods—and hence, the most important foods to buy in organic form—are strawberries, rice, milk, corn, bananas, green beans, peaches, apples, and oats and other grains. Root vegetables may also be particularly contaminated as they grow in the soil and are more likely to absorb toxins in the earth. Minimizing or eliminating meat and meat products will also help, because animals are high on the food chain, which means that pesticides and other toxins accumulate in their cells and thus make meat a concentrated source of these harmful chemicals. If you do eat meat and dairy, be sure they come from animals that have been raised organically.

one person can be the same as a half a bottle of wine or a six pack for another.

To make the transition easier, read labels and don't eat anything with an ingredient whose name you don't recognize or can't pronounce. If you must buy prepared foods because of a too-busy life, choose the low-fat, low-salt varieties that used to be sold only in health food stores, but which are becoming more widely available. Substitute tea for coffee, and fruit juice mixed with mineral water for alcoholic beverages.

Brain-Boosting Daily Eating Plan

To begin following the plan, keep a food diary for at least one week, writing down everything that you eat, including snacks and beverages. Then compare your daily eating habits with the foods and suggested amounts outlined in the next section, Daily Servings for a Healthy Brain. This first step will show you where your diet could use improvement, and indicate whether your memory or thinking problems could be, in part, diet related. How you introduce these ideal types and amounts of food into your daily meals is up to you. The choices you make about which foods to eat and when to eat them depend on your lifestyle, your body chemistry and metabolism, your taste buds, and, often, other people in your life. Trying to achieve an optimum diet is a gradual process. Make small changes slowly, as suggested above, rather than aiming for the kind of sweeping changes that are difficult to adhere to and cause more stress for you and your family. Very few people can change their way of eating in a matter of days or even weeks. Each person needs a transition period.

Daily Servings for a Healthy Brain

LOW-STARCH VEGETABLES

3 to 4 cups per day

Choose from the following: broccoli, carrots, spinach, lettuce, onions, celery, string beans, artichoke, summer squash, endive, cabbage, cucumbers, asparagus, chard, peppers, parsley, sprouts, and tomatoes. Be sure to include 1 cup of high-calcium leafy greens such as collards, kale, dandelion and turnip greens, or bok choy in your daily amount.

STARCHY VEGETABLES

½ to 1 cup per day

Choose from the following: potatoes, yams, sweet potatoes, parsnips, winter squash, turnips, beets, artichokes, taro, and jerusalem artichokes.

FRESH FRUIT

1 to 3 servings/pieces per day

Choose from the following: apples, apricots, berries, banana, cantaloupe or other melon in season, cherries, peaches, plums, oranges, grapefruit, grapes, and kiwi. The more colorful and deeply colored the fruit, the more loaded with brain-protective nutrients. Try to include one orange-colored fruit per day.

WHOLE GRAINS

At least 2 cups per day

Choose from the following: brown rice, oats, corn, millet, barley, buckwheat, amaranth, quinoa, wheat (couscous, bulgar, wheat berries, whole wheat cooked cereal), triticale, and rye. Add 1 to 2 slices of whole grain bread, if desired.

BEANS AND OTHER LEGUMES

1 or more ½-cup servings per day (up to 4 servings if your primary source of protein)

Choose from the following: soy products such as tofu, textured vegetable protein (TVP) foods, split peas, lentils, kidney beans, navy beans, chickpeas, adzuki beans, black beans, white beans, and mung beans. Cooked dried soybeans are not recommended because they contain a protein-inhibiting enzyme; however, edamame (fresh frozen soybeans in the pod) are an excellent choice.

MEAT, FISH, POULTRY

1 serving of 4 to 5 ounces or less per day

Choose from the following: cold-water fish such as salmon, tuna, mackerel, and herring, which you should eat twice a week. Eat fresh, lean meats such as organically raised free-range turkey or chicken in moderation. Eggs should be fresh, organic, free-range, and raised locally; limit yourself to 3 to 4 per week, but you may eat egg whites in greater quantities and more frequently.

MILK (DAIRY OR NONDAIRY)

0 to 3 servings of 1 cup per day

Milks and milk products derived from vegetables such as soy, rice, almonds, or oats are preferable to animal milks. I do not recommend dairy products except for plain organic yogurt (avoid fruit-flavored yogurts, which are laden with sugar), or sour cream as a condiment.

ESSENTIAL FATS

2 to 3 teaspoons of unrefined vegetable oils of flaxseed or sesame seed per day

Use only organic, expeller-pressed oils; refrigerate once opened. Do not cook with these oils; rather, add them to salads and vegetables as dressings, stir into vegetable soups, stews, and cooked grains and cereals after cooking, and blend into fruit shakes and smoothies. You may also use small amounts of olive oil, which does not have essential oils, but, unlike polyunsaturated oil, is not damaged by heat and can be used for cooking as well as in salads and dressings.

NUTS AND SEEDS

2 to 3 tablespoons per day, if a source of protein

A small amount of fresh, preferably raw, unsalted nuts and seeds, or nut and seed butter, if desired.

WATER

At least eight 8-ounce glasses per day; purified or natural spring water is preferred.

If You Have a Food Allergy

If your answers to the questions in the self-assessment in chapter 6 suggest you might have a food allergy or sensitivity, you can still follow my basic eating plan—you may just need to avoid certain specific foods. Be sure to have your symptoms checked by a physician to make sure you don't have an underlying medical problem. Then, on your own or working with your doctor, become a nutrition detective by using the simple elimination and challenge procedure. This is the simplest way to determine whether you have food sensitivities.

Interestingly, it is sometimes the very food that we are allergic to that we are also addicted to. I often ask patients, if you could take only one food to a desert island, what food would that be? Invariably, when a blood test is done it shows up as a major allergy. To begin, do not eat foods containing these top ten offenders: Eggs, corn, chocolate, dairy, wheat, soy, citrus, peanuts, and food additives and preservatives.

Avoid these foods for eight to nine days. Be sure to read food labels carefully—prepared foods contain many hidden ingredients, in particular wheat, soy, milk, and eggs. Incredibly, some egg substitutes contain egg white, and some nondairy creamers contain milk. Keep a daily food diary to record what you eat and see if your symptoms improve.

If symptoms do improve after seven to fourteen days, determine the specific foods to which you are most sensitive by reintroducing one food at a time, every other day, to see if symptoms return. If, after you've eaten a particular food, symptoms do return, continue to avoid that food as much as possible. (You may want to try reintroducing it again after three months to see if you are still sensitive.) If symptoms do not return after reintroducing a specific food, you may continue to include that food in your regular diet. If you do not see any improvement, and you still suspect food allergies may be a trigger for your thinking problems, repeat the elimination and challenge procedure with the following other common allergens: peanuts; fish and shellfish, including shrimp and lobster; chocolate; fermented or mold-containing foods, such as baked goods with yeast as the leavening agent, some cheeses, dried fruits, mushrooms, soy sauce; vinegar and foods that contain vinegar, such as pickles, ketchup, salad dressings, mayonnaise, relish, sauerkraut; also avoid smoked meats including sausage, hot dogs, and corned beef; buttermilk, sour cream; and beer, wine, and cider. If you still have a problem after eliminating these elements, consult a professional with expertise in food allergies.

Ten Delicious Recipes to Boost Your Brain Power

What follows is a sampling of delicious recipes for breakfast, lunch, and dinner to get you eating foods that will feed your brain and please your palate. Healthy eating doesn't have to be bland, and tasty dishes don't necessarily require long preparation times. While most of these dishes can be prepared in under a half hour, some require longer cooking times, so plan ahead.

Multigrain Pancakes

MAKES 16 PANCAKES

1 cup whole wheat pastry flour
¾ cup cornmeal
½ cup oat or barley flour
1 tablespoon baking powder
½ teaspoon salt
1 cup low-fat or soy, rice, or oat milk
⅓ cup honey
¼ cup canola oil
1 egg or egg white, beaten

In a large bowl, stir together the whole wheat flour, cornmeal, oat flour, baking powder, and salt. In a medium bowl, beat together remaining wet ingredients. Add wet ingredients to dry ingredients and stir just until flours are moistened. Heat a large, lightly greased griddle or skillet over a medium flame. Pour about ¼ cup of the batter for each pancake onto griddle and cook for 2 or 3 minutes or until top edges are bubbly. Flip and cook for 1 to 2 minutes more. Keep warm in a 200-degree oven while preparing the rest of the pancakes. Serve with additional honey or all-fruit preserves.

Spinach, Corn, and Quinoa Soup

SERVES 4

2 cups water
2 13-ounce cans chicken broth
½ cup quinoa or other whole grain, rinsed
2 cups (about 8 ounces) cooked diced chicken breast

4 cups coarsely chopped spinach
1 cup whole kernel corn (not canned)
½ cup chopped scallions
Salt and freshly ground black pepper, to taste
Hot pepper sauce, to taste

In a 3-quart saucepan, bring water and chicken broth to a boil over high heat. Stir in quinoa and cooked chicken and simmer, covered, for 15 minutes. Add spinach, corn, and scallions and return to a boil. Reduce heat and let simmer 4 to 5 minutes or until quinoa is tender. Season to taste with salt, pepper, and hot pepper sauce.

Brown Rice and Lentil Soup

SERVES 6

2 tablespoons olive oil
1 cup chopped onion
1 cup finely diced carrots
1 cup diced celery
3 cloves garlic, minced
4 cups chicken or vegetable stock
3 cups water
1 cup long-grain brown rice
1 cup lentils, picked over and rinsed
1 14.5-ounce can whole peeled tomatoes
½ teaspoon dried basil
½ teaspoon dried thyme
1 bay leaf
1 tablespoon lemon juice
¼ cup chopped fresh parsley
¼ teaspoon freshly ground black pepper
Salt, to taste

In a 5-quart saucepan, heat oil over medium heat and add onion, carrot, celery, and garlic. Cook 5 to 6 minutes, until vegetables are crisp-tender. Add stock, water, brown rice, lentils, tomatoes, basil, thyme, and bay leaf. Break up whole tomatoes with the back of a wooden spoon. Bring soup to a boil, reduce heat. Simmer, covered, for 50 to 55 minutes, until rice and lentils are tender. Remove and discard bay leaf. Stir in lemon juice, parsley, pepper, and salt.

NOTE: If soup becomes too thick, add more stock or water until it reaches desired consistency.

Grilled Tuna with Orange and Almond Couscous

SERVES 4

MARINADE:

> ¼ cup lite (sodium-reduced) soy sauce
> 3 tablespoons lemon juice
> 1 tablespoon Dijon mustard
> 1 teaspoon grated lemon zest
> 1 clove garlic, minced
> 1½ to 2 pounds fresh tuna or salmon, cut into thick steaks

Combine all ingredients except fish in large glass bowl. Add fish and set aside at room temperature, covered, to marinate for 30 minutes, turning fish once.

COUSCOUS:

> 1 tablespoon olive oil
> ½ cup chopped onion
> 1 cup couscous

1 cup orange juice
¾ cup chicken or vegetable stock
¼ teaspoon freshly ground black pepper
¼ cup slivered almonds, toasted
2 tablespoons chopped fresh parsley

In a medium saucepan, heat oil over medium heat and add onion. Cook, stirring frequently, 4 to 5 minutes, until onion is softened. Add couscous, orange juice, stock, pepper, and salt. Bring to a boil; reduce heat, and simmer for 2 minutes. Cover pan and remove from heat. Let stand for 10 minutes. Stir in toasted almonds and parsley. Season with salt and pepper, to taste. Fluff couscous with fork before serving.

FISH:

Preheat broiler or grill. Remove fish from marinade and place on heated broiler pan or directly on grill, 4 to 5 inches from heat source. Cook 4 minutes or more on each side, depending on thickness, until cooked as desired; brush with remaining marinade. (To test for doneness, make a small slit in fish with knife.) Serve over couscous. Garnish with orange and lemon slices, if desired.

Salmon-Garbanzo Salad

SERVES 4

 2 cups cooked or canned garbanzo or other beans
 3¾-ounce can salmon or tuna, packed in water, drained
 1 small red onion, diced
 ⅓ cup minced fresh parsley
 3 tablespoons fresh lemon juice
 2 tablespoons minced fresh mint leaves
 2 tablespoons olive oil
 1 clove garlic, minced
 ⅛ teaspoon salt
 ⅛ teaspoon crushed red pepper flakes

Combine ingredients in a medium bowl. Serve at room temperature or chilled, over mixed salad greens. Leaving the salad (without the lettuce) in the refrigerator for a day or two will allow the flavors to develop.

Grilled Tuna Steaks with Spinach and White Beans

SERVES 2

 ⅓ cup mango chutney
 ¼ cup plain low-fat yogurt
 1 16-ounce can small white beans, drained and rinsed, or
   2 cups cooked white beans
 2 4-ounce tuna or salmon steaks
 1 tablespoon canola or olive oil
 3 cups shredded, well-cleaned spinach
 Pinch salt and freshly ground pepper
 1 tablespoon minced fresh parsley or cilantro leaves

Puree chutney and yogurt in a food processor. Place in small bowl, and stir in beans. Set aside at room temperature. Brush fish steaks with 1 teaspoon oil and grill over charcoal or in a grill pan for 4 minutes or more on each side, depending on thickness, until cooked as desired. (To test for doneness, make a small slit in fish with knife and taste.) Toss spinach with remaining oil, salt, and pepper. Place spinach on dinner plates and top with fish and then bean mixture. Sprinkle with parsley or cilantro and serve immediately.

Scallops with Fresh Lime

SERVES 4

Nonstick cooking spray
2 tablespoons extra virgin olive oil
1 tablespoon unsalted margarine
2 cups cherry tomato halves
1 cup julienned peeled carrots
6 scallions, whites and most of green, thinly sliced
¼ teaspoon crushed red pepper flakes
1 pound bay or sea scallops, washed and drained on paper towels
8 ounces linguine (preferably green), cooked and drained
Juice of one large lime

Spray the inside of a large skillet with the nonstick cooking spray. In the skillet, heat the oil and margarine for 2 minutes over medium heat until very hot. Add the tomatoes, carrots, scallions, and red pepper flakes and cook for 3 minutes. Stir in the scallops and cook until just golden and sizzling (about 3 minutes for bay scallops and 5 minutes for sea scallops). Avoid overcooking! Spoon scallops and vegetables over the hot linguine. Sprinkle with fresh lime juice and serve immediately.

Shrimp and Black Bean Salad

SERVES 6
LIME-GINGER VINAIGRETTE:
    ½ cup chicken or vegetable broth
    ¼ cup lime juice
    3 tablespoons extra virgin olive oil
    1 tablespoon minced fresh ginger
    ½ teaspoon ground coriander
    ½ teaspoon salt
    Hot pepper sauce, to taste

Whisk together ingredients in medium bowl and let stand at room temperature.

SALAD:
    3 cups cooked or canned black beans, drained and rinsed
    2 small heads romaine lettuce, shredded and rinsed
    1 small bunch arugula, rinsed, large stems removed
    2 bell peppers, one red, one yellow, seeded and diced
    10 scallions, minced
    ½ cup minced fresh cilantro
    1 bunch radishes, trimmed and thinly sliced
    Juice of 2 limes
    1 pound cooked medium shrimp, shelled and deveined
    ¼ cup toasted pine nuts

Place beans in medium bowl and toss with vinaigrette, set aside. In a large bowl, toss together all remaining ingredients except shrimp and pine nuts; divide between dinner plates. Top with bean mixture, then shrimp and pine nuts. Serve immediately.

Raspberry Almond Bean Pie

SERVES 6

1 prepared pie crust, homemade or store-bought
2 cups cooked cannelini beans
¼ cup plus 2 tablespoons sugar
¼ cup low-fat milk
1 egg
2 teaspoons grated lemon zest
1 teaspoon almond or vanilla extract
1 12-ounce package frozen raspberries, slightly defrosted
1 tablespoon cornstarch
2 tablespoons sliced almonds

Preheat oven to 375°F. Prick bottom and sides of pie crust and bake until it is just beginning to color, 10 to 12 minutes. Remove crust from oven and reduce oven temperature to 350°F. Combine beans, ¼ cup sugar, milk, egg, lemon zest, and extract in a food processor and process until smooth. Toss raspberries with remaining sugar and cornstarch. Spread half of raspberry mixture on bottom of crust. Layer bean mixture on top and dot remaining raspberry mixture. Sprinkle with almonds. Bake for 50 to 60 minutes until filling is firm and lightly golden on top.

Ginger Baked Apples

SERVES 2

> 2 Golden Delicious apples, cored from stem end, bottoms
>   left intact
> 2 teaspoons minced crystallized ginger
> 2 cinnamon sticks
> ¼ cup unsweetened apple juice
> Pinch ground allspice

Heat oven to 350°F. Place apples stem end up in a 9-inch glass pie dish. Place 1 teaspoon ginger and 1 cinnamon stick in hollowed out core of each apple. Combine apple juice and allspice, then pour into center of each apple. Bake until tender when pierced with a fork, 35 to 40 minutes. Serve warm.

Eat Smart

I know that changing what you eat, how you eat it, and when you eat it is not always that easy. It can provoke conflict and resistance amongst your family members, and within your own psyche. We've all got our food baggage, and our excuses. But unless we cultivate a healthier relationship with food, we will never eat smart, and we will never be able to use our heads to override ingrained habits and skewed priorities. Without becoming obsessive about it, if we care about our minds and memories, we've got to make good food a priority and give it the time and attention it deserves.

Food is not only one of life's necessities, it is one of life's greatest pleasures. Yet, instead of the life-giving pleasant experience that it could be, preparing and eating food has become just another bothersome task to take care of. Leah, the harried university employee, has noticed that "everybody eats, but they don't eat together. We eat at our computers, we eat at our desks, while reading E-mail, and while talking on the phone." She says, "I'm trying to break the habit of eating and working at the same time. A friend of mine suggested I pay more attention to cooking and eating with 'grace.' Of course, I haven't yet figured out how to make the time to do it. But damn it! I'd love to come home at night knowing that my partner and I will share a meal. In Judaism, food is a blessing, and eating is a kind of ritual. The price we pay for cutting corners—not buying, cutting, preparing, cooking, and cleaning up afterward—is higher than we think. Whether it's secular or sacred, making a ritual of eating is important for demarcating work and rest, for becoming conscious of where one ends and the other begins."

So many of us perform so many mindless repetitive tasks on a daily basis that we just continue to eat in a mindless way. Just ask anyone what he or she had for dinner last night. Most people can't even remember. Can you? Do you wolf down food and barely notice what or how much you ate? Do you overeat beyond the point of physical satisfaction? This is not nourishing your body with the attention it deserves. That's why I recommend to my patients that they slow down. Give your brain the time (about fifteen minutes) to realize that your body has been fed and has a fresh supply of nutrients. Chew your food well. Enjoy eating. To do this right, it is best to eat without distractions like reading, television, and highly animated conversation. Take the time to focus on the smells, colors, textures, shapes, and tastes of the food you are eating. In other words, make eating a "mindful" experience.

And mind the clock. It may be chic, or it may be a habit, but many people eat too much, too late. When your body sleeps it must be permitted to do its housecleaning and maintenance, which is growth and repair. If you go to sleep on a full stomach, your body is so busy digesting that it becomes overworked and can't do either job well. So I recommend you allow three hours between the time you eat and the time you retire. Most people wake up more energetic and have a more restful sleep when they eat their dinner earlier rather than later, and do not make it the largest meal of the day packed with lots of high-fat, high-sugar foods.

To accomplish this feat, you may need to juggle and negotiate. I remember Karen, one of my patients, found that she was gaining weight. When I asked her to keep a food journal including the times of her meals, I noticed that she ate dinner at 8:00 P.M. or later. I found out that she waited for her husband to eat dinner, and often became so famished that by the time he got home she had already eaten the caloric equivalent of a meal in snacks of corn chips and cheese! I asked her when she would really prefer to eat if she weren't waiting for her husband, and she said 4:30 P.M. I suggested that she have half her dinner at that time, and then another half with her husband. When she came back for her follow-up two weeks later, she had not only lost weight but felt more clear-headed because she was not overeating or eating fatty snack foods.

The timing of meals was also a problem for Susanne, a classical ballet dancer who takes as well as teaches dance classes. She was having a problem knowing what and when to eat, as the rule is "you can't dance on a full stomach." So, she would have donuts and diet sodas for breakfast, and live on candy bars the rest of the day. She would finally eat a decent meal in the evening. She seemed to be doing okay for a while, but recently noticed that in addition to dips in energy, she was getting sick often and would frequently forget exactly what came next in the dance sequences she was teaching. Working around Susanne's tight and physically active schedule was a challenge, but we found that she did have time to eat very small amounts of high-quality foods between classes and during breaks. Baked tofu was a lifesaver for her as it kept her energy up, was portable, didn't have to be refrigerated, and tasted good. In addition, because it is high in protein and choline, a B vitamin critical for the brain, the tofu kept her mind working as well as her body.

As Leah, Karen, and Susanne have discovered, changing your diet is often the first step on the journey to renewed health and vitality. Remember, taking responsibility for the health of your brain means a commitment to change and often includes abandoning cherished lifelong habits. Most of us love our indulgences, and giving them up seems a terrible deprivation. But we cannot improve our health until we begin to place a higher value upon our health than upon the immediate gratification we get from certain foods. Health is not merely the absence of disease, but is a state of optimum well-being from which life seems to flow effortlessly. When our body is healthy, our mind is healthy, and our judgment is on target. We always seem to be in the right place at the right time. What we need comes to us easily, and our intuition becomes strong and enables us to function in harmony with our environment.

CHAPTER 9

Step Two

Brain-Boosting Supplements

Food is the foundation of my brain-boosting program, and eating according to the guidelines in the previous chapter will go a long way toward restoring and maintaining your mental ability. But few women find that food alone can supply all the nutrients they need for optimum brainpower. That's why I often recommend that my patients augment their diet with supplements of vitamins, minerals, amino acids, and other nutrients known to help the brain function optimally. The bonus is that the right supplements in appropriate amounts not only preserve and boost your mental capacity, but may also help to restore balance in many chronic health conditions.

Optimum amounts of all nutrients are important, but in this chapter I focus on those nutrients that help protect your neurons from damage due to stress, pollution, and other toxic substances; that increase energy production in your nerve cells; that support the production and use of neurotransmitters; that improve circulation to the brain; and that support balanced hormone production.

Why Take Supplements?

While a nutritious diet is still the mainstay of good health, many studies and surveys have shown that it's rare for the average person to obtain the Food and Drug Administration's Recommended Daily Allowances (RDAs) for all the vitamins and minerals. A large survey recently showed that less than 10 percent of the population eats the recommended daily minimum of five servings of fruits and vegetables. This fact alone makes achieving the RDAs impossible. Even if we know what's good for us, we don't always follow through. Life keeps getting in the way—we're too busy and too stressed to cook and eat right.

And even if by some miracle, we eat an optimum diet every day, it is unlikely that we are getting enough of the vital vitamins, minerals, and other nutrients we need to keep our bodies and brains humming. There are many reasons for this. As we age, our ability to absorb nutrients declines. As our metabolism slows, we may try to control our weight by eating less, or we may not eat with the gusto of our youth. If we have been ill, under stress, taking medication, or exposed to pollution, nutrients become depleted and our need for them increases.

Furthermore, the fruits, vegetables, and grains we eat are often harvested before peak ripeness and peak nutrition, and they are then stored and shipped, and stored again in the grocery store. We buy them and store them some more before we finally eat them. Studies show that these "fresh" foods lose nutrition all along the way. If we cook them, they lose more. You may not have the obvious physical signs of vitamin deficiency, such as pellagra or scurvy—but there's still a good chance that you are suffering from nutritional deficiencies. Such deficiencies have symptoms that are insidious and subtle or subclinical—we don't notice them or don't equate them with nutrition. But they affect many body organ functions, including the ability of the brain to remember and think.

The evidence is compelling. That's why I recommend that in addition to eating a whole-foods diet, my patients get at least the minimum requirements found in a broad-spectrum daily multivitamin and mineral supplement. The evidence shows that taking supplements in the amounts of the recommended daily allowance can correct obvious and subclinical nutritional deficiencies, and thus encourage better mental performance. Although it is better than nothing, consuming the RDAs may not be enough for optimum health of mind or body. In addition, there's evidence that taking supplements in a reasonable amount in excess of the recommended daily allowances can further improve brain function. I agree with the growing legion of respected authorities who no longer believe the RDAs are really adequate for every person. I have seen the many exciting new studies that show that higher amounts of certain nutrients, such as the B vitamins, vitamin E, choline, and selenium, enhance the nervous system and have many other beneficial effects as well.

Studies show that vitamin and mineral supplements have improved people's brain function, memory, moods, learning ability, attention span, reaction time, coordination, and even I.Q. test results. Most amazing—and troubling—of all, these effects occurred whether or not the subjects had obvious symptoms of vitamin deficiency. Other studies show that B vitamins and antioxidant vitamins can reduce the risk of age-related mental deterioration in middle-aged and older people; in many cases they can restore memory and thinking ability even after decline has begun. We could improve so many people's quality of life with just a few supplements.

It's likely that at least part of the mental decline we consider to be a "normal" part of aging is really due to nutritional deficiencies. As an example, consider the following studies:

- Dr. David Bonton, a British psychologist, gave 127 men and women aged seventeen to twenty-seven either a multivitamin supplement or a placebo. After a year of taking the pills, he compared the participants' pre-study scores on a battery of tests with their post-study scores. Those women who took the vitamin supplement had improved post-study scores in tests of reaction times and information processing. Interestingly, the women benefited more than the men.

- In a study of 260 normal, healthy older adults living in Arizona, researcher Dr. James Goodwin found that the higher the level of vitamin C and B vitamins in the blood, the better the scores on a test of mental function. For example, subjects did 20 to 25 percent better if their vitamin C level was in the 90th percentile, compared to those whose vitamin C was in the 10th percentile. Years later, other researchers went back to take another look at the people in the study. The results were the same—people who took supplements did better cognitively, with many of them scoring "as well or better than younger adults on verbal memory," according to the study.

• A study from Hawaii of 3,735 older Japanese men confirms the brain benefits of supplementation, especially of vitamins C and E, potent antioxidants that probably protected their brain cells from accelerated aging.

So many of my patients report that they feel better and think better when taking supplements in potencies higher than the RDAs that it's clear that some people need amounts well above the RDA. That's why I generally recommend that my patients take so-called "therapeutic doses" of a broad spectrum of nutrients in order to both treat and prevent memory problems, poor concentration and attention span, and learning problems—as well as many other illnesses.

The Nutrient Table of Vitamins and Minerals (page 162) gives a range of safe recommended dosages (in addition to the amounts ingested via food) for the best-known nutrients; it provides both the RDA, and the

NUTRIENT TABLE OF VITAMINS AND MINERALS

Nutrient	RDA*	Therapeutic Intake
Vitamin A	5,000 International Units (IU)	5,000–10,000 IU
Beta-carotene	none	8,000–10,000 IU
Vitamin B complex		
B$_1$	1.5 mg	25–50 mg
B$_2$	1.7 mg	25–50 mg
B$_3$	20 mg	25–50 mg
B$_6$	2 mg	25 mg
B$_{12}$	6 mcg	25–50 mg
Folic acid	400 mcg	400–800 mcg
Pantothenic acid	10 mg	25–500 mg
Biotin	300 mcg	25–200 mcg
Vitamin C	60 mg	500–2,000 mg
Vitamin D	400 IU	400–800 IU
Vitamin E	30 IU	400–1,200 IU
Vitamin K	80 mcg	80 mcg
Calcium	1,000 mg	1,000–1,500 mg
Magnesium	400 mg	500–750 mg
Iron	18 mg	15–18 mg
Selenium	70 mcg	50–400 mcg
Zinc	15 mg	20–50 mg
Copper	2 mg	2 mg
Omega-3	none	250–3,000 mg
Flavonoids	none	250–1,000 mg
Coenzyme Q-10 (CoQ-10)	none	60–200 mg
Alpha-lipoic acid	none	25–50 mg

Important Precaution: If you have any diagnosed health problem or special health needs, consult a physician on the proper and safe nutrient dosage for you.

*RDA values are for non-pregnant, non-lactating adults.

optimum (therapeutic) intake. The optimum intake amounts are based on the most current research studies published in professional journals and my own clinical experiences as well as those of other well-respected clinicians. More is not always better where nutrition is concerned. The range of optimum amounts recommended may seem high to those who follow the RDAs, but these dosages are beneficial for many people and are safe in basically healthy people. Some people may experience adverse effects with very high doses, but this is generally limited to people with certain medical conditions. If you have any questions or concerns, work with a knowledgeable nutritionist or physician who specializes in nutritional sciences.

Buying and Using Nutritional Supplements

How much is your mind worth? It is priceless, beyond value, and yet most people buy the cheapest brand of supplements they can find thinking they're all the same. Some will buy the most expensive, thinking that will assure them of the highest quality. Some experts believe that you should buy only "natural" vitamins because synthetic ones are less effective. Others feel you are paying extra money for nothing. Keep in mind that the accepted definition of a "natural" nutrient is one that has a chemical structure the same as that found in nature. We can synthesize such chemicals easily, yet they are labeled "natural" because it is believed the body can't tell the difference. However, some products are more biocompatible than others—that is, they are more easily absorbed and therefore better used by the body. For example, there is evidence that this is true of the naturally occurring form of vitamin E. There is also evidence that supplements that are concentrations of foods that are naturally high in certain nutrients are also better absorbed and utilized. However, in most cases, high potencies are difficult to get in natural form.

How to choose among the thousands of brands? While the bargain hunter may end up with worthless and ineffective supplements, the price of a product is no guarantee of quality either—you may be paying mostly for a pretty label and fancy marketing techniques. So, what's a supplement seeker to do? Your best defense is to know your manufacturers. I have included a list of the manufacturers that, to my knowledge, are the most reputable in Appendix B.

Your Individual Supplement Program

Although certain nutrients are better known for their brain-nourishing benefits, as a general rule it's best not to take a supplement of just one nutrient. Nutrients typically work synergistically and frequently depend on one another to work best. In addition, taking large doses of one nutrient can create an imbalance in your body. For example, all the B vitamins usually work best together. If you take only vitamin B_{12} for instance, it competes with other B vitamins for absorption into the intestine, and thus an excess of B_{12} can create a deficiency in the others.

Fortunately, gone are the days when we needed to buy dozens of bottles of individual supplements to get higher amounts than the RDAs. Now supplementation is easier and more convenient. Simply buy one of the good, broad-spectrum multivitamin and mineral formulas that contains at least the amounts specified in the table on page 162. This may be all you want to take, and you will still be ahead of the game. Alternatively, the formula product can act as your foundation for a program that is more specifically tailored to your needs, based on the self-assessment in chapter 6 and the information in the section on individual brain-boosting nutrients that follows.

To figure out what you need and how to get it from the products available, sit down with the nutrient table on page 162 and the results of your self-assessment. If your assessment results show that you have mild memory impairment and only a few contributing factors, look for a multi-formula that contains all the nutrients at the lower end of the optimum intake range specified in the nutrient table. If you have moderate memory problems, or many contributing factors, or both, look for a supplement with amounts closer to the higher end of the optimum range. To achieve the higher dose of the antioxidant nutrients (beta-carotene, vitamins C and E, selenium, flavonoids, and alpha-lipoic acid), you will probably also need to take individual supplements of these nutrients or an antioxidant formula that comes close to your total desired intake. For example, you would need to add a good antioxidant supplement in addition to your multi if you live in a polluted city or have a job where you are exposed to high levels of toxins. If stress is a major contributing factor, you might need to take a stress vitamin containing B complex and vitamin C along with flavonoids in addition to your multi. I always tell my patients that if they can't remove themselves from a stressful situation, then how their body manages stress will become paramount. And that stress-management includes supplementation with the appropriate vitamins and minerals. You also need to consider your medical history and that of your family, especially if you are already exhibiting symptoms of a familial disease. For example, if you have heart disease on both sides of the family, your cholesterol is in the high 200s, and your triglycerides are 700, I would recommend you get a total of 800 IU of vitamin E (preferably in dry form) and at least 500 mg of choline because they lower these blood lipids. This is, of course, in addition to appropriate dietary modifications and an exercise program.

I recommend that you give vitamin and mineral supplements a two-month trial and then assess the results. If your condition has not improved enough, you can increase the dosages into the upper levels of the optimum intake range, or add one or two amino acid supplements. Of course, if you have already been taking high-potency nutritional supplements you can start taking amino acids immediately. I would recommend acetylcarnitine and L-glutamine to start. Begin with the lower dose, assess the results after a one-month trial, and increase the dose if necessary. If these two don't work for you, try phenylalanine and aspartic acid in the same way. Bear in mind that your nutritional supplement program is not etched in stone. You need to experiment to see what feels best for you. The rule of thumb is to take the least amount possible to get the desired results. So start out with amounts in the low range, see how you feel, then increase the amounts or change the types of supplements you take to see if you improve.

Claire, for example, had been taking a low-potency daily multivitamin that provided the recommended daily allowance, but she felt that it was not enough. She decided that in addition to making important changes in her diet, such as removing sugary foods and eating more fish, she wanted to start a more sophisticated, targeted supplement program. Her self-assessment showed only mild memory and concentration problems, but high stress and a moderate exposure to urban pollution. So, she began with a high-potency multi-nutrient formula, plus an antioxidant formula to counteract the stress and pollution. Although after two months on this improved regimen she felt much better physically, psychologically, and mentally, she eventually decided to increase her supplement program. Because heart disease and Alzheimer's ran in her family, she eventually added 200 mg of CoQ-10 and 500 mg of choline daily, and to this she also added acetylcarnitine and L-glutamine.

Remember, nutritional supplements are just that—supplements to a healthful, balanced diet and active lifestyle. They are not substitutes. Taking supplements is not a license to slather butter on everything, lie around eating junk food, or smoke cigarettes.

If you have a diagnosed disease and/or are taking medication, consult a professional before taking supplements. Some supplements may interact with medication

---

**WHAT TO KEEP IN MIND
WHEN USING SUPPLEMENTS**

- Try to divide the dosage throughout the day to increase effectiveness. For example, if you are taking 1,500 mg of vitamin C, take 500 mg three times a day.
- Take most supplements with meals; this also increases absorption and prevents indigestion or "tasting" the vitamins later. Amino acid supplements should be taken on an empty stomach; iron supplements should be taken separate from calcium because these two nutrients compete for absorption in the digestive system.
- Store supplements in a cool, dark, dry place—not the refrigerator, which is damp. Supplements have a limited shelf life, so toss them after the expiration date.

---

or cause problems. The recommended dosages have been found to be safe in the vast majority of people; however, be alert for any possible side effects or unusual sensitivities.

The B Vitamins

There are several vitamins that belong to the group known as B complex. Each one has its own unique role to play in maintaining the health of your mind and body, but they have so much in common that it makes sense to think of them as a single nutrient. B vitamins work together and are found in many of the same foods. As supplements, they have been used for many years to treat problems of the mind—from schizophrenia to depression, anxiety to memory loss. The body's need for B vitamins increases when you are under any kind of stress, be it emotional or physical. According to animal studies, B vitamins taken in dosages that exceed the RDA enhance immune function, thereby providing protection against infections and diseases that can affect the brain. Several B vitamins also lower homocysteine, a substance that damages arteries and thus leads to cardiovascular disease and poor blood circulation to the brain.

B vitamin supplements play a key role in stabilizing and restoring brain function—from maintaining the nervous system, reducing the harmful effects of stress and depression, to resisting infection and protecting against cardiovascular disease. The best sources for B vitamins are unrefined whole grains, liver, green leafy vegetables, fish, poultry, eggs, meat, nuts, and beans.

B_1 (THIAMINE)

Various studies have shown that thiamine deficiency is common, and 4 percent of older Americans admitted to hospitals have a thiamine deficiency. B_1 helps neurons produce energy, is an antioxidant, and helps improve blood flow. B_1 has been known for decades to regulate mood. Thiamine deficiency invariably leads to fatigue, inactivity, diminished mood, and poor self-confidence. The good news is that thiamine supplements rapidly correct these symptoms. In one study of thiamine supplementation, it was found to be particularly effective in women, and even those who were not deficient benefited from extra intake. These women noted that they were more clear-headed, energetic, decisive, and had faster reaction times than those women who received a placebo.

Dosage: I recommend supplements in the range of 25–50 mg per day.

Supplements: Thiamine hydrochloride or thiamine mononitrate.

Adverse Effects: None known at any dosage.

B$_3$ (Niacin)

This B vitamin aids neurotransmitter production, improves blood flow, reduces cholesterol levels, helps neurons produce energy, and assists in the regulation of blood glucose. In a study of ninety-six healthy adults of all ages conducted in Amsterdam, those who received "megadoses" of niacin enjoyed remarkable benefits. Compared with the placebo group, their short-term and long-term memory improved by 10 to 40 percent.

Dosage: I recommend supplements in the range of 25–50 mg per day.

Supplements: Niacin or niacinamide.

Adverse Effects: None known at this dosage, except for a "flush" with nicotinic acid at doses of 100 mg or more.

B$_6$ (Pyridoxine)

B$_6$ helps trigger the production of a number of neuro-transmitters, including serotonin, dopamine, and norep-inephrine. And as in the case with folic acid, B$_6$ protects the brain's arteries from homocysteine, a substance harmful to your arteries. Studies indicate that most people get only about 50 percent of the RDA of B$_6$, and that after age forty you need 25 percent more B$_6$ than you do when you're younger. Low levels of B$_6$ are associated with mental confusion, poor concentration, and memory problems. In addition, because of its role in serotonin production, B_6 deficiency may contribute to depression.

Dosage: I recommend supplements in the range of 25–50 mg per day.

Supplements: Pyridoxine hydrochloride or pyridoxine 5 phosphate.

Adverse Effects: Nervous system problems are extremely rare in lower doses.

B_{12} (COBALAMIN)

B_{12} is needed for production of acetylcholine, a major memory neurotransmitter. It is involved in red blood cell formation and reactivation, which helps keep the brain supplied with oxygen and able to produce energy. B_{12} protects the nervous system against stress and is required in higher amounts during times of stress. As with folic acid and B_6, this vitamin fights homocysteine damage; this may explain why people who have low blood levels of B_{12} have four times the risk of developing Alzheimer's disease.

It is estimated that more than 42 percent of adults over the age of sixty-five are B_{12} deficient, and mental confusion is one of the major symptoms. In fact, many older people with vitamin B_{12} deficiency are misdiagnosed with incurable dementia or Alzheimer's disease. Studies show that over 60 percent of people with dementia enjoyed a reversal of their symptoms when treated with B_{12}. The blood test for B_{12} is not reliable, but your doctor can diagnose this deficiency by testing your blood for homocysteine and serum cobalamin.

Even if you eat a diet high in B_{12}, you may not be absorbing much. As we get older, we have trouble absorbing nutrients in general, making supplements a good idea. With age, our levels of a substance called intrinsic factor start to dip. Intrinsic factor is needed to absorb vitamin B_{12} in the intestine. That's why so many people become low in B_{12} as they age, and why supplement injections are more effective than pills. As an alternative, try sublingual (under the tongue) pills of B_{12}. Both the injected and sublingual varieties are absorbed directly into your bloodstream.

Dosage: The amount in a multivitamin supplement is usually sufficient (usually 25–50 mg), but some people may need to take more B_{12} than an all-in-one daily supplement provides. People over fifty may need between 1,000–2,000 mcg a day to overcome absorption problems.

Supplements: Cyanocobalamin.

Adverse Effects: None known at any dosage.

FOLIC ACID

Deficiencies in this B vitamin are associated with a breathtaking array of mental symptoms, from poor memory to dementia, depression, schizophrenia, and attention deficit disorder (ADD) in children. Folic acid is needed to produce serotonin and dopamine, two neurotransmitters in the brain, and is part of several chemical reactions that take place in memory cells. It is also used to produce red blood cells, which means it is needed to make sure your brain is getting sufficient oxygen. Folic acid also aids digestion, which provides nutrients to the brain. In addition, this mighty vitamin is needed to prevent buildup of homocysteine, which damages arteries, contributes to atherosclerosis, increases risk of stroke, and impedes blood flow to the brain. It may also help prevent Alzheimer's according to one study. Nearly 90 percent of Americans do not consume the recommended daily allowance.

Dosage: I recommend 400 mcg daily, in divided doses, for most people as a preventive. You may need up to 1,000 mcg a day if you are experiencing moderate memory problems, as diagnosed by self-assessment.

Supplements: Folic acid.

Adverse Effects: None known at any dose.

CHOLINE

We are mainly interested in choline because it is a building block for acetylcholine, a major memory neurotransmitter. It also helps facilitate the growth of dendrites and augments your capacity to learn. Choline, along with another B complex vitamin called inositol, seems to emulsify fat in the blood, and keeps cholesterol from sticking to artery walls. It thus helps keep blood flowing to your brain, supplying it with the oxygen, glucose, and other nutrients it needs for optimum function. Choline is stored in the nerve cells as phosphatidyl choline, where it becomes a structural component of the cell membranes. It protects the membranes and keeps them fluid so that nutrients and other substances can flow in and out of the cell freely. Some studies show that if cells lack choline, they will cannibalize their own membrane in a desperate search for it. Perhaps this is why Alzheimer's patients lose memory cells, and have very low levels of choline to boot. Phosphatidyl choline also protects your liver from toxins such as those in medication and pollution, and it helps to rebuild healthy tissue. It also enhances the nerve cells' production of energy from glucose.

Dosage: Take 25–500 mg as a preventive; 500–1,000 mg daily in divided doses as a treatment. People over the age of sixty-five may need more: 1–5 grams per day.

Supplements: Lecithin granules, oil, or liquid are the most common sources of choline in the form of phosphatidyl choline. But I have seen more improvements to mild short-term memory loss from a supplement containing only phosphatidyl choline.

Adverse Effects: Some people develop a fishy odor in their bodies when taking choline; can cause depression in people with a preexisting tendency to this condition.

The Antioxidants

Every moment, your body and brain are assaulted by cell-damaging free radicals. Your body's naturally produced antioxidants keep these harmful substances under control, but you need certain nutrients to form the antioxidant enzymes. Indeed, certain nutrients—such as vitamin C, vitamin E, and selenium—act as antioxidants themselves. Although food supplies these nutrients, it does so in insufficient quantities to counteract the high levels of free radicals in our environment. A study published in 2000 suggested that supplements of vitamins E and C can protect your brain from dementia, and actually improve memory, creativity, and mental activity. This study focused on elderly men who took both vitamins C and E together, and other studies have shown that these nutrients work synergistically. That's why I recommend that my patients take generous amounts of antioxidants. Antioxidant nutrients also have many other roles to play in protecting and restoring your memory.

VITAMIN C

We know this vitamin is crucial for brain function because it passes through the blood-brain barrier very easily and is highly concentrated in the brain. Vitamin C is a superb antioxidant and has been shown to protect cells, including brain cells, from free-radical damage, accelerated aging, and deterioration. Vitamin C also recharges other antioxidants, such as vitamin E, thus renewing their potency. This versatile vitamin also helps your body create neurotransmitters such as dopamine and adrenaline, and therefore facilitates the transmission of messages from one neuron to the next. As an antioxidant, vitamin C protects not only brain cells but artery walls, as a result reducing the risk of cardiovascular disease and its detrimental effects on the brain. Many studies show that the higher the intake of vitamin C from food and supplements, and the higher the levels in your blood, the lower the risk of cognitive impairment. In one study, the vitamin reduced the likelihood of impairment by 40 percent. People with Alzheimer's disease have much lower levels of vitamin C in their cerebrospinal fluid than do healthy young adults. In fact, in one study, none of the people taking vitamin C supplements developed the disease. The best food sources for vitamin C are green leafy vegetables, berries, citrus fruit, and tomatoes.

Dosage: Many nutritionists advise taking 2,000 mg a day; others suggest taking anywhere from 3,000 mg to 10 or 15 grams. Your body will let you know how much you need through a phenomenon called "bowel tolerance." The first time you take large doses of vitamin C, start with 1 or 2 grams a day, and add 1 gram each day until you notice symptoms of gas, bloating, or diarrhea. Then gradually cut back on the dosage until bowel symptoms disappear.

Supplements: Ascorbic acid; mineral ascorbates are buffered and gentler on the stomach.

Adverse Effects: Other than bowel symptoms, there are no confirmed adverse effects associated with taking large doses of vitamin C; earlier studies that suggested a possible occurrence of kidney stones have been disproved.

VITAMIN E

Vitamin E is another multitalented nutrient. As an antioxidant, vitamin E helps minimize free-radical damage. Since it is fat soluble, it is stored in the fatty parts of your cell membranes; thus, it is uniquely capable of preventing the fat molecules so abundant in brain tissue from turning rancid. Vitamin E protects both the fatty outer membrane and inner membrane of your nerve cells, thereby increasing your brain's ability to transmit messages from cell to cell, and create energy within the cells.

Vitamin E also reduces free-radical damage to your

artery walls, helping to protect you against cardiovascular disease and its choking effect on blood flow to the brain. Numerous studies show that vitamin E supplements reduce the risk of stroke by 53 percent. It also reduces the inflammatory effects of pollution toxins, allergies, and infections, which can eventually reach the brain and wreak havoc there. Autopsies have given us visible evidence that vitamin E deficiencies cause the delicate axons of nerves to degenerate. MRI (magnetic resonance imaging) studies show that low levels of vitamin E in the blood are associated with brain damage due to impaired blood vessels in the brain or free-radical assault. In these studies, subjects ranged in age from forty-five to seventy-five, and those with the lowest levels of vitamin E had seven times the damage of those with the highest levels. An amazing study of 341 patients with Alzheimer's showed that 1,000 IU of vitamin E slowed the progression of the disease in more than half the people who took it—the vitamin had even better results than the Alzheimer drug it was being compared to. In a Chicago study of 633 people sixty-five years or older, ninety-one people developed Alzheimer's. But none of the twenty-seven people who were taking vitamin E supplements (200–800 IU per day) developed it. Statistically, researchers would have expected four of them (15 percent) to have developed the disease by the end of the four-year study.

It's no wonder so many brain researchers are taking vitamin E themselves. And it's no wonder that the American Institute on Aging believes vitamin E shows such promise as a brain saver that it has launched a study to investigate its effects. The study involves 720 Americans aged fifty-five to ninety who have what is called mild cognitive impairment (MCI); the study is designed to determine if vitamin E will delay further memory loss and prevent or delay Alzheimer's in these people. About 75 percent of those with MCI are expected to progress to Alzheimer's. Even if vitamin E supplements only cut this rate in half, it will be a significant step toward reining in the occurrence of this devastating disease. The best food sources for vitamin E are cold-pressed vegetable oils, whole grains, nuts, dark green leafy vegetables, and legumes.

Dosage: I recommend supplements in the range of 400–1,200 IU per day, in divided doses.

SELENIUM

Selenium is a mineral that functions as a powerful antioxidant because it is a component of the body's natural antioxidant enzyme glutathione peroxidase. Thus, it protects against damage of nerve cells, especially the fat molecules that comprise so much of your brain. When your brain does not get an adequate supply of selenium, several neurotransmitters do not do their jobs. So, it's not surprising that studies show that extra-high selenium diets and selenium supplements improve mood, self-confidence, and clarity of thought—even if there is no obvious selenium deficiency. Some people's mood scores jumped 40 percent when they took selenium for five weeks. Selenium deficiency is associated with many diseases and conditions, including cancer, heart disease, and high cholesterol. It seems to detoxify heavy metals, including lead, which tamper with thinking and memory. Selenium protects the liver and immune system from free-radical damage, and helps regulate thyroid hormone, which plays a key role in maintaining memory and mental function in general. Good food sources for selenium include grains and meat (depending on the selenium content of the soil) and seafood. Generally, soils in the western states are higher in selenium than those in the east.

Dosage: I recommend supplements in the range of 50–400 mcg per day.

Supplements: Selenomethionine is the most easily absorbed and safest form.

Adverse Effects: None in doses up to 500 mcg.

ALPHA-LIPOIC ACID

Alpha-lipoic acid, or ALA, is such a potent antioxidant that it has been dubbed the "superantioxidant" by one researcher. It is unique in that it is a very small molecule, allowing it to pass through the blood-brain barrier easily, where it can protect your brain tissue. It also enhances the antioxidant effects of vitamins C and E, and replenishes them when they have become depleted so they can quench more free radicals. Alpha-lipoic acid further aids in the battle against free radicals by increasing levels of the powerful antioxidant enzyme component glutathione, which protects the fat content in neurons. Alpha-lipoic acid acts as a free-radical mop, and removes rancid fats and toxins in your cells.

In addition, ALA helps your liver process medications and other toxic substances, and boosts brainpower by helping your cells to produce energy from glucose.

Unfortunately, we do not have any human studies on the connection between ALA and brain function; however, animal studies show that older participants who received alpha-lipoic acid performed better on memory tests than did unsupplemented younger animals.

But the benefits of ALA don't end there. ALA also prevents stroke by protecting your cardiovascular system from free-radical damage, and it may reduce the neuron damage that results from stroke. Additionally, alpha-lipoic acid appears to speed up the post-stroke recovery process. In fact, ALA is used in Europe to prevent and treat nerve damage due to diabetes, and to improve the efficacy of insulin. Both diabetes and stroke are murder on brain cells, so if you are at risk for other conditions, consider adding this relatively unknown nutrient to your list of antioxidant supplements. Alpha-lipoic acid is found in significant amounts in only a few foods, including spinach, broccoli, and organ meats.

Dosage: I recommend supplements in the range of 25–50 mg per day, and up to 100 for significant memory loss.

Supplements: Alpha-lipoic acid.

Adverse Effects: None known.

Coenzyme Q-10

Coenzyme Q-10, or CoQ-10, as it is also called, behaves very much like vitamin E, but it is not a true vitamin. It reduces free-radical damage and therefore protects your neurons. It also protects and strengthens blood vessels and the heart itself, and thus keeps the brain supplied with oxygen and nutrients. CoQ-10 plays a critical role in the production of energy in the cells, including in that of the neurons in the brain. It is considered to be a "cellular spark plug" because of its ability to spur on a cell's energy centers, an ability that enables the brain to be in top form. Unfortunately, the body's levels of CoQ-10 dip as we age, and any cholesterol-lowering drugs we may take cause CoQ-10 to dip further. But supplements have been shown to restore youthful levels, at least in animals. Other studies have shown that CoQ-10 protects animal brains from damage due to Lou Gehrig's disease (amyotrophic lateral sclerosis, or ALS), a debilitating disease of the nervous system. Animal studies also suggest CoQ-10 as a promising therapy to treat and prevent Parkinson's disease, another nervous disorder. The best food sources for this nutrient are sardines, peanuts, and spinach, as well as beef hearts and chicken hearts.

Dosage: I recommend supplements in the range of 60–200 mg per day, in divided doses; take up to 200 mg if you are exposed to pollution or cigarette smoke or are at high risk for a genetic degenerative nervous system disease.

Supplements: Coenzyme Q-10.

Adverse Effects: Rare, even in high doses; some reports of gastrointestinal effects.

Omega-3 Fatty Acids

Omega-3 boosts brainpower in a breathtaking variety of ways. Because the typical American diet is deficient in omega-3 fatty acids, I usually recommend a supplement in addition to including increased consumption of deep-water fatty fish such as herring, salmon, tuna, mackerel, and shrimp. One of omega-3's major roles is to reduce the inflammation that can damage cells in the blood vessels and neurons in the brain. It also protects the health of the myelin sheaths that surround the axons of nerve cells, thus enhancing transmission of memory messages between cells. Furthermore, it maintains the flexibility of nerve cell membranes, which better enables cells to absorb needed substances and keep harmful substances out. This membranic flexibility also makes it easier for neurotransmitters to pass between two neurons, thereby improving communication. Omega-3 helps avoid free-radical damage of the fatty tissue in the brain. This antioxidant ability keeps blood vessels that supply the brain healthy and free of atherosclerosis so blood can flow unobstructed.

The omega-3 family includes fatty acids called *DHA (docosahexaenoic acid)* and *EPA (eicosapentaenoic acid)*. The latter two are found in fish oils, and supplements of these nutrients are derived from fish oils as well. Many studies link fish oil (consumed in fish) with improved cognition in old age. Several studies show supplements are effective, too, and may confer additional benefits. For example, fish oil supplements have relieved depression in people with bipolar disease (manic depression); 65 percent of people who took fish oil supplements in a study saw their depression improve, as compared with 18 percent of people who took a placebo. What's more, only a small fraction of those whose condition improved had a recurrence of depression.

Other studies show that the DHA form of omega-3 improved mental function in young women, especially their ability to concentrate and pay attention. DHA appears to improve your brain's efficiency by speeding up the transmission rate of a particular brain wave called P300. The rate of this brain wave is associated with the brain's efficiency when learning and remembering—the rate slows as we age and in people with dementia. Indeed, omega-3 supplements have been shown to improve the memory, mood, and other symptoms of Alzheimer's patients—in many subjects, in fact, there was dramatic improvement. There is additionally tantalizing evidence that suggests that fish oil is useful in treating attention deficit disorder, dyslexia, and other learning disabilities.

Dosage: I recommend supplements in the range of 250–3,000 mg per day, in capsules, or 2 teaspoons of cod liver oil per day.

Supplements: In capsules or oil. Cod liver oil is a cheaper alternative to capsules, but some people complain that it leaves a fishy aftertaste, even in its flavored varieties. An alternative for vegetarians is DHA that is derived from algae, and many health food stores now sell eggs that are high in DHA because the chickens are fed algae. These special eggs are, of course, more expensive than regular eggs.

Adverse Effects: None known, but some people notice a fishy odor and taste when taking high doses of EPA.

The Amino Acids

There are about 20 amino acids, or building blocks of proteins. Although your body can produce most of them, you must get the remaining ones from food or supplements—these eight to ten are known as essential amino acids. Your body produces proteins, hormones, and neurotransmitters from amino acids. If your body is depleted of essential amino acids, it cannot make the necessary essential proteins and important neurotransmitters, and, as a result, mental function declines. Amino acid deficiency can be caused by infection, trauma, stress, aging, problems with food digestion and absorption, and inadequate levels of other nutrients. Although the body produces amino acids from protein, eating more protein will not necessarily fix an amino acid deficiency. That's why I sometimes recommend specific amino acid supplements to my patients. Unlike most other nutrients, unless otherwise instructed, amino acid supplements should be taken on an empty stomach 45 minutes before meals containing protein so they do not compete for absorption with the proteins in your food. Conversely, eating carbohydrates such as fruits or vegetables will help your liver or other organs assimilate the amino acids, and taking them with vitamin B_6 will help the liver utilize them. I always start my patients on the lowest dose and then work up slowly over the course of a few weeks.

When buying amino acid supplements, look for the "L" form because it is more easily utilized, an important consideration as we age and nutrient absorption becomes less efficient. Also, stick to "free-form amino acids," which are of higher quality. If you take amino acid supplements, be sure you also take a broad-spectrum vitamin and mineral supplement that will help you metabolize the amino acids. Amino acid supplements are generally safe for most people; however, if you are taking an MAO inhibitor, such as Marplan, Nardil, or selegiline, do not use certain amino acid supplements unless supervised by a healthcare professional.

PHENYLALANINE

Phenylalanine is used to produce the neurotransmitters dopamine and norepinephrine. It is also needed to regulate blood sugar. This amino acid boosts energy, and improves long-term memory and mood. It's a great alternative to caffeine because unlike coffee it does not cause the jitters or irritability, and does not burn out your adrenals.

Dosage: I recommend supplements in the range of 250–500 mg, three times a day between meals. Do not take with milk or other proteins; best to take with water or diluted juices. Do not take with an amino acid supplement that contains tyrosine, valine, isoleucine, leucine, or L-tryptophan because they compete for absorption. Avoid this supplement if you are pregnant, or have high blood pressure, cardiovascular problems, skin cancer, or phenylketonuria (a metabolic disorder).

ACETYLCARNITINE

Acetylcarnitine is the preferred form of carnitine, which is not an amino acid per se—it is actually related to the B vitamins. But because it is very similar to amino acids, carnitine is usually grouped with them. Acetylcarnitine (ALC) helps the major memory neurotransmitter acetylcholine work. Its ability to slow the effects of aging on the brain and nervous system is being studied intensely. It is already being used to treat depression and other cognitive disorders, and studies show that ALC slows the progression of Alzheimer's disease. ALC offers protection from free radicals and increases the levels of antioxidants in your brain. Studies show ALC can actually reverse damage to neurons—particularly in the hippocampus, a major memory center in the brain, and in the prefrontal area of the cerebrum. It also appears to increase the ability of neurons to produce energy, and reduce the accumulation of lipofuscin, the aging pigment that can clog the brain. Studies of Alzheimer's patients showed that those who were treated with acetylcarnitine deteriorated more slowly, and studies of stroke victims showed that acetylcarnitine helped them to recover faster.

Dosage: If you have only slight memory loss, start with 750 mg in divided doses. If you have moderate memory decline, you may need a total of 1.5–3 grams per day. For severe memory problems, up to 4 grams a day may be needed. No serious adverse effects have been reported, but some people feel agitated when taking acetylcholine. To minimize this effect, take after meals, or reduce the dosage.

GLUTAMINE

This amino acid is known as "brain fuel." It is used to produce several natural chemicals needed to improve immune system detoxification for proper brain function, including GABA, an important neurotransmitter known for its calming effects on a brain "racing with thoughts."

Glutamine is used to neutralize waste products of brain metabolism that can cause fatigue, confusion, and an inability to concentrate. Supplements of glutamine have been used to treat many problems related to cognition, including depression, schizophrenia, and senility. This amino acid may be taken on a regular basis, or just before a particular occasion for which you want to be especially alert and clear-headed.

Dosage: I recommend taking 500 mg, twice a day on an empty stomach. Do not exceed 1,000 mg without consulting a healthcare practitioner.

TYROSINE

Tyrosine is needed to create the neurotransmitters norepinephrine and dopamine. Not surprisingly, tyrosine deficiency can cause depression. Tyrosine helps the adrenal, thyroid, and pituitary glands function, and low levels of tyrosine are associated with low thyroid, which can affect cognition. Tyrosine is especially effective in improving short-term memory, increasing mental alertness, and protecting the brain from environmental stressors.

Dosage: I recommend supplements in the range of 500–2,000 mg per day.

METHIONINE

This amino acid does not form neurotransmitters. Rather, its value lies in its ability to detoxify the brain of heavy metals, including mercury and cadmium, that the body absorbs from dental fillings and food such as fish and seafood.

Dosage: I recommend 500 mg per day, taken with food.

Tryptophan and 5-Hydroxytryptophan

Tryptophan is the primary building block for the "feel good" neurotransmitter serotonin. Not surprisingly, tryptophan therefore helps to keep your thoughts calm and more focused. It is also helpful for insomnia, but tryptophan can cause unwanted drowsiness during the day. The Food and Drug Administration banned it in the United States in the 1980s because tryptophan products produced by a Japanese company caused dozens of deaths and hundreds of cases of serious illness. Even though the culprit was contamination and not the amino acid itself, tryptophan remains available only by prescription. But 5-hydroxytryptophan (5-HTP) is available over the counter, and it may be an even more potent brain supplement. Your body converts tryptophan to 5-HTP, which is used to produce serotonin and then melatonin. Anything tryptophan can do, 5-HTP can do—and maybe better. Studies do show that 5-HTP reduces anxiety and depression and raises endorphins, the body's own painkillers. Adverse effects are rare, but include digestive upset; this may be reduced by taking the supplements with food, although it may slightly reduce the supplements' effectiveness.

Dosage: I recommend 500 mg of tryptophan at bedtime, which can be increased to 1,000 mg as needed. Or, try 100 mg of 5-HTP at bedtime. It should always be taken with 25–50 mg of B complex.

These nutritional supplements have made a huge difference in many women's abilities to remember, think, learn, and concentrate. However, some women may need the extra power provided by the herbs and botanicals discussed in the next chapter. Just remember that supplements and brain-boosting botanicals both work best when you also supply your body with optimum nutrition.

CHAPTER 10

Step Three

Beyond Ginkgo—
Herbs *and* Other Botanicals

Can herbs and other natural medicines really help you to remember and think better? Absolutely! Food, nutritional supplements, hormone balancing, stress reduction, and exercise, all help your body achieve optimum brainpower on its own. Botanicals are medicines from plants that add something more—they are gentle yet powerful chemicals that can more completely restore and protect your mental capacity, and perhaps boost it to a new level. So, if you have incorporated the other elements of my program into your life, and are not able to achieve the effect you want, you may decide to take advantage of the extra push that certain botanical substances can provide.

Most likely, you've read or heard about Ginkgo and other brain-boosting herbs, herbal formulas, and "smart drugs" in magazines, or on TV, the radio, or the Web; and it's also pretty likely that you still aren't sure what kind of herbs to take, or how much, or when to take them. Are they worth the time, money, and effort? Are they safe? It's hard to tell when companies around the world market every substance imaginable and do so without any government body regulating their claims of effectiveness. As the *New York Times* reported in a March 23, 1998, article, "Although difficult to quantify—no agency or organization tracks online drug sales—much of the trade is in experimental and unproven substances." And a spokeswoman for Health Action International, a nonprofit consumer rights group based in Amsterdam, has stated, "While consumers think they're getting objective information, what they're actually getting is promotion."

You need straight answers to make your way through these hyped-up products that promise more than they can possibly deliver. This chapter will provide you with these answers. I feature only the most effective and most-studied natural substances and products with which I have had personal and professional experience. Perhaps you've even tried Ginkgo biloba, the most-hyped brain-enhancing botanical studied thus far. But as you'll see in this chapter, Ginkgo is not the only herb that may improve memory—it's only the most well known. And although it helps many people, Ginkgo may not be the most effective botanical for any individual in a given situation. My own mother is a perfect example. She took Ginkgo but did not notice any difference in her memory.

I switched her to huperzine, another botanical, which worked beautifully.

For the most part, herbs and other botanicals are natural, and are available without prescription through the same sources that sell nutritional supplements. Another group of substances, the so-called "smart drugs" are in another league—they generally require a doctor's prescription and are often imported from Europe. I do not usually include them as part of a brain-boosting program, but I discuss them briefly here to give you an idea of what is available in case you want to try them under the supervision of a health professional.

Adding Herbs and Botanicals to Your Program

Using the results of your self-assessment test (chapter 6), choose the herb or botanical that best suits your needs. As you'll see, certain products are better for some types of memory loss than others. In addition, if you are interested in prevention, use a lower dose; if you have mild to moderate cognitive impairment, use a dose in the higher range.

Remember, just because something is "natural" it doesn't mean it is innocuous. Herbs and botanicals are generally safe to take—far safer than any drug you can name. But they may cause undesirable reactions in some people. The most common symptoms of herb intolerance are nausea, stomach upset, or diarrhea; however, these are rare. If you suspect an adverse reaction, stop taking the herb or botanical immediately and consult a professional.

If you have a diagnosed medical condition or are taking medication for any reason, be sure to consult with your doctor before taking any herbs. Avoid herbs and botanicals if you are pregnant or lactating. Be sure to purchase all of your products from reputable companies who use the highest quality of standardized extracts (see Appendix B for resources).

Unless otherwise indicated, it is best to divide the total recommended dosage into several smaller doses throughout the day—three times a day with meals is customary. Generally, you should give herbs and botanicals at least one month to see if they are effective before you decide to increase the dosage or switch to another product. And remember, herbs and botanicals are not a quick fix or magic bullet for memory problems. You should use them as complements to the more basic foundation of brain-boosting steps in my program. Good nutrition, exercise, and stress management enhance the botanicals' effectiveness; this, in turn, allows you to reduce the dosage, which reduces cost and the possibility of experiencing any adverse effects.

Once you start taking a remedy, be patient—natural remedies tend to work more slowly than synthetic drugs. I usually evaluate my patients after a few weeks to see how they feel. Generally, most people feel better on herbs and botanicals and notice that their memories and thinking have improved remarkably, provided that these herbs are addressing the underlying cause of their memory problems. If you suffer from hypoglycemia or another medical condition, or have a lack of B vitamins or certain amino acids, herbs might help, but will not be the answer to all your problems. Since there are no definitive tests to determine which herbs are best for any individual, it is often a process of trial and error.

June is a good example of someone who immediately responded well to herbal treatment. In her mid-forties, she said she was in for a "midlife tune-up." She walked into my office with a laundry list of problems: Her sex drive was way down, she was depressed, and her brain function seemed to be diminishing almost daily. It seemed that she was not only forgetting more, but was having difficulty concentrating, comprehending, and learning new skills and information at her fast-paced job as an assistant in an attorney's office.

I took a complete medical history and went over her diet, sleep and exercise habits, and vitamins and medications. She said, "I'm not a pill taker. I will take one thing only." I prescribed 120 milligrams of Ginkgo daily, to be taken at breakfast. At her two-week follow-up appointment, she expressed delight that not only was her brain function enhanced, so was her sexual desire, mood, and even social behavior.

Ginkgo was the single "magic bullet" for June—a rare occurrence! Most people are not so lucky. Often just one remedy will not do the trick, and herbs and other botanicals must be safely combined for greater effectiveness. In fact, I rarely prescribe just one herbal remedy. I generally use a combination formula (Memoractiv by Thorpe, which contains phosphatidylserine, Ginkgo, acetylcarnitine, vinpocetine, and the Ayurvedic herb Bacopa) along with a therapeutic strength vitamin and mineral supplement.

For example, a patient of mine named Susan recently started working again after being out of the workforce for thirty years. She had to go back to work because she recently became divorced and had to work to support herself. Even though she got an entry-level position as a receptionist, she was overwhelmed by all the new things she had to learn: computers, voice mail systems, billing credit cards, and so on. She was not a "machine person" and had a difficult time comprehending all the steps she needed to perform in order to do her job. Although she was taking Ginkgo, she was disappointed with the results. She came to me in tears and said, "Just look at me! I'm fifty-five years old. Who ever thought I'd be returning to work full-time? My supervisor is younger than my daughter! Can you help me?"

I put Susan on Memoractiv, the combination formula mentioned earlier, since it is a good source of the herb Bacopa. Bacopa is a hard-to-find herb that I felt she needed because of its ability to improve memory and concentration while soothing nervousness and anxiety. When Susan returned after two weeks, she had a big smile on her face. She said, "I'm not over the hill after all. I'm starting to learn and master the steps I need to operate all those machines. Even though I still don't like the technological age, at least now I can keep afloat."

Herbs

Herbs usually come in several forms: loose herbs that you steep in water to make into a tea; tinctures, which you add to a small amount of water; and capsules. Tinctures and capsules are the easiest to take and are the most standardized and reliable when it comes to potency and dosage. Standardization refers to an extraction method that guarantees a certain level of concentration of an herb's components which have been clinically shown to have beneficial effects in particular situations. "Standardized" herbs are gaining in popularity because their consistency allows medical professionals to achieve measured results. Indeed, standardized herbs are forms I usually recommend to my patients.

GINKGO BILOBA

This ancient Chinese herb is an extract made from the leaf of the Ginkgo tree. It is the most well-documented plant extract used to support brain function—there are more than 1,000 studies of Ginkgo biloba from all over the world. The consensus is that Ginkgo does help many people improve a variety of brain functions. It has been shown to minimize age-related memory problems (affecting learning, short-term memory, and recall), concentration problems, and absentmindedness. It may also help ease dizziness and vertigo, which often accompany forgetfulness, and tinnitus (ringing in the ears). A 1995 study found that high doses of Ginkgo helped Alzheimer's patients as well. Another very rigorous study published in 1997 in the *Journal of the American Medical Association* duplicated these results: Patients who took Ginkgo for one month enjoyed improved memory and attention span; this improvement was even more noticeable when patients took the herb for three months. However, many experts believe its more significant contribution may be as a preventer of cognitive decline than as a treatment. Ginkgo is very popular in Germany and France, where more than 10 million prescriptions are written every year; in the United States it is available without a prescription.

Ginkgo seems to accomplish its many miracles in several ways. In the first place, it increases the circulation of blood to the brain, which improves the supply of oxygen, nutrients, and glucose. This enables neurons to create the energy and other chemical reactions you need to think and remember. It also boosts circulation to the inner ear, thus explaining its power to help heal tinnitus and dizziness, a malfunction of the nerves in the ear. In the second place, Ginkgo protects against free-radical damage and reduces inflammation. This further improves circulation by keeping your cardiovascular system in shape, and also protects the nerve cells themselves.

Supplements: I recommend an extract standardized to 24 percent flavoneglycosides and 6 percent terpenelactones, or capsules of the dried herb.

Dosage: For prevention take 40 mg of standardized extract, or 120 mg of capsules daily, in divided doses. You may take up to three times this dose if you have mild to moderate symptoms. Some people notice an improvement within two to three weeks of beginning treatment, but, in most cases, you need to take Ginkgo for at least three months before you enjoy the full benefits.

Adverse Effects: Gingko biloba is essentially devoid of any serious side effects. Some people have reported mild headaches for a day or two when starting the herb, and some people have reported mild stomach upset. Do not take Ginkgo if you are on a blood-thinning medication, including aspirin or ibuprofen, because Ginkgo can add to the blood-thinning effect. For the same reason, avoid taking Ginkgo for two weeks prior to any surgery, including oral surgery.

GINSENG

Ginseng is a root herb that has been used in China for thousands of years, and in America since the 1700s. Ginseng is a native to China, Korea, Russia, and America. Each variety has slightly different characteristics, but all act as an "adaptogen"—a substance that helps you cope with all kinds of physical and psychological stress. Chinese medicine says it balances "yang energy" and Western medicine says it improves the function of the adrenal glands.

As far as the brain is concerned, ginseng's power lies in its ability to control and lower the release of the stress hormone cortisol, which, as I explained in chapter 3, is deadly to the brain. Many studies confirm ginseng's beneficial effects on the brain: subjects taking this herb made fewer mistakes, had speedier reaction times, improved their scores on standard cognitive function tests (by more than 50 percent on average), and increased mental and physical stamina. Ginseng is popular as an anti-aging tonic used by many women during and after menopause to relieve symptoms of vaginal dryness, hot flashes, insomnia, and reduced libido. A recent study showed that women taking ginseng experienced an improved quality of life and less depression.

Supplements: Panax ginseng is the most popular form

used today, but *Siberian ginseng* is the type most often included in products geared to improve cognitive ability. Quality among all the varieties of ginseng varies widely. When buying panax ginseng extract, look for a product that is standardized for 7 percent ginsenosides; when buying Siberian ginseng extract, choose a product standardized for 1 percent eleutherosides E. Ginseng may also be purchased as a whole root from herbal pharmacies, broken into small pieces and chewed. This is the way it is used in China.

Dosage: For prevention, take 100 mg of extract, or 500 to 1,000 mg of capsules per day. This dosage may be tripled if your symptoms are mild to moderate and/or you are under a lot of stress. Some herbalists advise that you follow a three-weeks-on two-weeks-off schedule.

Adverse Effects: Used in the recommended dosage, ginseng is generally safe. In rare instances it may cause overstimulation or gastrointestinal upset. People with hypertension should not use ginseng. Long-term use has been reported to cause menstrual irregularities and breast tenderness.

BACOPA MONNIERA ("BRAHMI")

This plant extract has been used for more than 3,000 years as an Ayurvedic remedy in India. Long known for its beneficial effects on the brain, which the Hindus consider to be the center of creative activity, this herb is also known as "Brahmi," after Brahma, the creator of the universe. Since 1951, the Central Drug Research Institute (CDRI), a premier drug research institute in India, has been researching the Brahmi plant. Various CDRI studies have shown that Brahmi extract facilitates the acquisition, consolidation, retention, and recall of learned tasks. Additional studies showed that people who took Brahmi learned better and more quickly, and retained whatever they learned for a longer period of time. In another study, students who took Brahmi enjoyed peak improvement in concentration in the study's first hour. In the second hour, their concentration level was reduced to 50 percent, and in the third hour, to 25 percent. Studies also looked at retention of information. In normal circumstances, retention is 55 percent—in other words, people forget one out of two learned tasks. After taking Brahmi for a period of three months, the retention level increased to 95 percent—in other words people forgot only one out of every twenty learned tasks. In real life, Indian students who take Brahmi regularly reportedly excel in their examinations, so it's no wonder that "all across India school children are popping little green and yellow pills" containing this herb, as reported in *TIME* magazine in May 1997.

Bacopa also helps to combat stress, improve reflexes, and increase mental and physical power. Research has shown that Brahmi reduces "markers," or biochemical substances associated with stress. Two specific stress markers are heat-shock protein and increased levels of lipid peroxides in various brain regions. Brahmi prevented these increases in all the regions of the brain studied, particularly in the hippocampus region which is concerned with learning and memory.

Within the last twenty years, Indian studies have also shown that in adults, Bacopa improves concentration, short-term or immediate memory, and work production. The subjects in a particular study made fewer errors at work and experienced a reduction in nervousness, anxiety, insomnia, and irritability; all of these improvements further strengthened brain function and mental performance.

Scientists are still investigating the mechanism behind Bacopa's remarkable effects; we believe that the active memory components are Bacosides A and B, which can enhance the transmission of impulses from one nerve to the next. Bacopa is also an antioxidant and removes excess heavy metals from the blood, thus protecting the nerve cells from free-radical damage.

Supplements: Bacopa has a bitter taste and in traditional Ayurvedic medicine it is generally used in the form of paste or juice to which sugar, jaggery, raw date sugar, or honey has been added. Some of the traditional preparations with Brahmi are *Brahmi Ghrita* (in ghee, clarified butter), *sarasvatarishta* (a decoction used as a brain tonic), *Brahmi rasayana* (a rejuvenating formulation with other herbs), *Brahmi taila* (medicated oil), and *Brahmi sarbat* (a cooling drink). It is also available as an oil, and in a powdered extract, which many Americans find easier to take. Contemporary products are often standardized to contain 20 percent Bacosides A and B. When I prescribe Bacopa to my patients, it is always as part of a combination formula that contains other brain-boosting botanicals, such as Ginkgo and vinpocetine.

Dosage: Dosage depends on the form of Bacopa you take, so be sure to follow the instructions on the label. For example, for powdered extract, take ¼–1 teaspoon, three times daily; for the oil form, recommended dosage is three to five drops, once or twice a day. Expect to see improvements within four weeks.

Adverse Effects: There are no known side effects or toxicity when Bacopa is taken at recommended doses. In fact, Bacopa monniera is used safely even by children in India.

HUPERZIA SERRATA (HUPERZINE OR HUPA)

This ancient plant remedy from China is derived from a type of moss. It has been used for centuries to treat inflammation and fever, but scientists recently found that it also increases the level of acetylcholine, the memory neurotransmitter. Huperzia serrata also protects against cell death due to stress. The extract has been heavily studied in China, and more recently by major research centers in the U.S., such as the Mayo Clinic and Georgetown University. In animal experiments, HupA improved learning retention and recall better than the Alzheimer's drugs Aricept and Cognex.

There are promising human studies as well. In tests performed on Alzheimer's patients in China, huperzine improved memory and cognition in 36 percent. And it did this without the dose-limiting and unpleasant side effects of currently used Alzheimer's drugs. In another rigorous study conducted in several centers, 103 patients with Alzheimer's disease were given 200 mcg of HupA or a placebo for eight weeks. Study results showed that about 58 percent (twenty-nine out of fifty) of patients treated with HupA showed significant improvements in their memory, cognitive, and behavioral functions, while only 36 percent of those who received the placebo improved. In a rigorous study of healthy Chinese teenaged students, thirty-four pairs of students complaining of memory and learning problems were given HupA (100 mcg taken twice per day) or a placebo for four weeks. At the end of the trial, the students who received HupA had significantly higher scores on memory and learning performance tests compared to the students in the placebo group.

Supplements: I recommend a purified extract because there have been isolated reports of possible liver and kidney toxicity associated with raw preparations. Huperzine occurs in forms "A" and "B," (-) and (+). The most biologically active form of huperzine is (-) huperzineA; this is often branded as "Memorzine."

Dosage: The generally recommended dosage is 50 mcg twice a day, although most studies used 200 mcg per day, and this appears to be safe.

Adverse Effects: The reported side effects are generally mild and include dizziness and headaches. However, no long-term safety studies have been conducted.

Other Natural Substances

This category of cognitive enhancers includes a fatty substance made from soybean oil, a medicine made from a plant, and a hormone.

PHOSPHATIDYLSERINE (PS)

Phosphatidylserine, or PS, is a form of fat that is part of all cells, but is especially concentrated in the brain cells.

We've known about the effects of PS supplements, derived from soy, since the 1970s: improved cognition in mature adults. Since then, more than two dozen studies of older adults have refined the results. In 1991 a landmark study showed that PS can, for example, improve your ability to learn and remember names and faces, and recall telephone numbers, misplaced objects, and paragraphs. It also proved to enhance participants' ability to concentrate. The researchers wrote that PS was able to "roll back the clock" by about twelve years. In other words, subjects remembered as well as people twelve years younger. Other studies with PS have also shown improved recall of events from the previous day and from the past week. In other studies, people in their sixties who were experiencing memory difficulties and took phosphatidylserine outperformed those who took Ginkgo biloba. PS has also improved young males' ability to cope with physical stress from athletic training. It has improved attention span, behavior, ability to learn, and mood in children, and shows promise as an adjunct to Ritalin therapy. In Europe, PS is used to treat Alzheimer's and other forms of senile dementia.

Phosphatidylserine affects many aspects of brain-cell metabolism. It strengthens the cell membranes and protects against deterioration of the cell structures and their functions. It helps nutrients enter the cell more easily and helps to remove the waste products of metabolism. PS helps the cell produce energy, and imaging techniques suggest it can revitalize and rejuvenate cell metabolism throughout the brain. It also increases the production of the neurotransmitter acetylcholine. Last but not least, PS increases the effectiveness of Ginkgo in improving circulation to the brain.

Supplements: PS is found in lecithin, but not in a pure form; a capsule supplement containing only PS is preferable.

Dosage: Take 100–300 mg daily for prevention and treatment of mild memory loss; take up to 600 mg daily for mood enhancement.

Adverse Effects: There are no consistent reports of significant side effects associated with PS, and no well-known drug interactions with phosphatidylserine.

VINPOCETINE

This plant-based medicine is derived from the periwinkle plant. It has been popular in Europe and Asia as a treatment for memory problems and epileptic seizures. Although there are more than 100 human studies using vinpocetine, this substance is not yet as well studied as Ginkgo. However, it seems to work in the same way and offer similar benefits. Some experts believe that with more study, we will find that vinpocetine surpasses Ginkgo in effectiveness.

Vinpocetine has been studied in young, middle-aged, and older people and in healthy individuals as well as those with diagnosed medical conditions. These studies provide evidence that vinpocetine can improve both short-term and long-term memory, and enhance alertness, ability to learn, speech, and language. Hungarian researcher Gedeon Richter has conducted a series of studies involving 882 patients with neurological disorders ranging from stroke to cerebral insufficiency. In these studies, 62 percent of the patients improved significantly overall. In one of the studies, cerebral insufficiency patients were asked to memorize a list of ten words. At the start of the study, they were able to memorize an average of six words. After a month of taking vinpocetine, patients memorized ten words on average.

The short-term memories of normal, healthy volunteers have also benefited from vinpocetine. In a double-blind crossover study, women between the ages of twenty-five and forty took a computer-administered short-term memory test called a Sternberg Memory Scanning Test. The test involved showing volunteers one to three digits on a computer screen. A moment later, they were shown a long string of digits. The women then indicated whether any of the first digits appeared in the long second string. Women who took 40 milligrams of vinpocetine took, on average, less than 450 milliseconds to respond when the first set contained three digits; the women who took the placebo took an average of 700 milliseconds to respond. That means vinpocetine doubled their memory power.

Vinpocetine has such remarkable effects on thinking and memory because it is a vasodilator—it relaxes the blood vessels and improves blood flow to all parts of the body, including the brain. As a result, your brain gets more oxygen and more glucose to create energy. Hence, sometimes vinpocetine is described as "Viagra for your brain." It also improves energy production more directly, protects nerves from free-radical damage, and "scavenges" heavy metals in the body. Studies show that through its effects on circulation, vinpocetine protects your heart and entire circulatory system. Some studies also demonstrate that vinpocetine helps minimize dizziness and tinnitus (ringing in the ears), and improves and protects your eyes in many ways. It may also reduce damage to the brain due to stroke.

Supplements: Until recently, you had to pay a high price for vinpocetine, as it was available only imported from Europe. It recently became available at relatively low cost in the U.S. through suppliers of natural supplements.

Dosage: 15–45 mg per day.

Adverse Effects: Adverse effects are rare, but include low blood pressure, dry mouth, weakness, and increased heartbeat if taken in very high doses. It appears to have no interactions with other drugs.

DHEA (Dehydroepiandrosterone)

You may never have heard of it, but DHEA is the single most prevalent hormone in the bloodstream. This major sex steroid hormone is produced by your adrenal glands and is a key player in your body's stress response. DHEA affects all hormones and your body converts DHEA to other hormones including estrogen, progesterone, and testosterone. DHEA levels begin to dip between the ages of twenty-five and thirty; by the time you are eighty-five years old, your DHEA may be only 5 percent of what it was in your youthful prime. So, the theory goes that use of DHEA therapy to restore levels to those of bygone years should also bring back youthful vigor and energy.

Studies seem to support this theory. Perhaps the most remarkable and most often cited is a human study that showed an association between DHEA replacement and an increase in perceived physical and psychological well-being in both men and women (including increases in lean body mass and muscle strength). Other studies showed that DHEA improves neurological function (including memory), immune function, and stress disorders. It is also useful in treating depression; one study showed a 60 percent improvement in middle-aged people—a far better result than conventional antidepressant medications. DHEA crosses the blood-brain barrier and can affect serotonin, the feel-good neurotransmitter; it also lowers levels of cortisol. Both of these actions can help elevate mood and improve cognition. In rats, DHEA has been shown to increase acetylcholine levels (needed for transmission of nerve impulses) in the hippocampus region of the brain, which is the primary seat of memory and learning. A study published in 1996 also indicated that DHEA could protect brain cells from the early changes associated with Alzheimer's disease.

Supplements: DHEA is available in health food stores in tablet, capsules, and liquid.

Dosage: The generally recommended dosage is 10–50 mg per day.

Adverse Effects: There are no reports of toxicity at doses that restore DHEA to normal, youthful levels. However, DHEA is a precursor to estrogen, testosterone, and progesterone, and adverse effects of an excess of

DHEA include elevated levels of one or more of these hormones. I agree with the many practitioners who feel it is not wise for women to take DHEA without medical guidance and careful monitoring of hormone levels.

Smart Drugs

In addition to the herbs and botanicals I recommend, there are other products used for cognitive enhancement. Known as smart drugs, many of these compounds were originally designed to help people with neurodegenerative diseases such as Parkinson's disease and Alzheimer's disease hold on to what they were losing. It didn't take long to figure out that healthy people—many of them in their twenties—could also use these drugs to turbocharge what they still had and gain an extra edge. Today, many health practitioners also recommend them to patients who complain of mild to moderate memory loss and failing concentration. Smart drugs have become a billion-dollar industry; we can expect to see more of them down the line as they emerge to satisfy the people clamoring for means to increase their mental vigor in order to keep up with the ever faster beating of the technological drum.

These "nootropics" (from the ancient Greek, meaning "acting on the mind") are derived from many different sources and act in a variety of ways. Some are derived from neurotransmitters and other chemicals your brain uses to process memory. Although my patients rarely need to use them, and I don't recommend using them without a doctor's supervision, you may want to consider them as an option. To give you an idea what's currently available, I've outlined below some of the drugs most commonly used today.

PIRACETAM (NOOTROPIL)

This is the original smart drug reported to improve memory, clarity of thought, alertness, concentration, problem-solving ability, and verbal skills. As the oldest smart drug, piracetam may be the most studied and most used. It is said to work by stimulating the production of acetylcholine as well as increasing the sensitivity of neurons to this neurotransmitter. It also helps cognition by improving the supply of oxygen, the metabolism of glucose (the brain's source of energy), and the connection and communication between the left and right halves of the brain. Some studies indicate that piracetam slows the progress of Alzheimer's disease; in one study, this drug markedly improved patients' memory test scores in as little as seven days. Piracetam has also been studied in healthy people—and both older people and young university students benefited. It has also benefited people with mild memory impairment. Piracetam is a popular smart drug that works best in conjunction with phosphatidyl choline and Hydergine, another smart drug, described below. Piracetam has not been approved for any use by the Food and Drug Administration and must be obtained from outside the United States.

Deprenyl

Deprenyl protects dopamine, the neurotransmitter involved in normal muscle movement, libido, and immunity, as well as cognition. Deprenyl is what's known as an MAO-B inhibitor; decades ago it was found to interfere with monoamine oxidase B (MAO-B), a chemical that breaks down dopamine. In addition, deprenyl increases the brain's supply of dopamine by stimulating neurons that produce it. Not surprisingly, deprenyl is becoming a mainstay in the treatment of Parkinson's disease, a condition in which there is a severe drop in the levels of dopamine. Parkinson's patients who take deprenyl not only experience fewer tremors and other physical symptoms, they also experience improved cognition. In several studies with Alzheimer's patients, this drug improved concentration, all types of memory, and the ability to complete sentences. Along with vitamin E, deprenyl is being studied as a possible preventer of Alzheimer's. Deprenyl is now a popular smart drug that is available by prescription, although the FDA has approved it only for use in treating Parkinson's disease.

Hydergine

Hydergine is an extract of a fungus and has a long history of treating various senile dementias. This substance improves blood flow to the brain, helps your body dissolve lipofuscin (fatty deposits that interfere with cell functioning), boosts metabolism of the neurons, and acts as an antioxidant. It seems to improve memory alertness and clarity of thought, mental response times, and mood and sleep. It is available by prescription in the U.S. and Europe.

GALANTAMINE

This is a supplement extracted from the common snow-drop or daffodil that helps increase the concentration and effects of acetylcholine, the primary memory neurotransmitter. Galantamine is used to improve memory, improve muscle function, and fight fatigue. It shows promise as a nontoxic way to reset your body's biological clock—a boon for frequent fliers and shift workers—and as a therapy for sufferers of chronic fatigue. This experimental drug is currently being studied in the treatment of Alzheimer's disease.

PHENYTOIN (DILANTIN)

This drug seems to improve intelligence scores and long-term memory. It is used to treat epilepsy and is believed to help people with obsessive depression. Studies show phenytoin helps balance hormones in the brain.

ONDANSETRON

Ondansetron is said to improve memory, "name face recall" in particular, by increasing levels of acetylcholine, a neurotransmitter.

VASOPRESSIN (DIAPID)

This hormone is said to improve memory and concentration, and increase attention span.

GEROVITAL (H3)

Gerovital is a combination of several compounds, including the anesthetic procaine. It appears to improve memory, mood, and energy. It is available as Gero-Vita (in form 6.H.3) in the United States.

ANIRACETAM

This is similar to piracetam, and is said to be effective in treating aging-related mental lapses.

ASPIRIN

Aspirin recently became a staple in the heart disease prevention cupboard, and it may be the next smart drug. New studies indicate that because of its blood-thinning ability, aspirin may reduce clots in the brain and thus stave off the tiny strokes that lead to senile dementia.

SAM-E (S-ADENOSYL-L-METHIONINE)

SAM-e is as effective as Prozac for depression, and without any adverse effects. But you don't have to be interested in SAM-e for its mood-elevating benefits to enjoy its memory-enhancing effects. Studies have shown cognitive improvement with SAM-e supplementation in people with dementia.

PREGNENOLONE

Pregnenolone is a steroid hormone that your body converts to DHEA, which in turn is converted into estrogen, progesterone, testosterone, and other hormones—hence its nickname, "the grandmother of all hormones."

Pregnenolone boosts the release of acetylcholine and improves transmission of nerve capsules. Studies also show that it can enhance memory.

Many of these drugs have been proven to work on animals. Today hundreds and thousands of people are taking smart drugs, and they report improvements and few side effects. But the animal studies are short-term, and therefore we do not know what kinds of effects these drugs might have on humans in the long run. What happens if you take the drugs for twenty or thirty years or more? What happens when you stop? What are the optimal safe doses? What if you combine them? These drugs are still controversial. They should only be used by people with severe memory problems, and only under the supervision of qualified healthcare practitioners with knowledge and experience in this area. I recommend you turn to these pharmaceuticals only if the natural therapies in this book do not help enough after a fair trial. And let the buyer beware: very few of these drugs have been approved by the FDA. Many are made outside the U.S. and must be purchased through the mail; as a result, they may not meet the quality control standards we have in this country.

We don't know what the future holds, but we can assume that there are more cognitive enhancers down the line. We can only hope that they will be even more effective and widely available, and that we better understand how to use them to obtain the best effect. In the next chapter, you'll learn about another approach that includes natural substances that help improve your brainpower in a different way—by restoring your hormone balance.

CHAPTER 11

Step Four

Hormone Replacement Therapy

*M*any of the women who see me professionally because of memory problems experience additional symptoms related to hormone imbalance. Science has recently begun to appreciate the connection between estrogen and the brain, so it's not surprising that if a physician pays attention to a midlife woman's complaints of memory problems, he or she tends to look at only this one aspect. I've had many women come to me after their physicians automatically prescribed estrogen replacement therapy, thinking it would take care of the problem. Happily, some women do improve when they receive estrogen therapy. Unfortunately, for most women, hormone pills, patches, or creams are not a panacea. Most women's brains and bodies are not that simple. For example, there are other factors that may coexist with hormone deficit, and which may also be directly or indirectly related to memory problems. Even if hormones are a factor, the hormone therapy may not be supplying the woman with the right type or amount of hormone or hormones.

Menopause is not a disease. The years surrounding it are a time of transition, a time when your hormones are changing in a way that resembles puberty in reverse. Today, women have many choices about how they will ease this transition. In this chapter, I discuss the pros and cons of hormone therapy in all its forms—including conventional hormone replacement therapy (HRT) with synthetic hormones, hormone therapy with natural hormone products, and other natural approaches that help your body find its equilibrium and restore thinking power on its own.

The Problem with Conventional Hormone Replacement Therapy

The most commonly prescribed estrogen replacement is a pill containing estrogen that is derived from the urine of pregnant mares (hence the name of the most popular brand, Premarin). Estrogen is also available in adhesive patches applied to the skin (usually the thigh or abdomen). Because the hormone is absorbed more slowly through the skin, rather than quickly (and in one dose) by the digestive system, patches are thought to cause fewer adverse effects than pills. Some women prefer the patch simply because it's easier to remember to change the patch twice a week than to remember to take their estrogen pills every day. There are also estrogen creams, which are usually applied to the vaginal wall. Creams are most often prescribed for women whose major complaint is vaginal dryness and uncomfortable intercourse. The estrogen in the cream is also absorbed into the bloodstream, by which it travels throughout the body.

What can estrogen therapy do? In my opinion, the benefits have been vastly oversold. Studies show that estrogen therapy does help with vaginal dryness and atrophy; it also reduces hot flashes and slows osteoporosis (this effect stops once you stop taking the estrogen). However, studies do not show that estrogen therapy improves sex drive. For that, you need testosterone, the sex drive hormone for men and women; but when testosterone is given to women it causes unwanted side effects such as excess body and facial hair. There are contradictory studies on whether HRT can improve mood swings, memory, and concentration.

What are the risks in exchange for this slender list of benefits? Recent studies show that rather than reduce the risk of cardiovascular disease, HRT can actually increase it. According to a 1999 article in the *Journal of the American Medical Association,* "there is no overall cardiovascular benefit to HRT; and there is a pattern of early increase in risk of coronary heart disease." Estrogen therapy also increases the risk of breast cancer, high blood pressure, and thromboembolism (dangerous blood clots in the veins).

There are more problems. Estrogen, when given

alone, causes the uterine lining to build up continuously, which increases the risk of uterine cancer. So, progestin, a synthetic progesterone, is also usually prescribed to women who still have a uterus. Like your body's natural progesterone, the progestin causes the uterine buildup to slough off, reducing the risk of uterine cancer. It does not eliminate it completely, however, and adding progestin to the regimen can cause temporary bleeding and PMS-like symptoms, such as bloating, to appear.

Why should HRT be fraught with so many problems? Isn't it just replacing what nature is taking away? Actually, no. In the first place, it does not replace all the dwindling and wildly fluctuating hormones. Estrogen and progesterone are not the only hormones that change at this time—testosterone, DHEA, and cortisol also are affected. Your thyroid may also slow down. Conventional HRT ignores these other key hormones. Furthermore, HRT is not "natural"—it replaces your estrogen and progesterone with horse estrogen, which is not human estrogen, and with synthetic progestin which isn't a perfect match to human progesterone.

Finally, conventional HRT does not take into consideration that women actually produce three forms of estrogen. *Estradiol,* the most potent form, is secreted by the ovaries and is the predominant estrogen during reproductive years. It is one of the driving forces behind your reproductive and menstrual cycle. It stimulates breast growth and the maturation of your other sexual organs, promotes fertility, and maintains pregnancy and lactation. It keeps your skin, muscles, and organs elastic, toned, and firm, and your bones strong. When your childbearing years are over, however, an excess of estradiol can increase your risk of breast cancer. *Estriol,* on the other hand, is the form of estrogen that naturally predominates during the postmenopausal years. If your body is healthy, it converts the estradiol it still produces to estriol, which confers similar benefits to your body but is safer and perhaps even protective of your health. There is compelling evidence to suggest that estriol acts as a cancer preventer by filling receptor sites and preventing other estrogens from lodging there (such as unconverted estradiol and harmful xeno-estrogens, discussed in the section on environmental pollution in chapter 4). In spite of this evidence, conventional hormone therapy includes only the estradiol form of estrogen, which is actually the most dangerous form for older women. The third type of estrogen is known as *estrone* and is mainly the interim step in converting estradiol to estriol.

HRT may help some women to some extent, but often it helps only a little, and other approaches may work better without adding the risk of side effects. Take Sharon, for example, who went back to college at the age of 39 and whose peri-menopausal symptoms were interfering with her academic performance. She began with Premarin pills and switched to an estrogen patch, which helped minimize her hot flashes and improve her moods, but did "nothing" to help her memory or the depression that was worsening her memory problems. She didn't want to take an antidepressant because she was concerned about the side effects. She wondered if she should start taking vitamin E supplements, because a woman she knows was having memory problems, too, but after taking vitamin E "became the best in the class." Or consider Sybil, age 49, who has experience with both the estrogen patch and oral Premarin. She says, "The hormones helped the short-term memory loss, but not completely. At least I could take the Post-its off my body and just stick them around the house instead! But even on the Premarin, I once found myself buying a magazine and thoroughly enjoying the whole thing from cover to cover. When I walked into my bedroom I discovered another copy of the exact same magazine, which I had bought—and read—two weeks before."

By the way, these days testosterone is being used for libido and the latest trend is to try it for cognitive problems. But I am not convinced it is effective, and women usually stop taking it fairly quickly because it makes them sprout hair in the wrong places, or lose the hair on their heads, or become too aggressive.

Natural Hormone Therapy

Recently, hormone products that are more natural have become available. Natural hormones are usually synthesized from soy or yam. Even though this means they are "semi-synthetic," they are still a closer match to your own hormones than either horse estrogen or synthetic progestin. In the case of estrogen, the products usually contain a more favorable balance of all three estrogens, not just estradiol, which is the least desirable form during menopause. Natural estrogen is available in a cream form that can be applied to the vagina or to other parts of the body where the skin is thin and the cream is easily absorbed. Natural progesterone is also available as a cream.

Some physicians believe that during peri-menopause and into menopause, progesterone deficiency, not estrogen deficiency, is the cause of menopause symptoms. They point out that estrogen is not the only hormone that fluctuates at these times. Brain fog, short-term memory problems, and a host of other physical and mental symptoms therefore have their origin in "estrogen dominance," which is related to a deficiency in another hormone—*progesterone.* When estrogen is "unopposed" by progesterone, estrogen therapy will not make symptoms better—it can actually make them worse. In my experience, very often a moderate supplementation of a natural transdermal (through the skin) progesterone will clear up or greatly modify many mental and emotional symptoms: fatigue, brain fog, mood swings, irritability, depression, crying jags, hypoglycemic reactions, mental exhaustion, aggression, insomnia, inability to concentrate, as well as many physical symptoms that accompany peri-menopause and menopause. Natural progesterone doesn't seem to cause the PMS-like symptoms that progestin does.

Many women find they do better on natural hormones. Anna, a nurse, felt like "the bitch from hell on Premarin." She says, "I was always looking for a fight, constantly irritable. I feel calmer on the Tri-est." Lynn, a civil-rights attorney, finds that she, too, gets better results with natural hormone therapy, although she is still not back to her old self. She says, "I don't have the brain fog anymore, but I definitely don't have the cognitive ability that I once did." Sybil concurs: "I felt better instantaneously on the natural hormones. The brain fog lifted—not completely—but I am so much better." Desiree, age forty-four, takes plant-based hormones and knows she is fortunate to have gotten such a dramatic result—she knows when it's time for her next dose "without looking at the clock," because she notices her thinking "starts to get fuzzy again."

However, women are highly individual, and some women actually feel worse on hormones, even when they are natural. Lucy says she found some relief with Estrace, but switched to natural Bi-est estrogen and natural progesterone. "My problem," she says, "is that the progesterone makes me so sleepy, and I am now more forgetful. I am a paralegal and cannot focus on the material enough to remember anything."

Natural hormone products are available through special pharmacies called compounding pharmacies. As is the case with synthetic estrogen, natural estrogen requires a prescription, but progesterone does not. These pharmacies can work with your physician to compound hormone preparations to meet your individualized needs. The cost of these products may not be directly billable to your medical insurance carrier, but some may reimburse you for these medications. Even though they are natural, you cannot use these hormones on your own; you need to work with a physician who is familiar with them. (See Appendix C for organizations that can help you find one in your area.) And remember, they are still not a substitute for a healthy lifestyle; in fact, they work better when you

LOOK TO YOUR THYROID?

Some physicians believe that an underactive thyroid may be a contributing factor to estrogen or progesterone imbalance and the cognitive problems that ensue. They say that even if a woman's test for thyroid deficiency comes back normal, thyroid hormone supplement should be given a try, because the test may not be accurate (see chapter 5). They find that the right thyroid supplement normalizes thyroid deficiency and thus enables you to make your own estrogen and progesterone in adequate amounts. I have found that thyroid hormone therapy may be a better choice than either progesterone or estrogen replacement therapy for some women who are experiencing menopause symptoms, including memory problems, cognitive changes, and brain fog.

also support your body and brain with good food, nutritional supplements, exercise, and stress management.

Using Hormones Wisely

If you are considering taking either synthetic or natural hormones, I recommend that you first get a comprehensive evaluation of your hormone status. Blood tests are the conventional approach but may not always be an accurate way to test the hormone levels in your tissues. Some practitioners prefer to use a saliva test, but I believe the test of choice today is twenty-four-hour urine collection. I and many other practitioners use test results as either guides or confirmations to make recommendations. Many experienced practitioners go more by symptoms.

If you do find a hormone imbalance, you should realize that most physicians are pro-HRT and often send a woman home with a sample of the latest estrogen that the drug sales representative gave him or her. I feel that even if you opt for conventional hormone replacement therapy, this knee-jerk one-size-fits-all type of prescribing is a mistake. You need to experiment. If you try HRT, give it three months and then assess the effects. If there is no improvement, change the dosage, the form, or the ratio between estrogen and progesterone. Right now, there is no single "right" regimen for all women, and no regimen tested to address cognitive problems specifically. Studies using half the regular dose of estrogen and/or progesterone are promising, and ultra-low dose regimens are also being tested.

Don't be afraid to voice your issues and concerns to your physicians and to expect individualized treatment. Lisa, a forty-seven-year-old legal secretary, was put on Premarin by her gynecologist, but when she found out what Premarin was made from, said, "I'm not taking that horse hormone." After four years of experimentation, she finally found a hormone replacement therapy—one that is yam and soy based and made by a compounding pharmacy—that suits her. Zelda, a fifty-year-old computer programmer, began with estrogen therapy and soon added a progesterone cream. She had her hormone levels tested and was found to have the testosterone of a seventy-year-old, so DHEA, which the body converts to testosterone, was added to the mix. "That gave me enough energy and clarity of thought to really start to work on my problem," she says. Zelda had been on thyroid medication for years, but her doctor had recently read studies showing that many women need a medication that contains two types of thyroid hormone instead of the single hormone most commonly prescribed. When she switched medication, within three days, Zelda felt as if her brain was "working better." She says, "It hasn't completely cured my problem, but my thought processes are faster, sharper. It takes me less time to get from thought A to thought B. I don't feel like I'm slogging through a thick swamp anymore."

Other Natural Approaches

Many women do not find either synthetic or natural hormone replacement therapy appealing—either because they cannot or will not tolerate the side effects, because they don't like the idea of using an artificial substance, or because it is too risky because of their personal or family medical history. If you are among them, there are other ways to balance estrogen levels besides a pill, cream, or patch. These are covered in other chapters and include diet, nutrition, herbs and other botanicals, exercise, and stress management. Incorporating these aspects of my program into your life will help you through this phase more comfortably, gently supporting your body in its own efforts to get back on an even keel. In addition, there are specific herbs to take and foods to eat that help balance hormones.

Hormone-Balancing Herbs

There are many herbs that can ease menopausal symptoms in general, often through their estrogen-like effects. You may find that a single herb is all you require; or you may find that a combination works better for you. Herbs can have many subtle effects and many women find they get the safest and best results when they work with a trained herbalist. Below are the most commonly used hormone-balancing herbs and the recommended dosages. Ginseng is also a very effective hormone-balancing herb; refer to chapter 10 for more information on ginseng and on herbs in general.

DONG QUAI

This Chinese herb has traditionally been used to treat menopause symptoms for centuries. It is thought to work through its mild estrogenic effect, and by stabilizing blood vessels, which protects the cardiovascular system.

Adverse Effects: This herb is not recommended for women who have bloating, heavy bleeding, diarrhea, fibroids, or any tenderness or discomfort in the breast. It should not be taken if you are on blood-thinning medication.

Dosage: 15–30 drops of tincture one to three times a day.

BLACK COHOSH

A Native American remedy for "female problems," black cohosh is a tonic for the nerves and helps restore hormonal balance by encouraging the body to rebalance itself. It mimics estriol, the best type of estrogen for women of menopausal age. Black cohosh is sold in a standardized potency under the name of Remifemin, and has been used by millions of German, Austrian, and Scandinavian women.

Adverse Effects: Do not take this herb if you are pregnant or experiencing heavy menstrual bleeding.

Dosage: Follow package directions for standardized tablets; or take 10–30 drops of the tincture, diluted in pure water (best if sipped throughout the day).

RED CLOVER

This herb has beneficial effects on the cardiovascular system and contains isoflavones, which are compounds with hormone-like activity. Soybeans (which I'll discuss later in the chapter) have been getting a lot of attention because of their isoflavone content, but red clover contains four types of isoflavones compared to soy's two.

Adverse Effects: Red clover is generally considered to be safe.

Dosage: Take 2 standardized 500-mg capsules three times a day, or ½ teaspoon of tincture three times a day.

I have gotten excellent results prescribing herbs to my patients, even in women with severe memory problems and hormone imbalances. For example, Linda is a very well-known healer and nutritionist who made an appointment to see me. "I've been to everybody," she said, "so you are my last resort." Ten years before, when she was forty-three, she had had a laparoscopy (an examination of the ovaries and fallopian tubes with a lighted tube inserted through a small incision in the abdominal area). After she woke up from the anesthetic, she felt as if "everything changed." She was thrown into instant menopause, was chronically depressed and fatigued, and was getting sick all the time. But worse than anything, she was afraid that she was becoming "brain dead" because her memory, concentration, and cognitive abilities were diminishing day by day. She had tried natural hormones and various herbs and vitamins, but nothing seemed to help. I took into consideration the totality of her symptoms and prescribed two to five grams of Siberian ginseng daily. She soon sent me an E-mail telling me how much better she was feeling. Her memory had definitely improved, and her concentration and her cognitive abilities had improved enormously. What's more, she was happy to report that she also had more energy and better circulation.

Hormone-Balancing Foods

Food can be another reliable source of phyto-estrogens, hormone-like compounds that function in several ways. These plants have estrogen-enhancing or estrogen-like effects, but are not the true estrogens that are produced by our bodies. These plant components are just beginning to be studied, but there is evidence that they help normalize or balance hormones. Sometimes they act like weak estrogens and lock on to the estrogen receptors of cells, which might protect breast cells from the harmful effects of the estradiol form of estrogen. This process could also protect cells from the cancer-promoting effects of *xeno-*

FOODS RICH IN PHYTO-ESTROGENS

Try to include more of these foods in your daily menu to boost your supply of natural estrogen:

- Soybeans and soy-based products, including tofu and soy milk
- Any and all beans
- Fruits, including apples, figs, dates, pomegranates, cherries, citrus, and apricots
- Plants and vegetables, especially alfalfa sprouts, garlic, sprouted green peas, fennel and anise seeds, parsley
- Cruciferous vegetables such as broccoli, cabbage, brussels sprouts, cauliflower, kale, and collard greens
- Nuts and legumes including lentils, split peas, cashews, peanuts, almonds, and flaxseed
- Whole grains such as wheat, oats, and corn.

---

estrogens—estrogen-like substances found in our polluted environment. Sometimes they seem to change the way our bodies react to our own estrogen. And sometimes they help our body's natural ability to convert estradiol to estriol. We are still not sure whether plant estrogens are a good idea for women with a personal or family history of reproductive cancers, including breast cancer. Plant estrogens such as those found in soy might stimulate the cancer, or they might block the cancer-promoting effects of the body's stronger estrogen. Too much estrogen from any source, like too much of anything, could be dangerous to your health.

I often recommend to my estrogen-deficient patients that they emphasize soy and other phyto-estrogen-rich foods that support and enhance estrogen production and use. Soy beans and soy foods are the best sources of the two most-studied plant estrogens, genistein and daidzein. It appears that soybeans themselves are the richest sources. Even though tofu is bland and tasteless, it is that quality that makes it so easy to disguise by adding small amounts of crumbled tofu to pizza, in chili, soups, stews, sauces, and casseroles, and even in oatmeal. Try some of the new soy food substitutes for burgers, burritos, and desserts. Below are several recipes from my book on soy cooking, *Yes Tofu, No Moo.* These were the favorites of my cooking classes at the Los Angeles City Colleges, where I taught for nine years. Because other beans are good sources of phyto-estrogens, I have included a few additional recipes using other beans as well.

Ten Hormone-Balancing Recipes

Pasta with White Beans and Clam Sauce

SERVES 4 TO 6

1 pound linguine, shells, or other pasta shape

1 tablespoon olive oil

4 cloves garlic, minced

2 8-ounce bottles clam juice

2 6.5-ounce cans minced clams, reserve juice

3 cups cooked small white beans, or 1½ 16-ounce cans, drained and rinsed

½ teaspoon dried thyme leaves
¼ cup chopped parsley
Salt and freshly ground black pepper, to taste

Cook pasta according to package directions; drain. In the meantime, heat oil in a large nonstick skillet over medium-low flame. Add garlic and cook, stirring, until tender. Stir in clam juice and juice from minced clams, then beans and thyme. Simmer for 5 minutes. Cool slightly. Transfer the mixture to a food processor and process until smooth. Return mixture to skillet. Add clams, parsley, and salt and pepper, to taste, and heat through. Toss with cooked pasta and serve.

Lentil and Orange Salad

SERVES 4 TO 5
4 cups cooked lentils, or 2 16-ounce cans, approximately
2 large oranges, peel and pith removed, sectioned
½ cup chopped red onion
¼ cup thinly shredded basil leaves
2 tablespoons apple cider vinegar
4 teaspoons extra-virgin olive oil
¼ teaspoon salt or to taste

In a large bowl, combine lentils, oranges, onion, and basil. In a small bowl, whisk together vinegar, oil, and salt. Toss vinaigrette with lentil and orange mixture. Serve at room temperature.

Tofu–Brown Rice Burgers

SERVES 4

Oil for baking sheet
1 pound tofu, drained and crumbled
2 cups cooked brown rice
2 tablespoons olive oil
2 cloves garlic, diced or minced
1 large onion, finely chopped
1 carrot, grated
½ cup wheat germ, or whole wheat pastry flour, as a binder
1 to 2 eggs or egg whites, as a binder
Tamari soy sauce, to taste
Olive oil (for sautéing)

Preheat oven to 350°F; oil baking sheet. Mash tofu in bowl. Add cooked brown rice. In a medium skillet, heat olive oil and add garlic, then onions, and sauté until golden and translucent. Add carrots and sauté until tender. Combine cooked vegetables with tofu and rice; add wheat germ. Beat egg or egg whites and combine with mixture. Season to taste with tamari. If too loose, add more wheat germ. Form patties and bake on oiled sheet at 350°F till brown.

NOTE: These burgers can be served hot or cold, and freeze well.

Incredible Rice Pudding

SERVES 6

Oil for casserole dish
1 pound tofu, well-drained
½ cup maple syrup
Juice and zest of 2 lemons
1 tablespoon vanilla extract
1 to 2 eggs or egg whites (optional)
1 cup cooked brown rice
1 cup unsweetened, finely-shredded coconut
½ cup raisins

Preheat oven to 350°F. Combine tofu and wet ingredients in a food processor and process until smooth. In a large bowl, stir together wet mixture and remaining ingredients. Pour into casserole and bake at 350°F for 45 minutes to 1 hour. Serve chilled.

Tofu Spinach Quiche

MAKES TWO PIES

2 tablespoons olive oil
2 cloves garlic, finely chopped
2 onions, diced
1 pound tofu, drained and broken into pieces
2 eggs or egg whites as binder
2 bunches fresh spinach, stemmed, washed, drained, and finely chopped
Tamari soy sauce, to taste
Garlic powder, to taste
2 9-inch pre-baked whole grain pie crusts
½ cup sesame seeds

Preheat oven to 350°F. In medium skillet, heat oil and sauté garlic and onions until golden and translucent. In food processor, combine tofu and eggs; process until smooth. Place tofu and egg mixture in a large bowl and fold in spinach. Season to taste with tamari and garlic powder. Divide spinach mixture between pie crusts, sprinkle with sesame seeds, and bake for 1 hour at 350°F, or until set. Serve hot or cold; this dish tastes even better the next day.

NOTE: Fresh spinach may be substituted with 2 packages of frozen chopped spinach, defrosted and water squeezed out. Eggs or egg whites may be substituted with 1 cup cooked rice.

Noodle Kugel

SERVES 6

Oil for baking dish
¼ cup light olive oil
¼ cup rice syrup
2 eggs or egg whites, beaten
½ cup seedless raisins, soaked in ½ cup warm water until plump, drained
½ cup chopped walnuts
½ teaspoon cinnamon
1 8-ounce package egg noodles, cooked and drained
½ pound tofu, drained, mashed with fork

Preheat oven to 350°F. Lightly coat baking dish with oil. In a large bowl, combine oil, rice syrup, eggs or egg whites, raisins, ¼ cup chopped nuts, and cinnamon. Add the noodles and tofu and mix well. Pour into oiled baking dish and sprinkle with remaining chopped nuts. Bake at 350°F for 30 minutes, or until firm. Serve chilled.

Corn Cakes

1 cup tofu, mashed well with fork
2 eggs or egg whites, beaten
¾ cup whole wheat pastry flour
Tamari soy sauce, to taste
2 cups whole kernel corn cut off the cob, or canned corn, well drained
¾ cup chopped scallions, whites and part of green
1 tablespoon olive oil, for frying
Guacamole or salad dressing, optional

Combine all ingredients through scallions in a large bowl; mix until doughy consistency is formed. Heat olive oil in a large skillet over medium heat. Drop corn cake mixture by tablespoon into skillet, flatten with fork, and pan fry to golden brown on both sides. Drain on paper towels and serve topped with guacamole or your favorite dressing.

Pineapple Cheesecake

MAKES TWO 9-INCH PIES

   1 pound tofu, drained
   ½ cup rice syrup or maple syrup
   1 tablespoon vanilla extract
   2 eggs or egg whites
   Juice and zest of 2 lemons
   1 8-ounce can unsweetened crushed pineapple,
      well drained
   ½ cup chocolate or carob chips
   2 9-inch pre-baked pie crusts

Preheat oven to 350°F. Combine first five ingredients in food processor; process and transfer to large bowl. Fold in pineapple and divide mixture between pie crusts. Bake at 350°F for 30 minutes. You may add chocolate or carob chips to tofu mixture before baking or use to garnish pies before serving.

Chickpea and Pasta Salad

SERVES 6

   3 cups cooked or canned chickpeas (garbanzos), drained
   3 cups cooked whole grain short pasta, like penne or elbows
   ½ cup chopped celery
   ¼ cup chopped red pepper
   ¼ cup chopped green pepper
   3 tablespoons chopped red onion
   ¼ cup plain low-fat yogurt
   2 tablespoons light or soy mayonnaise

1 tablespoon red wine vinegar
Salt and freshly ground pepper, to taste

Combine all ingredients in a large bowl. Toss well and serve.

Split Pea and Spinach Soup

SERVES 6

2 tablespoons olive oil
1 cup chopped onion
1 clove garlic, minced
1 tablespoon whole mustard seeds
1½ teaspoon powdered turmeric
1 pound dried split peas, rinsed and drained
5 cups chicken or vegetable stock
5 cups water
½ teaspoon salt
1 10-ounce package frozen chopped spinach, defrosted and drained
¼ cup lemon juice, or to taste
Salt and freshly ground pepper, to taste

In a 4-quart saucepan, heat oil over medium heat. Add onion, garlic, mustard seeds, and turmeric. Cook, stirring, until onions are tender and mustard seeds begin to pop. Stir in peas, stock, water, and salt. Bring mixture to a boil, reduce heat, and simmer, uncovered and stirring occasionally, until peas have disintegrated (2 to 2½ hours). Add spinach and lemon juice. Season with salt and pepper, heat through, and serve.

Look before You Leap

Before making a decision, women should thoroughly inform themselves about the pros and cons of hormones in general, and what hormones do to their bodies. Some women have been on Premarin and Provera for years and are doing fine, while other women tell me their mothers did nothing and they don't want to do anything. If a woman tells me she wants to take hormones, I usually recommend natural hormones from either a compounding pharmacy such as the Women's International Pharmacy or my office. It is my belief that women should take the minimum dose of the safest natural estrogen and progesterone that keep symptoms at bay, and then find natural adjunctive treatments for the rest of their symptoms.

I hope this chapter has given you at least a glimpse of what hormone therapy can and cannot do for your memory and concentration. For more details, you can refer to one of the many available books about dealing with menopause naturally (see Appendix D).

CHAPTER 12

Step Five

Stimulate Your Body *and* Brain

"I'm not much for exercising, even though I know I should do more. I just don't have the time," says Terry. "But I do notice that if I can start the day with a long brisk walk, my mind is clearer and I have more mental and physical energy. I'm more creative and I have better meetings with my clients. The day just somehow seems to go better."

*B*y now, we all know that exercise is good for the body, and many people realize it also gives them a psychological lift. But studies show that exercise is also an amazing brain booster. For all these reasons, I have made exercise an important component of my memory enhancement program. Whether you walk, run, dance, do headstands, the backstroke, or karate kicks—if you want to think and remember better, you've got to move. In this chapter, I explain why exercise is so good for your brain and how to tailor your exercise program to your specific needs, preferences, and time constraints. I'll also discuss the whys and ways of mental exercise, another proven technique to keep you from losing your mental muscle.

Dumbbells—or Smart Belles?

Aren't we lucky to live in an era when women no longer have to be soft and weak to be considered attractive and sexy? Gone are the days when women didn't sweat—they "misted" and delicately dabbed their dewy foreheads with a lace hanky. Today, smart women work out. Exercise is good for the body, and what's good for the body is good for the brain.

Exercise improves health in general. It also prevents many of the conditions related to memory failure—cardiovascular and blood sugar problems, hormone imbalance, depression, stress, and insomnia. Regular exercise also helps minimize symptoms of chronic disease, and even reverses them, and therefore should be part of a comprehensive treatment program for these conditions.

How good is exercise for the brain? Well, it may be the closest thing we have to a fountain of youth, suggests a study reported in 2000. Researchers at the University of Illinois compared a group of eighteen- to twenty-eight-year-olds with a group of sixty- to seventy-five-year-olds. They gave both groups cognitive tests at the start of the experiment. Then for six months the older subjects either did an aerobic workout or a gentle toning and stretching session three times a week. When they were re-tested, the aerobic group improved their scores in the tests of "executive control processes" and approached the scores of the younger group. They were better able to plan schedules, make and remember choices, and quickly reconsider them if circumstances changed.

What's more, studies show that people who exercise regularly are at lower risk for developing Alzheimer's. Numerous studies show that even walking is good for your memory, especially as you age. In one study, elderly people were either put on a walking program or allowed to remain sedentary. The walking group significantly improved their memories, but the sedentary group remained forgetful.

Exercise works its magic in several ways. Physical exercise boosts your metabolism, so body processes move along at a brisk, efficient pace, and toxic substances are processed and excreted more effectively. This includes the metabolism in your neurons, increasing the amount of oxygen and glucose available to produce the energy required to take care of all the cells' activities. By improving the blood circulation to the brain, exercise also improves the availability of nutrients and enzymes needed to maintain and repair neurons, including antioxidants to protect against free-radical damage. A better blood supply also helps rid the cells of waste products created by metabolism. About 25 percent of your body's blood supply gets pumped to your brain, even though your brain accounts for only 2 percent of your total body weight.

Exercising your body not only builds and tones muscles, it builds and tones your brain itself. It whips into shape the parts of the neurons responsible for producing neurotransmitters, including dopamine and norepinephrine. It increases the ability of your body and brain to absorb oxygen, which gives life and energy, and can make all the difference in your capacity to think. It enhances the production of *nerve growth factor* and *neurotrophic factor,* two chemicals that support brain function. In animal experiments, rats that ran on treadmills produced more growth factor and thus stimulated the growth of neurons in many parts of the brain, including those that govern thinking, memory, learning, and reasoning as well as physical movement.

Exercise reduces stress. It is especially helpful for people whose natural tendency is to cope with stress primarily by responding physically—for example, by pacing, or by cleaning house. If you are fidgety and jiggle your foot, tap a pencil on your desk, and toss and turn in bed, exercise is the release valve that helps you let go of physical tension. It also enhances mood, instilling a feeling of well-being and calm for four to twenty-four hours after the activity, and enabling you to better weather the ups and downs of life. Many studies show that exercise is a balm for depression and is a useful adjunct to psychotherapy. In one study of people fifty years old or older, exercise compared favorably with Zoloft, a popular antidepressant. In the long run, exercise actually did a better job of keeping symptoms at bay.

Exercise also burns calories, gives your metabolism a boost, and controls appetite. It helps you control your weight and improves your nutrition by allowing you to eat more wholesome, brain-supporting food and improving digestion and nutrition absorption.

A Balance of Mind and Body

It seems likely that a lot of the cognitive decline we equate with getting older is really related to our overwhelmingly sedentary lives. Evolutionarily speaking, we are designed to be active and to balance activity with rest. You may have devoted your time and energy to developing your intellect, your career, your finances, and have left little time to your physical bank account. While we can abuse our bodies when we are young, it eventually catches up with us. It's one thing for a twenty- or even thirty-year-old to spend hours in front of a computer or TV set. It's another for a forty-, fifty-, or sixty-year-old. It may look like "resting" but rest must be balanced with physical activity, or it is in truth hard on the body and the mind. What are you resting from? Being physically active can actually rest the mind, by giving it a break from the usual thinking tasks and patterns.

The fitness boom and our obsession with the latest diet notwithstanding, Americans are fatter than they ever were, perhaps the fattest people in the world. The baby boom generation is also the least fit, and the least physically active, in the history of the country and the world. Gee, do you think there's any connection? Few of us would want to go back to the drudgery of the "good old days." But back then life did offer some advantages.

Everyone was physically active for several hours a day. For many people, earning a living required muscle, sweat, and movement. As did relaxing. People (including women) hauled laundry, groceries, and coal; we farmed or worked in factories and on piers; we walked to and from work and friends and family. We chopped food and washed dishes—by hand! And when we relaxed, we danced, we played games, and above all, we strolled.

Today, we ride, we sit, we click. So, we have to make an effort to set aside time to be physically active and fulfill our evolutionary requirements, to keep our brains and bodies truly alive and vital. And age is no barrier—or excuse. There are many studies that show it's never too late to begin to be active (or to be active again), and that muscles, lungs, and heart respond beautifully once asked to work the way they were designed to. For example, in a study, fifty- to seventy-year-olds were put on an exercise program. After only four months their ability to absorb and use oxygen efficiently—an indication of their cardio-vascular fitness—increased significantly. And not surprisingly, they scored higher on cognitive tests, particularly in their ability to process information quickly and to focus.

Your Activity Program

You enter a health club. You see row after row of span-dex-and-sweatband-clad exercisers, eyes glued to the TV monitor or lost in their own worlds while tethered to their personal CD or cassette players. They walk, run, cycle, stair step up to heavenly bodies. They are surely getting a good workout—hearts pumping, sweat flowing, lungs expanding, muscles toning. In fact, my current favorite is the elliptical glider, which I use while watching TV to make the time pass faster.

But if these don't appeal, there are plenty of other ways to get your body working and boost your mind and memory. The good news is that you don't have to become a marathoner or a cyber-stepper to improve neurological functions. You don't have to be super fit to be super smart.

Studies show that moderate activity is sufficient to improve physical and mental health. In fact, too strenuous a workout schedule can actually harm your immune system, increase free-radical activity, and cause damage to your body, especially your joints. It's enough just to walk for about half an hour a day to reap the physical and mental benefits. But we are not talking about low-key stroll here. (Although that, too, would be better than nothing.) You need to set a pace that will allow you to cover at least three miles an hour. To keep motivated, try to vary the route; and don't use bad weather as an excuse. Bundle up in cold weather; hit the malls when it's too hot.

The most important thing is to choose an activity you like. Walking might be your starting point, or your mainstay. Variety keeps you interested, gets more parts of your body moving in different ways, and reduces the chance of overuse injuries. You may decide to pump up the volume and add jogging or running to your regime, or aerobic or ballroom dancing, in-line or ice skating, swimming, bicycling, team sports, skiing, yoga, or martial arts. Just remember to start slowly and gradually increase the length and/or intensity. Having a regular exercise partner or buddy can make working out more fun and motivating, plus the guilt factor of bailing out on your friend can help keep you committed. Find something you will do at home such as an exercise videotape, or a piece of equipment (although, honestly, this usually ends up as a very expensive clothes hanger).

Think about other ways to add activity to your life outside of a formal exercise program. Take a brisk short walk during a lunchtime break; if you can, walk, bike, or skate at least part of the way to your workplace or when running errands; take the stairs instead of the elevator; garden on the weekends; play with a child; help restore a natural habitat or park; fly a kite; go kayaking. And remember to take frequent mind-and-body breaks if you have a sedentary job. Get out of your chair, stretch, walk around, and get those physical and mental kinks out.

I have noticed that almost everyone resists exercising. And most people still resist exercise until twenty minutes into it—that's the point at which it starts to feel good! I have been exercising for eighteen years, and I still resist it. I find I need to get to the gym to do it, and the hardest part is getting there. If you can deliver your body, you've won half the battle. I usually bribe myself with a steam bath or a soothing soak in a hot tub afterward. One thing that helps is to vary your routine, change your workouts, and take a class so you can just follow instructions. My co-author is a big fan of aerobic dance classes. Not only does she love the dance-like movement, but learning and following the choreography challenges her brain in a way totally unlike her work—and she's relieved to let someone besides herself tell her what to do for a change.

If you can't find something you like, try, and then try again. One of my patients is an actress who leads a very busy life and needs to make herself available for auditions. She is very weight- and diet-conscious, but when she reached her late fifties, she put on a few pounds that stubbornly would not come off with her usual techniques. I broached the topic of exercise, and she became very defensive and said, "I hate exercising," "I hate to sweat," and "I just won't do it!" We spoke a little more and I found out she lived in the Hollywood Hills and had fabulous hiking trails behind her house. I asked if she would be willing to take a walk with a friend in the hills, and she said she would try it. Well, to make a long story short, seven years later she still hates to "exercise" but wouldn't miss her hike in the hills to which she is now "addicted." Perfect! My goal is to have my patients become "addicted" to exercise, and to remind them that variety or cross-training is the spice of life.

Start out slow, do your workout, and then cool down. If you are in pain for days afterward, you've done it too intensely. I have seen too many patients with exercise burnout, chronic injuries, exercise bulimia, and weekend athletic injuries. Stop or slow down when you've had enough rather than force yourself beyond your limitations. It's so much better to leave yourself hungry for more and looking forward to the next time. Treat your body with respect and listen to that inner voice that will always tell you what it wants.

You can expect to see results soon, in body and mind. Just ten weeks, according to one study, is enough time to

---

ARE YOU WORKING HARD ENOUGH?

To get an aerobic effect and improve your cardiovascular system and circulation to the brain, exercise needs to be of a certain intensity. To see if you are exercising strenuously enough to enjoy this effect, use a simple formula. First, determine your target heart rate: Take 220, subtract your age, and then multiply the difference by 70 percent. For example, if you are 50 years old, you would multiply 170 by 70 percent to get a target rate of 119. Second, compare your target rate to your heart rate during exercise. While exercising, stop or slow down a moment to take your pulse, using the tips of the first three fingers. Place the tips on your neck, about one inch below your ear, or at the inside of your wrist, one inch above the crease. Press lightly until you feel the throbbing of your heart; count the beats for 6 seconds, then add a zero to find the rate per minute. If it is below your target rate, you need to increase your intensity; if it is too high, slow it down.

---

notice significant results in fluid intelligence, learning ability, and mood. Twenty-six days was all it took for another group of exercisers to improve their scores on tests of verbal fluency, concentration, and abstract reasoning. In this case, the study subjects were an average of sixty years old and walked or jogged six to ten miles a day.

Mental Exercise: Use It or Lose It

Is your brain getting flabby? Are you using some parts too much and others too seldom or not at all? Research shows that "neurobic exercise"—mental gymnastics and stretching—are as important to a thriving brain as physical activity.

Animal experiments have shown amazing results. Laboratory rats living in rich, stimulating environments, full of thought-provoking activities and things to do and explore, were compared with rats living in boring cages with little or nothing to do. The rats living in the "Disneyland" version of life—with toys, treadmills, climbing tubes, running wheels, and novel food—differed remarkably from their "cage potato" cousins. Their brains exploded with growth; they had bigger, fatter cells and more of them, more synapses, thicker, longer dendrites, and new blood vessels to transport glucose and oxygen. This translated into better performance in finding their way through mazes and other things lab rats do. In other words, the mentally stimulated rats were smarter and learned and remembered better. Old rats and young rats alike got brainier—the old rats' brains just took longer to change.

Interestingly, women who have gone to college stay mentally and physically fit longer than women who have not gone on to higher formal education. They live longer, too, and are at lower risk for Alzheimer's. Could it be that college-educated women are better fed or enjoy other benefits of a higher socioeconomic status? Perhaps that's part of it. But another part is that mental stimulation beginning at an early age lays down a more plentiful foundation of brain cells and connections, so if you lose some cells later on, it doesn't deplete your "account" as drastically as that of a woman whose earlier life was less stimulating. (This is similar to osteoporosis, which is delayed in women who lay down more bone tissue in their youth.) Researchers have also discovered that people with intellectual hobbies—doing crosswords, playing a musical instrument—had a lower risk of developing Alzheimer's.

Your brain craves new things, new challenges. Like your body, it needs activity to stay healthy and vital, and to grow. And although it develops most impressively in your youth, it also continues to grow as you get older, allowing you to continue to compensate for any cell damage and cell death you encounter on your journey through life.

Of course, there is such a thing as too much stimulation, which becomes overwhelming and stressful and is no longer enjoyable. But studies show that the more we use our brains for thinking, reasoning, learning, and imagining, the bigger and better they become. So, get your brain out of its rat cage of dullness and sameness. Office workers: get up and learn to tango. Dancers: learn to play chess. Sales reps: learn to paint. Stay-at-homes: become a museum guide. Vary your routine. Use all your senses to stimulate more areas of your brain. Neurobic exercise involves the new, the unexpected, along with the use of more senses than you are accustomed to. The idea is not how difficult it is to do something, but how different it is from what you normally do. If you surprise your brain, it will surprise you. Whatever turns you on and is novel in your life will also turn on the growing mechanism in your brain. And who knows? You may even learn a skill that you can use in your work, giving you a double benefit.

Answers from the East

Can a karate kick help you concentrate better on the job? Can a headstand help you remember where you put your keys? Many Eastern cultures have practices that are specifically designed to exercise and unite the mind and body. Yoga, karate, tai chi—Western culture has no parallels, but we are fast adopting and adapting these treasures.

Martial arts' track record for improving intellect and ability to focus is so impressive that they are the latest complementary therapy for children with attention deficit disorder. Dr. John Ratey, an associate professor of clinical psychology at Harvard Medical School and an expert on the disorder, says, "martial arts help these kids more than an ordinary sport like soccer or baseball." He admits that no one knows what is happening for sure, but he says that he has no doubt that "something in the brain is changing." He theorizes that the repetitive, slow, structured nature of martial arts demands a kind of concentration that force coordination of the attention centers of the brain. Says one twelve-year-old with ADD who was quoted in the *New York Times,* "I learned that you have to concentrate . . . to get the movements right. And that just carried over into school and everything changed." Dr. Ratey adds that dancing or gymnastics might have similar benefits. And perhaps similar benefits can be reaped by older adults who have trouble concentrating and remembering as well.

If martial arts are not your style, something gentler such as tai chi or yoga may fit the bill. Many of my patients give their yoga practices major credit for restoring and maintaining their mental capacity. Dharma Singh Khalsa, M.D., writes in his book *Brain Longevity* that mind-body exercises such as yoga can have specific influences on the biochemistry of the brain, partly by increasing blood flow and energy flow to the brain, and partly because they release beneficial brain chemicals including neurotransmitters.

Yoga builds physical and mental strength, flexibility, balance, and grace. It helps you reach a state of awareness, tranquillity, and well-being. Practicing yoga regularly helps balance and rejuvenate your nervous, endocrine, reproductive, digestive, and circulatory systems. The calmness and focus achieved during yoga practice carries over into the rest of your life, and the practice of yoga knows no age limits.

Take One Small Step

Exercise can be your first step in saying "no" to a mental treadmill that could be killing your brain. Take Sherry, for example, who began as one of my most challenging patients. She worked for an attorney and found herself constantly stressed out because her job entailed not only a very fast pace, but a lot of overtime. She never seemed to have time for herself. By the time she got home, she was too exhausted to exercise or even make herself a decent meal, and so she grabbed what was fast or had pizza delivered. This caused her to gain weight and feel very depressed that she wasn't taking care of herself. Sometimes she would have some cheese and a few glasses of wine, and would wake up feeling hungover. It was a vicious cycle that she could not seem to break. I suggested that on the weekends she take just one yoga class, and go for a walk. She found a yoga teacher she loved and was inspired to squeeze another class in during the week. The yoga class and the walking sparked her energy, lifted her mood, and motivated her to make the effort to eat better, too. She started thinking about dinner before she went home and would pick up some chicken, a yam or potato, and a salad. This simple maneuver broke the cycle of putting herself second. She also began to set boundaries at work and to take a lunch break to eat the nutritious dinner leftovers she brought from home. Exercise was the catalyst for these changes and made a huge difference in Sherry's life, mood, and ability to think. It was also a key factor in reducing her stress levels, which is the topic of my next chapter.

CHAPTER 13

Step Six

De-Stress *and* Streamline Your Life

Stress is often a key player in brain burnout, but, ironically, forgetfulness itself can add yet another layer of stress by wreaking havoc on your self-confidence, self-esteem, and faith in the future. Forgetfulness can be exceptionally difficult to bear if you are accustomed to being in charge of your life. You may be at a key point in your life: perhaps you have struggled to make it and want to hold on to your position, or perhaps you are still scrambling to achieve and the climb is getting harder every day. Does it stress you out even more to be reminded that stress is a major factor in as many as 80 percent of all major illnesses from heart disease to cancer, and that it leads to anxiety and depression—as well as affects memory loss and the ability to think clearly?

Isn't it time to do something about it?

The self-assessments in chapter 6 helped you determine the physical gaps and flaws in your current lifestyle and pointed the way to using nutrition, nutritional supplements, and exercise to tailor my brain-boosting program to your individual needs. These physical approaches will definitely go a long way toward helping you cope with stress in general. Eating a balanced diet such as the one I recommend in chapter 8 nourishes your brain and keeps your nerves on an even keel. Nutritional supplements counteract the nutrient deficiencies caused by your "revved up" nervous metabolism, and perhaps stave off the physical and mental ailments that might result. A good multivitamin-mineral formula in the doses recommended in chapter 9 usually supplies the nutrients you need to counteract nutrient depletion and feed and calm your nervous and endocrine systems. Vitamin C and the B vitamins are particularly important for the nervous system and the adrenal glands. And exercise is a superb tension reliever, but it only works against stress and depression if you do it regularly. Unfortunately, in times of stress healthy habits often fly out the window as we revert to unhealthy comforts. We may turn to junk food to relieve anxiety and stress, drink gallons of coffee and diet soft drinks to keep us going long after we are exhausted, and perhaps indulge in cigarettes, alcohol, or other prescription or recreational drugs. We may not have the time or energy to take supplements or exercise regularly. Yet, these are the worst times to indulge in quick fixes and lapses because they ultimately bite back and further stress your system, including your brain. No question, these physical approaches are essential to any de-stressing program. But they are only part of the picture.

In this chapter, I suggest approaches that are mental and psychological—life-altering steps that go more directly to the heart of the matter. Are there ways you can change your situation to fix or eliminate certain stresses? Can changing your attitude about stress help you minimize its effect on your ability to think straight? Can resetting priorities help you slow down, streamline, and simplify your life? This chapter guides you toward finding answers to these questions; it also provides tips on getting a good night's sleep and using simple, tried-and-true relaxation techniques to help you break the vicious cycle of stress begetting forgetfulness begetting more stress. Like many women, you may find it most effective to use a combination of several of these approaches. For example, you may want to start with relaxing herbs or calming meditation. These approaches may help you get to the type of self-examination that will allow you to get to the roots of your stressful state of mind.

Try Calming Herbs

Conventional medicine treats stress with anti-anxiety and tranquilizing drugs such as Valium, but these may be habit-forming and impose unwanted side effects. Instead, you may want to treat stress and its cousins, anxiety and insomnia, with natural herbal remedies that are gentler on the system and can be just as effective. Ginseng, because of its ability to help your body adapt to stress, is also a good choice at this time (see chapter 10). These herbs are available at health food stores and many pharmacies. If you are or may be pregnant, or are nursing, or have a diagnosed medical condition, consult a professional before taking any herbs.

KAVA-KAVA

This herb calms the mind as well as the body and is a superb anti-stress and anti-anxiety remedy. It is often included in herbal sleep formulas along with valerian. Take up to three times a day in the following dosages:

500–700 mg of the dried root in capsule form
½–¾ teaspoon liquid extract
150–230 mg of an extract standardized for 30 percent kavalactones

Adverse Effects: May cause drowsiness if taken during the day. Should not be combined with alcohol or taken by anyone suffering from depression or taking certain medications.

VALERIAN

This is the most popular and traditional herbal sedative, and is used widely in Europe. Studies have shown that this herb improves the quality of sleep and helps people fall asleep faster. Instead of making you drowsy in the morning as conventional sleeping pills do, valerian actually increases morning alertness. Studies show it works as well as small doses of Valium or barbiturates. Take about 45 minutes before bedtime in the following dosages:

1,000 mg of the dried root in capsule form
1 teaspoon of liquid extract
150–300 mg of an extract standardized for 0.8 percent valeric acid

Adverse Effects: Do not combine with alcohol.

CHAMOMILE

This herb is known for its soothing qualities and is helpful during times of stress and anxiety, and also helps calm a nervous stomach. Take in the following dosages up to three times a day:

500 mg of the dried herb in capsule form
½–1 teaspoon of liquid extract

Adverse Effects: Do not take with alcohol or sedatives.

Get a Good Night's Sleep

Getting enough sleep isn't a waste of time! Depriving yourself of sleep fuels your stress. If you need an alarm clock to wake up instead of waking up naturally, you are shortchanging your body and mind of the rest they need to face the day. Unfortunately, alarm clocks are not the only things that disturb our sleep. Even women who have slept deeply and soundly all their lives may be suddenly bothered by insomnia at midlife. Nearly one-fourth of midlife women report that they have trouble sleeping—twice as many as young women. Midlife stress and fluctuating hormones can deregulate your biorhythms and lead to anxious, fitful sleep. Exhaustion leads to more stress and stress leads to insomnia in a vicious cycle that can be frustratingly resistant to change. Night sweats, the evening equivalent of hot flashes, can make things worse by disrupting sleep.

If you suffer from occasional, acute insomnia, or sleep fitfully and wake up tired, following my program should help you to restore a normal sleep schedule. In addition, you may want to adopt some of these sleep-supporting habits.

- Avoid all stimulants such as coffee, sugar, alcohol, nicotine, and cola, especially after 4:00 P.M.
- Establish a regular bedtime and waking time that remain the same for weekends and vacations.
- Create your own bedtime ritual to cue your body that it's time to wind down and disengage from daytime problems and thoughts. Many women are able to relax by reading, taking a hot bath (especially with certain aromatic oils as explained later), or listening to music.
- Avoid aerobic-type exercise in the last two hours before bedtime because it is stimulating. Yoga and gentle tai chi may be just what you need to calm down before bed.
- Try to eat a light supper; you may find it relaxing to eat a snack such as toast or a small bowl of cereal an

hour or so before bedtime. Some studies show that eating a high-protein meal late in the day is detrimental to sleep, while carbohydrates encourage drowsiness. There's some evidence that eating a diet rich in tryptophan, an amino acid, encourages normal sleep patterns. (Over-the-counter tryptophan supplements were taken off the market in the United States because of toxicity problems due to contamination during manufacture by one supplier; however, they are now available by prescription.) You can also get small amounts of this calming nutrient by eating tryptophan-rich foods, including turkey, bananas, figs, dates, and yogurt, at your regular meals.

- Wear earplugs if your bedroom is noisy. Use a sleep mask and cover windows with heavy blinds or drapes if too much light comes through. Make sure the room temperature is comfortable and that there is adequate air circulation.

- Keep the bed for two things—sleep and sex. Using the bed for working overtime or paying bills signals the mind for activity, not relaxation.

- Experiment with naps. Some people find daytime naps helpful, while others find they make it more difficult to sleep at night.

- Take extra calcium and magnesium at night—they are helpful sleep inducers when taken together. Divide your total daily supplements to include at least 500 mg of calcium and 250–500 mg of magnesium before bedtime.

- Try using a relaxation technique (see page 262),

which you can use both during the day and at night before retiring.

- Use aromatherapy for sleeping difficulties. Essential oils should help if in your nighttime bath or on your pillow. The most effective oils are lavender, chamomile, and neroli because of their sedative properties. Benzoin is helpful when worries are keeping sleep at bay; bergamot is best when depression is the cause.

- Have your hormone levels checked if you are experiencing other menopausal symptoms. High cortisol, low DHEA, or an imbalanced estrogen-progesterone ratio may be a marker for stress-related insomnia, and you may want to consider hormone replacement therapy.

- Take calming herbs before bedtime (see page 256).

- If night sweats are disturbing your sleep, emphasize foods and supplements that contain vitamin E (up to 1,200 IU per day), which has reduced daytime and nighttime flushes in one-half to two-thirds of the women who've used it. Citrus fruits, which are rich in bioflavonoids, are another natural weapon against hot flashes. Or take a supplement of up to 900 mg of bioflavonoids per day. Cut out refined sugar, sweets, chocolate, and caffeine—these can all worsen hot flashes and night sweats. Most importantly, eat foods that are high in plant hormones every day, such as soybeans, grains, peas, yams, and alfalfa. Herbs also help balance hormones. (See chapter 10 for more information about balancing hormones.)

Mind-Body Techniques

Mind-body techniques calm and clear your mind. They range from deep breathing to taking a walk in nature, from gardening to quiet meditation. What follows are some simple techniques that you can do at home or in the workplace. What binds them together is their ability to relax the body and calm and focus the mind. They also help prepare your mind and spirit for the de-stressing steps discussed below.

Breathing Techniques

Of course you have noticed how the simple act of taking a deep breath helps you calm down. It's instinctual. The practice of yoga has developed breathing into a fine art and a highly effective tension-taming technique. In yoga, the breath is called "prana" and is believed to be the life force entering your body with each breath, rejuvenating you with the energy of all creation. Specific breathing exercises are said to help balance consciousness, make you more creative, and allow you to feel joy, peace, bliss, and love. If you practice yoga, you can incorporate breathing into the poses or do these breathing exercises while sitting comfortably on the floor (preferably cross-legged) or in a chair. You can also do them to prepare you for meditation.

DEEP ABDOMINAL BREATHING

This is a simple technique that helps reduce anxiety, depression, nervousness, muscle tension, and fatigue.

Dark, quiet surroundings help, but once you have the hang of it, you can do this anywhere, any time you need "time out." All it requires is that you pay attention to your breath. Only the inhalation should require any effort—allow the air to flow out on its own as you let the weight of your chest and abdomen relax.

1. To begin, rest one hand on your abdomen and one on your upper chest. Breathe in slowly through your nose, attempting to fill your abdomen first by lowering your diaphragm. This may take several tries for some women—imagine your torso is a balloon, expanding from the bottom up.
2. Once your abdomen is filled, keep inhaling and fill your chest, allowing it to expand in the front, back, and sides.
3. Exhale slowly through your mouth, first emptying your chest and then your abdomen.
4. Repeat the inhalation and exhalation, trying to slow the breath even more. This should feel like a wave of air, rhythmically entering and leaving your body. Enjoy the turnaround times between the ins and outs of your breath—this is your "still point" or "gap" of higher consciousness and deeper relaxation.

ALTERNATE NOSTRIL BREATHING

This kind of breathing is marvelously rejuvenating. It brings energy and clearness to the mind. For best results, use Deep Abdominal Breathing, described above, for the inhalations and exhalations.

264 • Female and Forgetful

1. Using your right hand, place your thumb next to your right nostril and your middle finger next to your left nostril. Gently but firmly close off your right nostril with your thumb. Inhale through your left nostril.
2. Release your right nostril and close off your left nostril with your middle finger, exhaling through your right nostril.
3. Keeping your left nostril closed, inhale through your right nostril.
4. Close off your right nostril and exhale through your left nostril.
5. Inhale through your left nostril, and so on. Repeat this breathing pattern twelve times.

TOTAL BODY MUSCLE RELAXATION

This is another basic technique that builds on the Alternate Nostril Breathing exercise. It is based on alternately tensing and relaxing your muscles. It effectively slows your breathing and heart rate, leaving you rested and refreshed. Give yourself a half-hour to begin, and, as you become adept, you may reduce the time to twenty or fifteen minutes. Begin in a warm, quiet room; disconnect the telephone if possible.

1. Lying down, close your eyes and take a few deep breaths. Begin the Deep Abdominal Breathing exercise described on page 262 and try to maintain it throughout the relaxation.
2. Focus your attention on your right foot and point your toes very hard. Hold for one slow breath and

then let it go completely limp. Work up your right leg by flexing and relaxing your foot, tensing and relaxing your calf, and then tensing your thigh until your kneecap slides up toward the thigh. Then let it go, enjoying the contrast between the tensed and relaxed sensations. Do the same with your left foot and leg.

3. Squeeze and relax the rest of your body, moving up from your buttocks, to your waist, back, chest, right hand and arm, left hand and arm, shoulders, neck, and scalp. Include your face, opening your mouth and eyes wide, then scrunching them tight before completely relaxing those muscles.

4. Stretch your arms and legs to their longest length, and elongate every muscle in between. Relax.

5. Return your attention to your breathing and surroundings, and open your eyes.

Meditation

Meditation is not a religion, although it is an integral part of many religions, including Roman Catholicism, Jewish mysticism, and Tibetan Buddhism. Meditation has many techniques, goals, and effects. One thing many meditations have in common: they allow the mind to settle into a pool of welcome calm, where mental chatter ceases, at first for moments, and then, with practice, for minutes at a time. During these moments, you experience the state of pure being, of oneness with the universe. New worlds open up within you and without you, as you take your consciousness and mental powers to a new level.

Meditation alters brain waves to enhance those associated with improved cognition and deep, creative, insightful thinking. It also enhances your ability to learn. As you become more grounded and centered, you feel clearer and your thinking becomes more fluid and flexible. Studies have shown that meditation is deeply relaxing and rejuvenating. It lowers respiration, oxygen consumption, and metabolic rates. It reduces the blood levels of stress hormones, which are associated with aging and brain neuron death. New research shows that meditators have up to nearly 50 percent higher levels of DHEA— the "youth hormone"—than nonmeditators. Some long-term meditators have been found to be five to twelve years younger biologically than they are chronologically, as indicated by their blood pressure, visual acuity, and hearing.

There are many schools of meditation, but one of the easiest and most common techniques is the inward focusing of attention by concentrating on (meditating upon) rhythmic breathing, an object, or a word, thought, or mantra such as the word "om." Meditation is a different experience for each person and each session is different as well. The following exercise will help you get a glimpse of what meditation feels like. If you want to know more or explore this practice more deeply, there are many books and schools available.

1. Sit in a comfortable position that you can hold for 10 to 15 minutes, in a quiet place where you won't be disturbed by the phone or other people.
2. Close your eyes; you may prepare yourself by

doing the Deep Abdominal Breathing exercise described on page 262. If you are very tense, do the Total Body Muscle Relaxation exercise on page 264.

3. Choose a word or phrase to focus your mind on, such as the ancient Sanskrit mantra "Ham Sah," meaning "I am that"; or, repeat the word "one" to yourself, or "I am love, I am joy, I am one." As you silently repeat the focus word(s), thoughts will enter your head. When you catch yourself on a random thought chase, be grateful to your "observer self" for its observance, and then let the seductiveness of your mental chatter recede. It is normal—no matter how many years of practice you have—for the mind to be caught chasing its own tail.

4. You can time your words or phrases with your breath, keeping the inhale broad, deep, and easy and the exhale silent and effortless.

5. You can easily lose track of time in deep relaxation, so you may need to set a timer or stopwatch if you don't have unlimited time.

6. When you stop meditating, remain seated for a minute or two with your eyes closed, and then open them.

If you are energetic, nervous, and hyper, don't be surprised if you can't sit quietly and if your mind jumps around "like a monkey," in meditation parlance. Keep with it, and don't be too hard on yourself if you feel you aren't "doing it." Meditation feels good once you get the hang of it. Even if you think you're not doing it "right," the relaxation response will still most likely occur. Even beginners soon notice that they feel more peaceful. And the more they practice, the more adept they get and the better they feel. Aim to meditate once a day; twice, if possible. It's a great way to start the day, and a great way to end it, too. The best time is upon waking, when your mind is the most uncluttered and "suggestible." Some people meditate when they get home from work, as a buffer of calm to ease the transition from business to personal life. Instead of a martini, reach for your mantra.

Taming Your Stressors

One of my patients recently told me how she had completely rearranged her jam-packed day to leave her car at the mechanic's. Like most Americans, she was paralyzed without her wheels, so she arranged to have a friend give her a ride to work from the repair shop and then back again to pick up her car at the end of the day. Her car was supposed to be ready that evening, but she arrived at the shop to discover that it wasn't ready and wouldn't be ready for another day. What did this very capable, professional, sophisticated woman do? She burst out crying in frustration.

Of course it wasn't just the car that was the problem—it was her cluttered and harried life. The car was just the last straw. The techniques discussed above will soothe your nerves and help you face your stresses with equanimity. But they do not really get to the heart of the matter: an overly stressful life. To do that, you must examine yourself and then bring about a deeper change that gets at the root of your stressful state of mind—a state of mind that is ruining your memory and concentration.

Get Balanced

Women who are over-stressed feel their lives are out of control and tipping way out of balance. They have too much work, perhaps too many social obligations, and too many family responsibilities. Where is the time for themselves—to relax, to have fun, to hang out with their friends, to just "be"?

If you are like so many other overloaded women, you need to let go of trying to "do it all" in order to restore balance to your life. Most likely, you have been taught to take care of others and put other people's needs ahead of your own. You may consider admitting to being stressed out—and the importance of this—an admission of failure, or feminine weakness. In a sense, overloaded women can be considered "stressaholics." Like any addiction, the first step to recovery is to get past any feelings of shame and denial.

Not only do we not have to do it all, but we don't have to do it all at once. Leah often finds herself overwhelmed. She often finds herself "trying to read [her] E-mail, talk to [her] mother on the phone, look out the window, and keep one eye on the clock because [she] need[s] to run off to a meeting in five minutes." All this to "save time." But, she asks, "How much do we gain by multitasking? It may be so inherently inefficient that we are gaining nothing at all because we drop so many stitches along the way that each task must be redone individually. I usually have to read the E-mail three times if I'm doing something else at the time. Actually, I think there's an elegance and grace in doing one task at a time. So what if I can manage six things at once? Big deal. Does it make my life any more efficient? Maybe, maybe not. And what of the quality of life while I'm racing around doing six things at once but not paying attention to any one of them?"

Some people do seem to thrive on speed and multitasking. But others, like Leah, do not. She continues, "People have different rhythms and different energies. I am a person who likes to move in the world very slowly. My students tell me that I speak slowly—sometimes annoyingly so. I take lots of pauses so that I can collect my thoughts and choose my words carefully. . . . For me there is pleasure in moving slowly. It's a strategy for learning to pay attention and staying alert. It's also an aesthetic ideal. Slowing down is not a luxury. Everyone deserves to move at their own pace."

Ask yourself, Am I moving at my own pace? Or at someone else's? Who's the boss here? Am I doing too many things at once? Am I doing too many things in general? Do I need to take a break? Taking time out is not necessarily the sign of a malingerer—it can be a vital act of self-care and self-renewal. Take the weekends off. Take vacations. Enjoy yourself, take your mind off your stress and keep it on the present glorious stress-free moment. Pursue a hobby—this is a proven stress-buster. Enjoy good food, the great outdoors, a movie, sex, music, a good joke, the company of others, your own company.

You say you can't slow down? You can't simplify your life? You're afraid of slipping down the slope of life to a lower level that will make you more miserable? Well, ask yourself, how happy am I? Will that Lexus or status school for your child make you or your child happier? And if so, is it worth the price? Are there more important aspects to your life than doing, getting, spending? Who says busyness is a virtue? Not the Chinese! The Chinese word for "busy" is a combination of the characters meaning "heart" and "death." In other words, if you are too busy, you neglect your heart until it dies.

You don't have to retire to reap the benefits of retirement. Taking it easier doesn't mean you have to put your brain in mothballs. When researchers studied people who had just retired, they discovered that people who sat around in their easy chairs had significantly less blood flow to their brains, compared with those who kept working or pursued new hobbies and interests. Sometimes just a change of scenery and type of work will give your psyche and brain enough of a break to return to your "other life" renewed and refreshed.

Change the Situation

Take the time to sit down and evaluate the stresses you experience. Write them on a piece of paper and take a good hard look at the list. For each stress, ask yourself: Can I change this? Can I fix it or eliminate it? How? If

272 • Female and Forgetful

you are working outside the home and come home to a second shift, why not hire some help if your partner will not pull his or her own weight? If rush hour traffic is wearing you down, can you shift your work schedule slightly, listen to tapes while driving, or carpool? If you are responsible for taking care of an aging, ailing parent, can you convince other relatives to share the burden? Is something in your social or family relationships unsatisfying or irksome? If your computer skills are not up to date and this is causing problems at work, can you take a course that will bring you up to a more comfortable level? If you are trying to accomplish tasks that are not really suited to your skills, can you assign the work to someone else who is more adept at it? Do you live and work surrounded by time sinks—colleagues who chat too long, phone calls that interrupt your flow, people who are always asking you to do "little" favors? Do others seem to depend on you and not on themselves? Do they take up your time with idle, meaningless chatter that you could live without and that takes you away from what you really want to be doing? Can you say no? Can you say goodbye?

Look at how you spend your time. Again, write things down—you may be surprised. How important are these things? Prioritize. Know what you can give up, and then give it up, knowing what you are gaining in exchange. Are you stretched too thin because you've been taught to think of others first? How much of your overload is due to striving for material things—keeping up, acquiring more, newer, cooler things? How much of your stress comes from taking care of your new possessions?

Can you live with less? Can you simplify your life, your wardrobe, your cooking, and your shopping?

Investigate time-management and organization techniques. They really can help you simplify and streamline. For example, how many times do you handle a single piece of paper? Do you move things from one pile to another or from one side of your desk to the other? Do you continue not to deal with them? One classic piece of advice is to never touch the same piece of paper twice: once it is in your hands, you must act on it, file it, or throw it away. Another simplifying tip is to use technology appropriately. Do you really need to reply to a fax with another computer-generated and printed fax, or can you simply handwrite your response on the bottom of the fax and send it right back? This saves time, and is better for the environment. Organizing and putting order into your physical environment will help reduce the stress of forgetting and misplacing things, people, and appointments.

Remember, though, that these tricks and techniques for managing time and tasks teach you how to squeeze more productivity out of your day and yourself. This can help—it greases the wheels—but it cannot be the whole answer.

Change Your Attitude

Stress is an unavoidable fact of life. You can't get rid of every stressful thing, nor can you put everything away neatly in a drawer. But you can change the way you react to stress. Stress is *change*—it may be good, it may be bad—

and your reaction to it can be tempered so it does not create chaos in your life.

Some people are more resistant to stress than others. Such "hardy personalities" are able to weather the ups and downs of life with equanimity. A setback in life such as losing a job or spraining an ankle may make them sad, but it doesn't throw them into a major depression. They may even turn it into a challenge to be met with energy and enthusiasm, and a vehicle for personal growth. Such an attitude may be partly genetic and partly the result of childhood experiences and lessons learned. But anyone can become hardier and more optimistic and serene at any age.

This doesn't mean you should deny or repress your feelings. This will only cause problems later, when they resurface in a strange or disguised form. Be sad when a bad thing happens. Feel the sadness fully, let it fill you and then pass through you. Similarly, don't deny yourself the fullness of a joyful experience or a happy piece of news. Be glad you can feel these very human emotions, and then move on. No one who saw the movie *Broadcast News* can forget the scene in which the Holly Hunter character sets aside a specific time in her frenetic day to close the door and cry. Or Scarlett O'Hara's famous line "I'll cry tomorrow." As long as tomorrow does come, and we do let it out, this is a fine way to deal with stress, anxiety, and sadness in a world in which we can't always express our emotions every minute of the day because it just isn't appropriate or productive.

Even worry warts can benefit from this approach. A study out of the University of Pennsylvania found that chronic worriers who set aside a certain time each day to do nothing but worry actually reduced their level of anxiety. All it took was thirty minutes a day to focus on their woe and the resolve to not worry during the rest of the day.

What kinds of stories do you tell yourself as life rubs up against you? Do you think in all-or-nothing terms? Do you think every situation is the same as the last? Do you worry about the worst possible outcome? Is the glass half empty rather than half full? Are you a perfectionist? Do you assume the blame for things that are out of your control? Do you reprimand yourself for making an honest mistake, for failing if you did your best? These inner dialogues only make for more stress. Be aware of such negative self-talk and then tell these useless, inaccurate thoughts to get out of your head. Replace them with something more reasonable and positive, or at least more fair and neutral.

Vacations, weekends, pleasurable exercise—these are not wasted times. They give your busy life balance, and provide you with the physical and mental energy you need to make life a joy, not a drudgery. The steps in this chapter are tools for dealing with stress, for mental "housekeeping." By keeping your mental house in order, you are clearing out the extraneous materials from the very organ you'd like to perform better. It may be difficult, but it's a key step in helping your mind and memory to function as well as possible.

CHAPTER 14

Coping Strategies and Quick Fixes

My program works, but it takes time to correct the underlying chemical imbalance that causes memory impairment. What to do in the meantime? What to do if you don't get back 100 percent of your memory? This chapter provides you with tools that I and other women have used to get through this period of time. These include practical solutions for saving face (for example, when you've just completely lost your train of thought mid-sentence) and physiological quick fixes (such as choosing the best snack to restore mental acuity temporarily). You'll also find a section on "memory tricks"—tried-and-true methods to coax the most out of your uncooperative mind. I hope that you'll find these useful until the effects of my program take hold and your memory and mental sharpness have been more fundamentally restored. I also include some thoughts on handling memory loss psychologically. Nature, in her infinite wisdom, rarely takes something away without giving something in return. As we mature, we are given a different type of intelligence, which some call "crystallized intelligence," and which bestows us with abilities that our younger counterparts can only dream of.

Saving Face

You've just made the most ridiculous mistake and called Bill by the name of Alan; or you obviously can't think of a word and your companions are exchanging uncomfortable glances with each other; or you've done something silly like put your laundry in the recycling bin. There's nowhere to turn, nowhere to hide. How do you handle it?

Many women call on their sense of humor, and encourage or accept such mental faux pas with grace when others tease them. Many women simply blow it off as just another "menopausal moment," or say "excuse me, I'm having a senior moment." Sally has found that "it's best if you can joke about it or laugh or let it go, knowing you will remember it later. If you become flustered and embarrassed, it will make the incident far more important than it really is, and only serve to draw attention to that very thing you want people not to notice." JoAnn's creative solution is to hit the bottle—of hair dye. She says, "I started going gray very young and I've been coloring my hair since my twenties. I recently bleached my hair blonde and now when I am particularly forgetful or ditzy, I just tell people that I am having a blonde day."

If she loses her train of thought mid-sentence, Alice stalls—she just keeps talking and eventually she finds her way back. If that doesn't work, she can just be up front and say, "now, where was I going with this? What were we just talking about?" She explains, "memory lapses are becoming so common that most people will be able to relate, and help you out."

If all else fails and you really can't be up front, create a diversion—drop your keys, your purse, fake a sneeze. The memory you seek may emerge in the interim.

Quick Fixes

You're in the middle of the day, in the middle of a task, and your brain just short-circuits or fogs up. You've got to keep going and sharpen up. Here are the most effective quick fixes I know.

- Keep aromatherapy or essential oils on hand for a quick pick-me-up. Scents that help restore alertness include jasmine, lily of the valley, and strawberry. Also try mint and eucalyptus.
- Eat a potato. Glucose is the major fuel for your brain, but your brain can't store it. Estrogen helps keep glucose available to your brain cells, but because your estrogen may be low, you may have as much as 30 percent less glucose available in your

brain. Candy bars, sodas, sugar-laden coffee will give you a quick fix, but a quick letdown, too. Your best bet is a slow-but-steady-acting carbohydrate—and the lowly potato fits the bill perfectly. So keep boiled or baked potatoes on hand.

- Invert yourself. Part of the problem when your mind feels sluggish, dull, and confused may be poor circulation. If you have been sitting or standing for a long time, all your blood is pooled in your legs. There are several yoga positions that reverse gravity's pull and give your brain a blood rush. These include the plow, the shoulder stand, and the forward bend. Yoga is my co-author's favorite solution to the mind-dulling desk doldrums that affect anyone who sits all day. You can also buy an inversion table that allows you to safely and comfortably hang upside down to reverse the effects of pooled blood and spine compression. A good one is available from Living Arts for about $300 (www.gaiam.com or 800-254-8464). They also sell other items to aid in yoga, meditation, and self-massage.

- Take a quick stretch break or a brisk walk if you have hit a mental wall. Try this easy stretch for the spine, which wakes up the brain: Place your hands, palms down and shoulder width apart, on the edge of a table, sink, or counter that is waist level. Walk backward until your body forms an L-shape, with your back parallel to the ground and at a right angle to your legs. Hold the stretch for a few deep breaths.

Pay Attention

Sometimes we forget things or act absentmindedly because our minds are indeed "absent." We are so preoccupied with other things that we might as well be sitting on the other side of the world. Information just doesn't sink in or sinks in as shallowly as a message written in the sand. As Leah says, "Why don't I remember a name that someone has told me twenty seconds ago? Because I'm not paying attention. Just because my fingers aren't stuck in my ears doesn't mean that I am actually listening."

Sometimes this inattention can come back to bite you, as Marie, a fifty-one-year-old travel agent found out.

A relative of mine was involved in a lawsuit and she'd call me from time to time to keep me up to date, since she thought I might be called as a witness. I didn't take notes or focus on the details of the conversations since I thought she would settle out of court, and I had a lot of other things going on in my mind—my own business, a new home that I was remodeling, and a serious health problem. But I *was* deposed and under questioning I was unable to recall so many things, or I was unsure about them, or downright wrong. I was afraid they'd think I was a hostile witness or lying and covering up for my cousin, which would harm her case. At the very least it was embarrassing. How could I not recall such simple things as "when did you first learn about the litigation?" I couldn't tell the lawyers—perfect little Ally McBeal wannabes sitting

around the table—that I was going through menopause and was under a lot of stress. That seemed like
such a lame excuse.

When inattention is due to sensory and mental overload,
as is often the case, you can change your environment to
make it less stimulating, less noisy, and more serene in
order to give your attention span and powers of concentration a fighting chance. Although we don't always have
control over our environment, we can always make the
effort to be in the "here and now," to actively pay attention to what others are saying, to what we are doing, and
to what we are going to do. We can cut down on multitasking, which by definition divides our attention. But
you may decide that some of these little details are not
important enough for you to notice and remember. You
may consciously decide to filter out unnecessary information and focus instead on taking in and remembering
what you feel is really important. You may ask yourself,
Why am I cluttering my mind with junk?

Another effective way to stay aware is to say your
thought silently to yourself, or even out loud if you are
alone. Claire says this method works well for her. She
finds herself saying "I am going to the bedroom for a tissue" or "I am putting my notebook on top of the TV."
This helps her stay focused on the moment and the task
at hand. It can help you remember where you put things
because through verbalization and repetition, you create a
stronger memory. When someone tells you a name or a
number or some other little factoid, you can repeat that
to yourself, too.

Another approach that can make a big difference in your overall mental alertness and productivity is to pay attention to your own biorhythms. When you plan your intellectual day to coincide with your biorhythm peaks, you are likely to perform 30 to 40 percent faster and more accurately than during your valleys. Most people are at their mental best early in the day. So, reserve the hours between 9:00 A.M. and 2:00 P.M. for the brain-busters—tasks that require the most concentration and focus. Save the brain-dead late afternoon for smaller, less demanding tasks and mindless tasks like clearing out your computer files, going through the mail, and answering letters. And if you must sleep shorter hours to complete a certain project on deadline, it's better not to burn the midnight oil. Rather, go to bed at your usual hour and rise earlier. This keeps you on your biological schedule and supplies you with the most restorative sleep.

Get Organized

"Where did I put my . . . ?" Just fill in the blank. I wonder how some people can find anything because their environment is such a jumble. Or they don't have set places to keep things, so their lives are a series of treasure hunts. Getting clarity and order in your physical world will help cut down on forgetfulness because there will be fewer new things to remember. In the world of memory, neatness counts because it makes things more manageable and, therefore, the things you need to remember more accessible.

Start by cultivating certain habits. For example, decide on fixed permanent locations for things you use and move every day—papers, eyeglasses, writing implements, to-do pads, keys, gloves, wallets, day planners, watch—and always, always, always put them there and keep them there. This way you will not frustrate yourself looking for misplaced objects, and the answer to "Where did I put my . . . ?" will be "Where I always put it."

You may need to remind yourself of your intentions. Claire, a big fan of creating an orderly personal world, says, "I have found that as I'm doing something foolish, like putting my keys on the table instead of the bookcase in the entryway, my usual dumping place, I catch myself. I say, 'Is that really where you want to put them?' I have become aware of this flaw and become more astute at not creating those situations." Claire is also adamant about desk clutter. "As soon as I have two pieces of paper on the same subject I make a file folder and in they go, and then away they go in my filing cabinet."

While we all like spontaneity, variety, and freedom, routine is a good thing for forgetful people and you may need to create more of it than you did in the past. Try to schedule regular appointments and do many things at the same time each day, or the same day of the week or month. That way, you won't be racking your brain trying to remember where to be, what to do, and when.

Write things down. Almost every woman interviewed for this book said that this was her number one way of coping with poor memory. Make lists—and remember to refer to them and bring them with you, if appropriate. It may help to organize tasks into categories;

"to do," "to call," "to buy." One woman swore she was single-handedly supporting the 3M Company, the manufacturer of Post-its. Put these handy reminders anywhere—your computer, your phone, refrigerator, door—wherever you will see them so they will jog your memory. Make it a habit to write down key points of phone conversations. Keep these jottings, with the date, in a special notebook you keep by the phone. You may also want to make a note of important points in a conversation or meeting when you get home or to your office. Writing things down not only provides you with a tangible record to which you can refer, but the very act of writing things down forces you to pay closer attention and gives you two more avenues of remembrance—a motor memory as you write something down, and a visual one when you see what you have written.

At one memory center, they advise clients to keep a "memory notebook." This should be big—standard looseleaf size—so you don't lose it. Use it to write down everything that you need to do each day, making a note of how long each task will take. Customize your notebook to your lifestyle and personality. For example, many women use organizing tabs to demarcate a calendar section and address book, sections for birthdays, personal data, and medical information such as last doctor's appointment, mammogram, and pap test, and directions to key places. Why not include instructions for programming a VCR or using shortcuts on your computer? This master notebook will help provide structure and certainty and rein in a chaotic day of doings and details. As one woman said of her notebook, "each day becomes a piece of art I create and then can see in my mind's eye all day long."

Memory Tricks and Techniques

There are many memory tricks. They all work to a degree, but some work better than others and some people respond better than others do. You may want to give one or more a try, and use them consistently until they become second nature.

A popular method of improving memory is by using associations. If you are in the shower and realize you need to call Shari, think of something to associate with that name. Shari sounds like "cherry," so you may picture a bowl of cherries, eating them and tasting their sweet and sour juice, spitting out the pits, and being covered in red cherry juice. The more outrageous or extreme the image, the better. Or, if you are introduced to a man named Bill, you might picture him dressed in a suit made of dollar bills.

Another method is called "chunking," which is designed to help you remember lengthy numbers or lists. It works this way: your mind can only grasp a certain amount of information at one time, so by dividing bigger chunks into smaller ones, your mind can digest and recall the chunks more easily. Take, for example, a shopping list—chunk together the vegetables, the household items, and so on. A telephone number is naturally chunked already into groups of three or four digits—isn't it much easier to remember "213-926-4103" than "2139264103"?

Often when you try to think of the name of someone or something, you have the feeling that it is right on the tip of your tongue. When this happens, start with the letter "A" and go through the alphabet to see if the name begins with any of the letters. This works an amazing number of times. Sometimes it works behind the scenes—after I've gone through the whole alphabet to no avail, the name will pop out a few minutes later.

Finally, I recommend a version of tying a string around your finger. If you need to remember to bring or do something and you can't get to a pen and paper to write it down, throw a nearby object on the floor, or place it in an odd position. When you see the strangely placed object, it will remind you that you need to do something, and although it won't tell you what it is you need to do, it will start you working on the memory. This is particularly useful if you wake up in the middle of the night, and, for example, realize you need to pick up the dry cleaning in the morning. Nancy, my co-author, keeps a Beanie Baby monkey in her bedroom for just such occasions.

From "blonde days" to "senior moments," yoga headstands to notebook organizers and Post-its, these quick fixes and strategies are a testament to the resiliency of women who may have forgotten where they put their keys, but who have not lost their ingenuity. While this chapter may provide you with specific ideas, I hope it will also stimulate you to invent imaginative solutions of your own. As you work on the underlying causes and notice your memory and concentration improve, you'll find you rely on these crutches less and less and on your brain-power more and more.

Remembering Yourself

My brain-boosting program is targeted toward restoring your memory, but it does more than that. Forgetfulness is annoying and troubling, and possibly dangerous to your job and your well-being and that of others. But for many women it is also a much-needed wake-up call. Yes, the six steps of good nutrition, supplementation, stress reduction, herbal therapy, hormone balancing, and physical and mental exercise are all aimed toward improving your mental power. But in following my program you are also taking the steps needed to take control of your life and your mental and physical health overall. Because the program is holistic and natural, it is likely you will see improvements in every facet of your being. No matter how successful my program is in restoring your memory, it is also my hope that you will come to see the life change called forgetfulness as a tool for development.

Many women who have become forgetful have been changed by the experience. They have become advocates of their own health and well-being. They have a never-say-die attitude. They have learned how truly individual and special they are, and how precious their life and their health are. Forgetfulness has prompted many to ask big questions about life and about themselves. It has made them feisty and philosophical. It has made them grow.

JoAnn, who has suffered from memory loss and brain

fog for many years, has learned that you need to "follow your own intuition. When you feel that something is wrong, you begin your own journey of discovery and research into what can help you." JoAnn is a language teacher, and not surprisingly sees the body-mind as being "like a language with all its own idiosyncrasies and subtleties. It is up to each of us to learn the language of our own bodies to understand how we as individuals function and how to help ourselves. It's a lifelong process, but a rewarding one." She continues, saying, "This belief is the wonderful thing that I've gotten out of all of this." Being able to read the language of her own inner workings has helped JoAnn refuse to settle for one-size-fits-all medical treatment, and, as a result, find the best treatment for her.

While reflecting on the challenges and benefits of this struggle, Alice, the actress, reminds us of Marcel Proust's view of memory.

> Proust calls it the vast structure of recollection—memory and the universe of memory is life itself. Anything that impedes that is a diminishing of the life force. One should value every possibility that one has. Don't be passive. We women get wounded emotionally. Healing is a very complex journey—a lifetime study. Everyone wants a shortcut, a quick fix, but it can't be handed to you on a plate. When it comes to aging, I think the single most important component is vision in the large sense—vision of your understanding of the universe and yourself, vision of what you want to be. Some people accept growing old. They say, 'so you lose a little memory, you lose your sight. I shouldn't com-

plain.' Or they are fighters, and they have a reason other than their own narcissistic needs for maintaining those things—a reason for staying young. I have a higher purpose that really informs my drive. One of them is to be a powerful example to my children; [the other is] to be a powerful example to my profession.

This drive continues to give Alice the incentive to fine-tune her memory program and integrate more physical activity into her life, which was something she was never very fond of.

Engaging in a battle to find a diagnosis of and good medical care for her memory problems has made Diane savvy and "feisty." She says she is normally a quiet, kind, low-key type of person, but things have changed. She explains, "I've been through so much with these docs. I feel I've been knocked around by the system. One doctor told me I should let my physicians know right off the bat that I have a Ph.D. and that I'm familiar with research techniques, so they don't treat me the way they would treat some average housewife. It sounds terrible, but if I start feeling the arrogance of a physician, I do this. And they do usually treat me with more respect."

Diane has also found that necessity really is the mother of invention, and that a "limitation" can spur you to creative thinking. "We had a faculty workshop and the dean put me in charge of one of the presenting groups," she says. "We were supposed to identify some of the major theorists and researchers in our area. And the leader of the group was supposed to stand up and talk about all of the researchers that the group had agreed on. But I knew I wouldn't be able to do this, so for my group I came up with something else: each member of the group would pick a researcher and talk about that one. Our group decided to use a more cooperative method. None of the other groups did it this way. And I *had* to do it this way. I had no choice."

As Diane discovered, just because we are losing something doesn't mean we are losing "it." It's comforting to know that we can usually compensate for eroding aspects of our mental hardware by using what we've got more efficiently and relying on other mental skills. This type of mental ability is sometimes referred to as "crystallized" intelligence. It is unique and to be cherished because it incorporates a lifetime of experiences, a well-stocked memory bank, a polished judgment, and thoughtful articulation. It does not have the youthful "fluidity" needed to deal with a never-ending stream of new information, but it is a valuable skill to have. Like our relationships, our comprehension and retention of information grows deeper, richer, and more meaningful with maturity. We may not be able to compete with remembering trivial details, but we are better at remembering information that is personal and meaningful. Studies report that older people remember the gist of a story better than young people do—perhaps because they are better able to focus on the essentials. As they get older, the work of many visual artists becomes simpler. Matisse, Monet, O'Keefe—they eliminated or ignored the fussy little details and painted or photographed or sculpted bolder, simpler shapes that somehow conveyed the essence much more powerfully than highly detailed works.

Leah boldly asks, "Why do we need to have instant recall of every detail that crosses our paths? What if we stopped expecting other people to remember the inessentials?" She wonders if we are being "too narrow in our definition of memory. The view that a healthy person's memory should be perfect, that 'normal' retention is absolute and complete, is unfounded. Given all the stimuli coming at us, to become increasingly forgetful is, statistically speaking, normal and adaptive in a culture racing against itself."

Jessie, too, says, "Maybe there is a way to give yourself permission to forget. Why do we always have to achieve?" Why, indeed. A little farther down this path we find Lynn, who says, "I'm not as fast as I used to be, but I'm trying to be gentle with myself about it. I work with people with cognitive disabilities so I see that there are different ways of being in the world." Shoshanna also wants us to be kinder to ourselves. "As we age," she observes, "we all have losses in one area or another and it is part of the life cycle that memory loss happens. Don't spend too much time on what you don't have—enjoy today what you do have. This is how I'm trying to live my life."

In forgetting some things, we may remember others, such as joyous aspects of ourselves that we have long ignored. Diane, who blames her mental decline on undiagnosed depression and extreme job stress, can barely contain her amazement at her new self. "I decided to pull myself out of the mothballs and go back to something I did thirty years ago—flamenco dancing! I take lessons twice a week and practice on a piece of plywood I lay on the floor of the laundry room in my condo complex."

She laughs merrily when she adds, "I also became the lead vocalist of a rock band with a bunch of other miserable professors. My job is a viper's pit, but thank God I have my flamenco and my singing. Those things keep me going. But," she says, "prayer is probably the most helpful. I prayed for the gift of music and the songs just started pouring out."

In my work with so many women patients, I have discovered that it is important to understand that we are dynamic entities. Our bodies are constantly changing, and just because there is a change that you don't like doesn't mean you have to live with it forever. Our bodies ebb and flow like the cycles of the moon; our hormones and biochemicals ebb and flow as well. Because the essence of the universe is change, a healthy person is a resilient person who can flow with change. I always think of Miss Havisham from Charles Dickens's *Great Expectations*—the bride eternally waiting for a fiancé who never comes. A sorry sight indeed. What are we waiting for?

It is imperative that as a woman goes through the various stages of life she gets in touch with her essence, which may not be the image she portrays to the world. During the years that a woman is menstruating, she is preparing to assume the role of lover, wife, mother; and later, when menstruation stops, to assume the role of grandmother, matriarch, and so on. So we can view each role as just another phase of fulfilling our biological imperative. Not less, better, or worse, than another, but merely different from the former.

I've learned how important it is to turn to each other and talk to other women for support, knowledge, sharing, and comfort. A best friend, women's groups, or therapy can help us make these transitions as smoothly as possible. I have had many women cry in my office simply because I listened to them without judging them or making them wrong. I have known scores of women who have said, "I came to see you because you're a woman and have gone through this yourself. My doctor and husband just don't understand."

Attitude is everything, and a compassionate attitude of loving kindness toward ourselves, like charity, begins at home. I have found that most women push themselves far too hard, and are their own worst critics about their bodies, their careers, their relationships, and their parenting skills. Often they have unrealistic or unattainable expectations, and when they make a mistake, have not achieved a particular goal, or are less than perfect they beat themselves up mentally. Look at all the hats women need to wear: wife, mother, lover, cook, teacher, organizer, and chauffeur. Answering the inner critic with "I'm doing the best I can, I'm doing the best I know how right now" really helps.

Take a cue from Roberta Peters, the world-acclaimed soprano who, in her mid-sixties, is still singing opera and loving it. She remarked that although she no longer performs certain arias because she cannot hit the higher notes, other pieces of music are now within her reach because of the maturation and deepening of her voice. While we may rue the loss of some of the "notes" in our memory banks, we can revel in the deepening and richening of our own well-earned memory repertoires.

GLOSSARY

Acetylcholine. An important neurotransmitter needed for memory and thinking.

Adaptogen. A substance that helps the body to adapt to stress and return it to a more balanced state.

Adrenal glands. The two small glands that secrete stress hormones adrenaline and cortisol.

Adrenaline. A hormone released by the adrenals during times of stress that stimulates the brain cells to set the stress response in motion.

Alzheimer's disease. A brain disorder that causes impaired memory and thinking.

Amino acids. Molecules that are the building blocks for complex proteins, including neurotransmitters.

Amygdala. The portion of the limbic system that processes emotions.

Antioxidants. Nutrients taken in with food or as supplements, enzymes made by the body, and other chemicals that reduce or prevent damage to cells by free-radical molecules.

Arteriosclerosis. A thickening and hardening of the arteries that hampers blood flow to the brain.

Atherosclerosis. A type of arteriosclerosis that is caused by a buildup of fats on the inside of the blood vessel walls.

Axon. The part of the nerve cell that sends electrochemical impulses to the neighboring nerve cell.

Botanicals. Medicines derived from plants.

Brain stem. The part of the brain that relays information from the five senses and controls body functions, including breathing and heartbeat.

Cerebellum. The part of the brain that coordinates your body's movements.

Cerebrum. The "thinking" part of the brain; it is divided into two hemispheres, each of which is divided into four lobes.

Corpus callosum. The bridge of fibers that connects the two halves of the cerebrum.

Dendrite. The part of the nerve cell that receives electrochemical impulses from neighboring nerve cells.

Endocrine system. The system of glands that secrete hormones, the chemical messengers of the body.

Estrogen. Any of a group of "female" sex hormones produced in the ovaries, adrenal glands, and fat cells that affect all systems of the body, including the brain and nervous system.

Free radical. An unstable molecule that is missing an electron and that steals an electron from a neighboring molecule thereby causing damage to cells, including nerve cells.

Hippocampus. The portion of the brain's limbic system that processes unemotional short-term memory and determines whether to send it to the cerebrum for long-term memory storage.

Homocysteine. An amino acid found in the blood that can damage artery walls and is a contributing cause of poor circulation and heart disease.

Hormone. A chemical produced by the endocrine system that is carried by the blood to parts of the body where it signals the cells to perform in a certain way.

HRT (Hormone Replacement Therapy). Therapy administered to take the place of hormones no longer produced by the body due to either natural or medical menopause.

Hypothalamus. The part of the brain that regulates the autonomic nervous system (which controls automatic body functions such as breathing and heartbeat), sleep, immune function, mood, hunger, pituitary hormone production, and other functions.

Hysterectomy. Surgical removal of the uterus; a total hysterectomy also removes the ovaries, cervix, and fallopian tubes and results in instant menopause.

Limbic system. A group of neuron clusters that governs emotional reactions to experiences.

Memory. The process and result of retaining information and experiences that is the basis of learning.

Menopause. The cessation of menstrual periods.

Mitochondria. The energy factories inside the cell body, including that of a nerve cell, that power all cell functions, including memory and thinking.

Myelin sheath. The protective coating around the axon of a nerve cell.

Neuron. Cell of the brain and nervous system that processes memory and thought.

Neurotransmitter. A brain chemical that is responsible for carrying electrochemical messages from one nerve cell to another.

Peri-menopause. The period of time around the menopause that may last from five to ten years in some women.

Phytochemicals. Chemicals found in plants that have many beneficial effects—including antioxidant properties—on the cells of the body. (Also called "phyto-nutrients.")

Phytoestrogens. Chemicals found in plants that have an estrogen-like or estrogen-enhancing effect on the body.

Plasticity. The ability of the brain to change over time and grow in its capacity to think and remember.

Receptor. A "docking site" on neurons and other cells that a chemical molecule locks on to, enabling it to pass a message to the cell.

Synapse. The tiny space between the axon of one neuron and the dendrite of another, across which messages are carried by neurotransmitters.

Thalamus. The part of the brain that governs information gathered by the senses.

Sources for Supplements, Natural Hormones, and Smart Drugs

Supplements

Mail order sources for supplements and natural hormones:

Pacifica Women's Health Care
(310) 840-5755
ELottor@aol.com

Life Extension Foundation
(800) 841-5433
www.lef.org

Capitol Drugs
(800) 819-9098

Whole Foods Market
http://wholefoods.com/
(310) 274-3360

Merit Homeopathy
(818) 831-1727

Whitaker Wellness
Institute
(800) 826-1550

Total Remedy and
Prescription Center
(310) 473-5003

Santa Monica Homeopathic
Pharmacy
(310) 395-1131
www.smhomeopathic.com

Dixie Health
(800) 767-9232
www.tidesoflife.com

Healthy Hotline
(800) 603-0339

Montiff-Don Tyson's
Advanced Nutraceuticals
(310) 820-4483

Places to buy supplements and natural hormones for those who do not do mail order. Many also sell natural progesterone and estrogen. Call for locations near you:

Erewhon Natural Food
   Market
(323) 937-0777

Co-oportunity
(310) 451-8902

Wild Oats Community
   Market
(800) 494-Wild
www.wildoats.com

Great Earth Vitamins
(800) 527-7965

Kayser's Nutrition
(805) 682-3747

Lazy Acres
(805) 564-4410

Lassen's Health Food
(805) 495-2609

Supplement sources for healthcare practitioners:

Terrace International
   Distributors
(800) 824-2434
www.tidhealth.com

Thorne Research
(800) 228-1966
www.thorne.com

Scientific Bio-Logics
(714) 847-9355
www.healingedge.net

For quality natural brain boosters: Lecithin, Ginkgo biloba extract, acetyl-L-carnitine, Coenzyme Q-10, NADH, pregnenolone, DHEA, cognitex, melatonin, and Life Extension Mix.
Life Extension Buyers' Club
(800) 544-4440

For high-quality vitamins, minerals, amino acids, herbs, botanicals, and other smart nutrients at good prices as well as links to information and other sources, go to www.iherb.com.

For Memoractiv, the combination herbal memory enhancer I use most often. It is a combination of phosphatidylserine, Ginkgo, acetylcarnitine, vinpocetine, and the Ayurvedic herb Bacopa. To purchase on-line or find a natural pharmacy near you, visit the Thorne Research Web site: http://www.thorne.com/.

For Bacopa monnieri (Brahmi) in oil form, contact Louisville Botanical Co., 1936 Eastview Ave., Louisville, KY 40205, (502) 459-7401; E-mail: mike_ky@webtv.net.

Natural Hormones

Contact the following compounding pharmacies for natural progesterone and the three forms of estrogen. Many of these products require a physician's prescription.

Women's International
   Pharmacy
(800) 279-5708

Apothecure
(800) 969-6601

Bajamar Women's Health Care
(800) 255-8025

Belmar Pharmacy
(800) 525-9473

International Academy of
   Compounding Pharmacists
(713) 933-8400;
(900) 927-4227

Lloyd Center Pharmacy
(800) 358-8974

College Pharmacy
(800) 888-9358

Delk Pharmacy
(615) 388-3952

Smart Drugs

For a list of overseas companies that provide piracetam, Picamilon, Pyritinol, Hydergine, Deprenyl, and Centrophenoxine. (Hydergine and nimodipine must be prescribed by a physician.) Call (800) 544-4440.

Sources for Information and Treatment

Web Sites

The Internet is a portal to information and support. If you want to contact me, visit my Web site at www.findings.net/hormones.html. Be aware that not all the information on the Internet is reliable, so take whatever you find with a grain of salt. I have found the following sites to be among the most reliable. However, this is just a sampling of what was available at the time this book was written. I urge you to explore—there are new sites and new information posted all the time.

For women experiencing early menopause due to any cause: www.earlymenopause.com

For women experiencing surgical menopause: http://www.findings.net/sansuteri.html

For people interested in brain-booster supplements, memory enhancements, and aging prevention in general, the Life Extension Foundation site offers mail-order supplements and informative articles: www.lef.org

For information about alternative medicine check out OneMedicine: http://www.onemedicine.com

For more information about aging and neurological disorders: National Institute on Aging, (800) 222-2225; Alzheimer's Association, (800) 272-3900; National Institute of Neurological Disorders and Stroke, (800) 352-9424.

Alternative Health Professional Referrals

To locate an alternative health professional in your area, contact one of the groups below.

American Association of
   Naturopathic Physicians
P.O. Box 20386
Seattle, WA 98112
(206) 323-7610

American Institute of
   Homeopathy
1585 Glencoe Street #44
Denver, CO 80220
(303) 370-9164

American Holistic Medical
   Association
4101 Lake Boone Trail
Suite 201
Raleigh, NC 27607
(707) 556-9728

Memory and Wellness Clinics and Spas

There is a growing number of memory clinics, many of them university-based, that will perform a diagnostic workup and recommend an appropriate treatment program. These include

The Johns Hopkins School of
   Medicine
600 N. Wolfe Street #157
Baltimore, MD 21287
(410) 955-5000

Memory Enhancement Program
Mount Sinai School of
   Medicine
New York, NY 10001
(212) 241-2665

Memory 101
Beth Israel Deaconess Medical
   Center
Harvard Medical School
294 Washington Street
Boston, MA 02108
(617) 426-5500

WellMax Center for
   Preventive Medicine
La Quinta Resort and Club
Palms Springs, CA

Hilton Hawaiian Village
Honolulu, HI
(800) 621-5263
www.wellmax.com

APPENDIX D

Selected Bibliography

For more information about topics discussed in this book, see the following resources.

Books

Balch, James, and Phyllis Balch. *Prescription for Nutritional Healing*. Garden City Park, NY: Avery Publishing Group, 2000.

Barbach, Lonnie. *The Pause: Positive Approaches to Menopause*. New York: Dutton, 1993.

Brenner, Keralyn, and Deborah Gordon. *Perimenopause, the Natural Way*. New York: John Wiley and Sons, 2001.

Bruning, Nancy. *The Natural Health Guide to Antioxidants*. New York: Bantam, 1994.

Carper, Jean. *Your Miracle Brain*. New York: HarperCollins, 2000.

Chopra, Deepak. *Ageless Body, Timeless Mind*. New York: Harmony Books, 1993.

Crook, Thomas H. *The Memory Cure*. New York: Simon & Schuster, 1998.

Chu, Chin-ning. *Do Less, Achieve More.* New York: HarperCollins, 1998.

Domar, Alice. *Self-Nurture: Learning to Care for Yourself As Effectively As You Care for Everyone Else.* New York: Viking, 1999.

Green, Cynthia. *Total Memory Workout.* New York: Bantam, 1999.

Herrmann, Douglas J. *Super Memory.* Emmaus, PA: Rodale, 1990.

Higbee, Kenneth L. *Your Memory.* (2nd edition.) Upper Saddle River, N.J.: Prentice Hall, 1988.

Hudson, Tori. *Women's Encyclopedia of Natural Medicine.* Los Angeles: Keats Publishing, 1999.

Khalsa, Dharma Singh. *Brain Longevity.* New York: Warner Books, 1997.

Lieberman, Shari, and Nancy Bruning. *The Real Vitamin and Mineral Book.* Garden City Park, NY: Avery Publishing Group, 1997.

Lorayne, Harry, and Jerry Lucas. *The Memory Book.* New York: Stein and Day, 1974.

Northrup, Christiane. *Women's Bodies, Women's Wisdom.* New York: Bantam, 1994.

Packer, Lester, and Carol Colman. *The Antioxidant Miracle.* New York: John Wiley and Sons, 1999.

Regelson, William, and Carol Colman. *The Superhormone Promise.* New York: Simon & Schuster, 1996.

Sahley, Billie J., and Katherine M. Birkner. *Healing with Amino Acids and Nutrients* (no publisher available).

Simple, Molly, and Deborah Gordon. *Menopause, the Natural Way.* New York: John Wiley and Sons, 2001.

Walsleben, Joyce. *A Woman's Guide to Sleep: Guaranteed Solutions for a Good Night's Rest.* New York: Times Books, 2000.

Warga, Claire. *Menopause and the Mind.* New York: Simon & Schuster, 1999.

Weil, Andrew. *Natural Health, Natural Medicine.* Boston: Houghton Mifflin, 1990.

West, R. *Memory Fitness Over Forty.* Gainesville, Fla.: Triad Publishing, 1985.

Wolfe, Sidney. *Worst Pills, Best Pills II.* Washington, DC: Public Citizen Health Research Group, 1993.

Yutsis, Pavel, and Linda Toth. *Why Can't I Remember?* New York: Avery Publishing Group, 1999.

Articles

Geary, James. "Should We Just Say No to Smart Drugs?" *Time,* 5 May 1997, Internet edition.

Kidd, Parris. "Review of Nutrients and Botanicals in the Integrative Management of Cognitive Dysfunction," *Alternative Medicine Review* 4, no. 3 (1999): 144–61.

Mitchell, J. "Nowhere to hide: the global spread of high-risk synthetic chemicals," *World Watch* (1997): 10:26–36.

Singh, H K, and B N Dhawan. "Neuropsychopharmacological effects of the Ayurvedic nootropic *Bacopa monniera* Linn. (Brahmi)," *Indian Journal of Pharmacology* 29, 5 (1997): S359-S365.

Tierney, John. "Sharp Women Left Holding the Remote," *New York Times,* 19 February 2000, B1.

Johns Hopkins Health Information, "Different Wiring in Male and Female Brains," 21 April 1999. Available from www.intelihealth.com.

Maguire, E A, et al. "Navigation-related structural change in the hippocampi of taxi drivers," *Proceedings of the National Academy of Science,* 14 March 2000.

Borghese, C M et al. "Phosphatidyl serine increases hippocampal synaptic efficacy," *Brain Research* (1993): 31:697–700.

Crook, T., et al. "Effects of phosphatidyl serine in age-associated memory impairment," *Neurology* (1991): 4:644–9.

———. "Effects of phosphatidyl serine in Alzheimer's disease," *Psychopharmacology Bulletin* (1992): 28: 61-6.

Wecker, L. "Neurochemical effects of choline supplementation," *Canadian Journal of Physiology and Pharmacology* (1986): 64:329-33.

Index

Page numbers of illustrations appear in italics.

About the Authors

DR. ELISA LOTTOR is a board-certified naturopathic physician with a Ph.D. in nutrition. She completed her undergraduate and graduate work at Michigan State University. She also holds advanced degrees in homeopathy from the Hahnemann College of Homeopathy in England. She has been in private practice for seventeen years and currently sees patients in Los Angeles, Santa Barbara, and Ventura counties. She is the author of *Yes Tofu, No Moo* and *A Dietary Approach to the Treatment of Cancer* (both self-published) and many newspaper and magazine articles. She has been a member of the American Naturopathic Medical Association, the Price Pottinger Nutrition Foundation, and the California Council on Wellness.

Dr. Lottor's expertise lies in the fields of nutritional and botanical medicines and women's health. She is a much in-demand lecturer and seminar presenter both nationally and internationally on a variety of health-related topics, including memory loss, menopause, and the food-mood connection, and has taught classes in the Los Angeles Community College district. Her Web site, www.findings.net/hormones.html, is the winner of numerous awards and was featured on the *Oprah Winfrey Show.*

Dr. Lottor has a wide following in the greater Los Angeles area not only because of her holistic approach—she looks at the patient, not the disease—but, more importantly, because of the care, compassion, and nurturing she incorporates into her treatment protocols. Presently, Dr. Lottor lives with her husband and cat at a beach in Ventura County, California, where she is writing another book.

NANCY P. BRUNING has authored or co-authored more than twenty books, most of them about health and ways to integrate conventional and natural medicines. They include *Natural Relief for Your Child's Asthma; Effortless Beauty; Ayurveda: The A–Z Guide; Natural Medicine for Menopause and Beyond; Healing Homeopathic Remedies; Coping with Chemotherapy; The Real Vitamin and Mineral Book; The Natural Health Guide to Antioxidants; Breast Implants: Everything You Need to Know; The Methylation Miracle;* and *Swimming for Total Fitness.* Her most recent book is *Rhythms and Cycles: Sacred Patterns in Everyday Life.*

58 60
69

72, 3
78 cell
82, 3
94
, 01

218 3 fum
istreg
269
270-
274